Spirit and Trauma

Spirit and Trauma

A Theology of Remaining

Shelly Rambo

WESTMINSTER
JOHN KNOX PRESS
LOUISVILLE · KENTUCKY

First edition
Published by Westminster John Knox Press
Louisville, Kentucky

10 11 12 13 14 15 16 17 18 19—10 9 8 7 6 5 4 3 2 1

Book design by Sharon Adams
Cover design by Lisa Buckley
Cover art © iStockphoto.com

Library of Congress Cataloging-in-Publication Data

Rambo, Shelly.
    Spirit and trauma : a theology of remaining / Shelly Rambo.—1st ed.
        p.   cm.
    Includes bibliographical references (p.   ) and index.
    ISBN 978-0-664-23503-1
    1. Suffering—Religious aspects—Christianity. 2. Psychic trauma—Religious aspects—
Christianity. 3. Spiritual life—Christianity. 4. Bible. N.T. John—Theology. 5. Holy Spirit—
Biblical teaching. I. Title.
    BT732.7.R34 2010
    248.8'625—dc22

                                                                              2010003676

PRINTED IN THE UNITED STATES OF AMERICA

♾ The paper used in this publication meets the minimum requirements of the American National Standard for Information Sciences—Permanence of Paper for Printed Library Materials, ANSI Z39.48-1992.

Westminster John Knox Press advocates the responsible use of our natural resources. The text paper of this book is made from 30% post-consumer waste.

To Jody, *twin spirit*

Contents

Contents

Foreword

I am relieved that Shelly Rambo's book is now available for all to read. I found myself already referring to it in frequent and divergent contexts. These rather random instances from church and academy suggest the scope and the magnetism of this book.

Speaking with the pastor of an emergent church, I found myself urgently discussing Rambo's insight into the nonlinear temporality of trauma, with its stunning, subtle reading of the Gospel of John. Half of the members in this pastor's congregation are known, to her, to be recovering from some kind of abuse. It fit this pastor's sense of her congregation's allergy to the triumphalism often accompanying the narrative of cross and resurrection.

Soon after, I was discussing with seminary students how the present emerges from its past, lured to a new possibility. One student then wondered theologically, pastorally, about the traumatic collective pasts: how Hiroshima and the Shoah remain with us still. I shared Rambo's insight into trauma's refusal to recede into the past—how it interrupts any theology that would leap right from the crucifixions of history to the hope of resurrection. I explained how she unfolds the undervalued symbol of Holy Saturday as a liturgical opportunity for "confrontation with something of death remaining and extending into the territory of life."[1]

Then in the headier atmosphere of a PhD seminar at Drew University during the same week, her new language of "the middle," with its liturgical rhythms, began at once to lend a theological spirit to the philosophical notion in Deleuze of the pulsing "between" site of all becoming "always in the middle, between things, interbeing, *intermezzo*."[2]

---

1. See p. 46 of this volume.
2. Gilles Deleuze and Felix Guittari, *A Thousand Plateaus: Capitalism and Schizophrenia* (Minneapolis: University of Minnesota Press, 1987), 27.

In a fourth context, talking with some fellow theologians about how we read Scripture in postmodern and pluralist settings, I was struck by the relationalism of John's image of the vine. And this brought home to me the fruitfulness of Rambo's theological exegesis. The imperative to "remain in me as I remain in you" is linked to a new reading of the Spirit: its witness now places the disciples as "tenuous witnesses" at "the cusp of death and life." By translating the Greek *menein* as "remaining" rather than "abiding," she inspires an interhuman capacity to stand by each other in our sufferings—especially those who cannot be victoriously fixed.

It isn't often that a work of theology has such multilateral impact, yet this work unfolds like a luminous vine, branching, curling, connecting with the livelier edges, and deeper practices, of Christianity. The intensity of this fresh theological vision challenges the limits of one's own theological perspective. I, for instance, had no particular interest in the theology of von Balthasar, let alone the lost liturgical potential of passion week. Nor had I been working on theories of trauma. Yet I was fascinated when Rambo read von Balthasar's counterposition of the harrowing-of-hell tradition to his female friend's mystical visions, and found "a straightforward trajectory from death to life" that "introduces a new vocabulary of the between: residue, chaos, weary love, and trickling impotence." And she links Cornel West's meditation on Holy Saturday as a resistance to triumphalism into this interstitial space. Perhaps my own reflection on creation at the edge of chaos, with its potential to destabilize colonized orders of gender, sex, and sovereignty, had led me to the edge of her own problematic.

What is emerging here, under her sign of the "middle Spirit," is a pneumatology that may actually hold up in the face of personal and collective suffering, for it frees us from the dishonest resolutions, the grim guarantees, the disappointing promises. This Spirit breathes, witnesses, and remains, and it lures us as well. In a history haunted by unresolved (and sometimes unresolvable) loss, Rambo is mapping—with exquisite care—not a harrowing but a healing pathway through trauma. On this forking, multidimensional way, the Spirit is not (as in Moltmann, for example) simply *identified* with life—at least not the life that is opposed to death. Between Good Friday and Easter, between death and life, between the exhale and the inhale, between the future and the past, this middle Spirit vibrates, delicately. And, dramatically, it reopens the vining interconnections of the Johannine site of love. In the subtle power of this love's "remaining," it "is not only tied to death, it is marked by an *unknowing*." In both trauma and theology, a language capable of minding its effects falters. This spirit, vibrating still upon the face of the deep, witnesses to our most tormenting depths of loss, violence, and despair. "Love is a new commandment, and it calls witnesses into the abyss." In Shelly Rambo's writing, this spirit appears new indeed. It quiets the breathless wordiness of so much Western piety. Yet here, it is not mere silence, but a language edged with silence, a language that only such deep breathing allows.

One senses in this work a new voice and a new genre. But consistent with its own sense of history, its newness and futurity do not arise in opposition to the past. Rambo's critique, for instance, of the standard binary fixation on crucifixion and resurrection bears no resemblance to twentieth-century anti-patriarchal dismissals of the cross. Yet it embodies a ripe feminist sensibility. This theology is new precisely in its way of remaining with both biblical and theological traditions. Such theology—which, I sense, happily heralds a new wave—represents not an orthodox return, but instead solicits, one might say, polydox possibilities in and about orthodoxy itself. These possibilities are activated by transdisciplinary discourses, such as those supplementing theology with recent pastoral, psychological, and social deployments of trauma theory. At the same time, throughout the book, the practice of a mystical breathing, a spirited theopoetics, seems to permeate the exemplary clarity of Rambo's prose. This is a work disclosing theology's own power to remain.

Catherine Keller
New York City
November 21, 2009

Acknowledgments

We carry each other. If we don't have this, what are we?[1]
Anne Michaels

I ask him how he can do the kind of work he does. A psychiatrist assigned to provide psychological evaluations in death-row cases, he enters the courtroom at the last stop in the criminal justice system. His work is to review a life in its entirety in order to make a plea for the inmate's life to be spared. Before a trial, FedEx trucks arrive at his house, delivering boxes of papers that contain comprehensive documentation of a person's movement through family systems and societal institutions. Over the next weeks and months, he studies the documents and interviews friends, family members, and teachers—all those who can speak to the progress of a life, from child to convict. From grade-school report cards to first felony offense reports, he scans the documents that make up a life. Stepping into the courtroom, he makes his case, providing for the judge the survey of a life at this final juncture. In essence, he tells me that he testifies to the layers of trauma that construct this man to be an offender, a man standing on death row. This plea for mercy, at its best, ends in a sentence of life imprisonment; at its worst, it ends in death.

I ask him how he can do the kind of work he does. I expect to hear an inspiring statement about his vision for justice or his belief in personal transformation. Instead, he says, "I am not the same man I was before I started this work." And that is it. There is no awe-inspiring statement. There is no turn for the better in his words. They are heavy and full of despair. His words haunt me, but I understand them. When you enter certain worlds, they do not let you go. My work as a theologian does not take me into courtrooms, but studying trauma has changed the way I move in the world. I feel the fragility of the world more acutely than I did ten years ago. I view persons as more vulnerable in it, and the earth more wounded by our heavy footprints. I feel its weight. I have come to

1. Anne Michaels, *Fugitive Pieces* (New York: Vintage Books, 1998), 22.

believe that we are connected in ways that we cannot account for and consti-tuted by much that we do not know.

Because of this, I also believe that I am not the sole author of this book. The spirits of many have both weighed me down in the writing process and carried me through the process of writing it. Although my study of trauma began with book study, my education has expanded in ways that I could not have imagined. Through conversations with military chaplains, survivors of sexual abuse, com-munity leaders working in postdisaster areas, and urban leaders wrestling with the realities of immigration enforcement and street violence, I witness the unique dimensions of trauma as it touches persons and communities. I am grateful for the honesty and urgency in these conversations. They have, I trust, kept this book honest to the experiences of trauma and urgent in its theological proposals.

If it were not for the students at Boston University School of Theology who gathered weekly around seminar rooms, probing the most difficult questions of God and human suffering, this book would not have made it into print. Thank you for going to the depths in your studies. Multiple communities have also inspired and sustained me through the writing process. I want to thank my mentors and friends at the Oregon Extension, the community of women scholars gathered at the Women's Studies in Religion Program at Harvard Divin-ity School in 2006–7, Churches Supporting Churches, and my colleagues at Emory University and Boston University School of Theology. I am also grate-ful for the editing hours and expertise of Bronwyn Becker, Adam Wallis, Carlo Schmidt, Don McKim, Dan Braden, and the editing staff at Westminster John Knox Press.

It is an art to read works in progress and to see the inchoate beauty in them. I want to thank the multiple artist-teachers who witnessed this book in its mul-tiple incarnations: Serene Jones, who saw a theologian in me before I did; Don Saliers, whose life is a dance of gratitude and ideas an orchestra of possibility; Cathy Caruth, who continually gives me eyes to see my own field differently; Wendy Farley, who counters my sighs of failure with theological inspiration and challenge; and Mark D. Jordan, who tells me to keep writing, believing it is the most faithful and the most subversive act I can perform. His generous intellec-tual spirit and wise counsel permeate each page.

There are those who walk the daily path of life with me, carrying me in ways too numerous to name. To my parents, Ruth and David Rambo, who gave me a rich theological tradition and a love for books and ideas. To my family members and those who have become family: Ty, Helena, Wyeth, Beth, Mark, David, Stephen, Matthew, Kate, Ingrid, Barb, and Julie. This book is dedicated to my twin sister, Jody, who carries the world with me.

Introduction

The storm is gone, but the "after the storm" is always here.
Deacon Julius Lee, New Orleans

I am standing in Deacon Julius Lee's backyard. There is nothing there, except for the cement sidewalk pieces and remnants of a washed-out foundation. As I look to the right, I see a house standing on its side after being carried by the floodwaters and winds to the edge of the property. As I look to the left, I see what they call "Pink City," the stand-in homes symbolizing the celebrity-sponsored housing project under way. Looking straight ahead, I see the new levee wall. The Lower Ninth Ward is Lee's neighborhood and one of the areas of New Orleans hit hardest by the storm.

It is twenty-nine months since Hurricane Katrina struck the Gulf Coast. I am with a group of students from Boston University School of Theology who have come to New Orleans to do some rebuilding. We were invited to participate in a monthly meeting of Churches Supporting Churches, a working group of New Orleans ministers and sponsoring church leaders who are actively discerning their role in rebuilding communities in the aftermath of the hurricane. Julius Lee, a retired member of the United States Air Force and a deacon at Greater St. Luke Baptist Church, speaks up at the meeting. He tells us that there is a great push to claim that New Orleans is back to normal. The language of restoring, rebuilding, can make people forget the existing reality of what people are

1

experiencing. Things are not back to normal, he tells us. "People keep telling us to get over it already. The storm is gone, but the 'after the storm' is always here."

"Is always here." These words have stuck with me, perhaps more than any others in my decade of studying trauma. A profound truth about trauma is encapsulated in his words. Deacon Lee was attesting to the fact that Hurricane Katrina is not simply a singular event that took place in August 2005. It is an event that continues, that persists in the present. Trauma is what does not go away. It persists in symptoms that live on in the body, in the intrusive fragments of memories that return. It persists in symptoms that live on in communities, in the layers of past violence that constitute present ways of relating. It persists in the symptoms that fuel present wars. He is also speaking about public uneasiness with trauma and the push to move beyond it—an impatience with suffering, revealing a timeline on public attention and sympathy.

Life after the storm, people in New Orleans can tell you, is not life as they once knew it. It is life continually marked by an ongoingness of death. This ongoingness, the return, is the enigma of traumatic suffering. How do you account for an experience that was not fully integrated and, thus, returns? How can you heal from trauma?

Paul Womack is a three-tour veteran of the U.S. military. He served in Vietnam, Desert Storm, and Iraq. I met him after a workshop I led for ministers seeking ways to respond to the needs of returning veterans. Paul, now a minister in New York state, listened with two ears, one as a civilian minister and the other as a military veteran. The session focused on what religious leaders need to know about trauma. After the session, Paul approached me. "I know I probably have all the symptoms of everything you are talking about, PTSD and all that, but mostly it just feels sad. I feel sad all the time." It is a sadness that does not go away. Paul says, "The church didn't provide me a place to bring my experience." He is heartened to see the attention that is being focused on soldiers in Iraq and Afghanistan, but he says that for many veterans, like him, their experiences have never been addressed. When we talk about military trauma, he urges us to remember that a lot of history is buried that has never been addressed, either in our homes or in our religious communities. The wounds of war often lie below the surface of daily work and relationships. He claims that his deepest experiences remain untouched by the practices and teachings of the Christian faith; instead, they are met with theological silence. In the few moments that I spoke with Paul, I realized that he had a longing to have the sacred story meet his story. He wants the gospel—the good news—that he preaches and teaches to speak to his story and not erase it. He wants it to be heard for the truth that it speaks, a truth that he cannot fully bring into words.

These are two very different situations. But each reflects the inheritance of trauma and the challenges that trauma poses to the ways in which persons and communities live and move in the world in the aftermath of overwhelming violence. The nature of life following an overwhelming event(s) of violence is fundamentally changed. Life is never the same again. Philosopher Susan Brison writes about the experience of the aftermath as an experience in which death and life are unbounded: "The line between life and death, once so clear and sustaining, now seemed carelessly drawn and easily erased."[1] She refers to life in the aftermath of trauma as a "spectral existence." In the aftermath of trauma, death and life no longer stand in opposition. Instead, death haunts life. The challenge for those who experience trauma is to move in a world in which the boundaries and parameters of life and death no longer seem to hold, to provide meaning. The challenge for those who take seriously the problem of trauma is to witness trauma in all of its complexities—to account for the ongoing experience of death in life.[2] The challenge, for both, is to forge a path of healing amid all of the complexities.

Both Deacon Lee and Paul struggle to reconcile their present experience of life—reconfigured through trauma—with their experience of faith. Deacon Lee notes a general impatience of persons, even religious communities, to rush past Katrina, to proclaim the good news before its time. Paul notes the ways in which his tradition has failed to provide a theological diagnosis for the wounds of war that still live inside him. These responses reflect the ways in which religious narratives and particular interpretations of them can fail to attend to the ongoing realities of a death that does not go away. Can theology witness to what remains? What resources do theologians offer to Deacon Lee and Paul?

TRAUMA

The phenonemon of trauma is not new. There is no time in history when we can say that trauma began. Yet the study of trauma is relatively new, spanning a little over a century. Judith Herman's classic book, *Trauma and Recovery*, traces this history, beginning with the studies of "hysterical" women in the work of Charcot, Freud, and Breuer at the end of the nineteenth century. Studies of soldiers and the aftereffects of combat have dominated trauma studies, and the cycles of war in the twentieth century have taken posttraumatic stress disorder (PTSD) out of the private sphere and identified it as a political and national diagnosis.[3] Innovative technologies have also changed the shape of trauma studies and treatment. From expanding technologies in brain research to modifications in

1. Susan Brison, *Aftermath: Violence and the Remaking of a Self* (Princeton, NJ: Princeton University Press, 2002), 9.

2. See Cathy Caruth, "Preface," in *Trauma: Explorations in Memory* (Baltimore: Johns Hopkins University Press, 1995). Caruth writes, "But the study and treatment of trauma continue to face a crucial problem at the heart of this unique and difficult phenomenon: the problem of how to help relieve suffering, and how to understand the nature of the suffering, without eliminating the force and truth of the reality that trauma survivors face and quite often try to transmit to us" (vii).

3. See Edward Tick, "The Soul of the Nation," in *War and the Soul: Healing Our Nation's Veterans from Post-traumatic Stress Disorder* (Wheaton, IL: Quest Books, 2005). In that chapter he describes PTSD as a national diagnosis.

diagnoses of trauma disorders, we have more information about the impact of violent experiences and their effects on persons and communities. The study of trauma has also moved away from an exclusively individual look at the psyche to a study of cycles of history and the global and political effects of ongoing violence. The study of trauma has expanded to account for multiple levels of trauma: historical trauma, institutional trauma, and global trauma.

In each of these cases, the study focuses on the ways in which an overwhelming event or events of violence continue in the present, returning and impacting the present and future in unaccounted-for ways. In the past century, the study of trauma has circled around this enigma of the return of the past. Students of trauma attempt to discern and witness the marks of an event—a wound—that remains long after a precipitating event or events are over. These studies attempt to account for the marks of violence on human persons and communities. Trauma is often expressed in terms of what exceeds categories of comprehension, of what exceeds the human capacity to take in and process the external world. To think of this historically entails thinking about the ways in which events like genocide, mass natural disasters, wars, and foreign occupation of territories continue to shape and reshape communities and nations in the aftermath.

A central way of expressing this excess is in terms of the relationship between death and life. Trauma is described as an encounter with death. This encounter is not, however, a literal death but a way of describing a radical event or events that shatter all that one knows about the world and all the familiar ways of operating within it. A basic disconnection occurs from what one knows to be true and safe in the world. The event comes to be understood as a radical ending past which it is difficult, if not impossible, to conceive of life. The term "survival" captures something of the suspension of life in the aftermath of a traumatic event. The event becomes the defining event beyond which little can be conceived. Life takes on a fundamentally different definition, and the tentative and vulnerable quality of life in the aftermath means that it is life always mixed with death. This more mixed picture of death and life is present in Deacon Lee's statement; it is the "always here." No life after the storm is conceived apart from the storm. There is no access to life as it was before the storm. Instead, the storm is always present. The "always here" makes it impossible to see life and death in any straightforward relationship. Life and death are inextricably linked. The push to move beyond the event, to a new and pure place, is not just a misconception about traumatic survival; it a dangerous move that threatens to elide the realities of traumatic suffering. This move also makes possible suffering's repetition.

THEOLOGY

Theologians have always engaged the perennial questions of human suffering. In the face of the claim that the divine is in relationship with the world, the question is how to account for the suffering in the world. Is God responsible for the suffering? Does God will it? If God is all-powerful, why doesn't God fix the situation? Questions about God's will, power, and presence are all central for religious persons interpreting their experiences of suffering and the suffering around them. The most familiar theological discourse about suffering is known as theodicy, the theoretical practice of reconciling claims about the goodness of God with the presence of evil in the world. While theodicies provide logic for thinking through religious claims about God's nature and human suffering, they do not function effectively to address and respond to suffering. While theodicies might provide explanation, the degree to which explanations are helpful to the healing process is unclear.

In the mid- to late twentieth century, the question of suffering—divine suffering—was at the forefront of contemporary theology. Theologian Jürgen Moltmann revolutionized Christian interpretations of the crucifixion by claiming that God did not stand outside of the event of the cross but, rather, experienced the suffering. Reformulating the concept of the Trinity and dismantling notions of divine impassibility, Moltmann provided a Christian theological response to the Holocaust.[4] He was representative of many theologians trying to account for the violence and atrocities of the twentieth century. Classic affirmations about God are set alongside the extremities of human experience. Womanist and feminist theologians also countered traditional theologies of the cross, arguing that theologies of the cross have glorified suffering and provided sacred validation for the perpetuation of oppressive systems for persons and communities on the margins. While contested, the cross was understood to be the site from which questions of suffering and violence are primarily engaged.

Yet the rise of trauma studies, and theological engagement with it, calls attention to new aspects of the conversation about suffering. More recently, theologians following the conversations about trauma have started to think that trauma calls for a distinctive theological articulation. Unique dimensions of trauma move theology in new directions. If we are witnessing suffering in a new key in trauma, how does this change the discourse of theology? The work of theologians such as Flora Keshgegian, Serene Jones, Cynthia Hess, and Jennifer Beste suggests that trauma poses unique challenges, transforming the discourse about suffering, God, redemption, and theological anthropology in significant ways.[5] Their work testifies to the fact that trauma is not simply a category that can be confined to the fields of psychology and counseling; it had broadened to present profound challenges to epistemology, constructions of the self, and theological understandings of time.

4. Jürgen Moltmann, *The Crucified God: The Cross of Christ as the Foundation and Criticism of Christian Theology* (New York: Harper & Row, 1974).

5. See Jennifer Beste, *God and the Victim: Traumatic Intrusions on Grace and Freedom* (New York: Oxford University Press, 2007); Serene Jones, *Trauma and Grace: Theology in a Ruptured World* (Louisville, KY: Westminster John Knox, 2009); Flora Keshgegian, *Redeeming Memories: A Theology of Healing and Transformation* (Nashville: Abingdon Press, 2000), and *Time for Hope: Practices for Living in Today's World* (New York: Continuum International Publishing Group, 2006); and Cynthia Hess, *Sites of Violence, Sites of Grace: Christian Nonviolence and the Traumatized Self* (United Kingdom: Lexington Books, 2009).

While theologians have expanded our understanding of familiar terms such as "grace" and "hope," one aspect of Christian theology remains unexplored: the central narrative of death and life. I claim that trauma returns theologians to our primary claims about death and life, particularly as they are narrated in the events of cross and resurrection. Trauma disrupts this narrative, turning our attention to a more mixed terrain of remaining, one that I will identify as the "middle." By reexamining the relationship between death and life as it is narrated theologically, I am seeking a picture of redemption that adequately accounts for traumatic suffering, that speaks to divine presence and power in light of what we know about trauma. This picture of redemption cannot emerge by interpreting death and life in opposition to each other. Instead, theology must account for the excess, or remainder, of death in life that is central to trauma. This reconfiguration of death and life, viewed through the lens of trauma, unearths a distinctive theology that can witness the realities of the aftermath of trauma.

Stories of redemption span the Hebrew and Christian Scriptures and contribute to a sweeping vision of creation, fall, and restoration. The events of Jesus' cross and resurrection are often interpreted, in Christian theology, as the climax of a grand redemptive narrative. How do we interpret these events? This narrative of death and life becomes the basis for articulating God's redemptive work on behalf of the world. It also serves as a template for orienting Christian believers in the life of faith. The events of Jesus' death and resurrection provide a lens through which Christian identity is forged. These Gospel accounts of Jesus' death and resurrection—taught, preached, and practiced within Christian communities—are understood to speak to the many deaths and rebirths, endings and beginnings, that human beings experience. They provide meaning to these experiences. The Christian claim is that through these events, redemption is achieved.

Traumatic experience, insofar as it reconfigures the relationship between death and life, challenges familiar interpretations of redemption. Death is not something concluded and life a fresh start and a new beginning. Insofar as the redemptive narrative is read with death and life at opposite poles, it will fail to witness the experience of trauma. The redemptive narrative of cross and resurrection is often read in a linear fashion in which life (resurrection) is victorious over death. While this outlook can provide a sense of promise and hope, the linear reading of life over-and-against death runs certain dangers. It can gloss over difficulty, casting it within a larger framework in which the new replaces the old, and in which good inevitably wins out over evil. Death is concluded and new life is ushered in. Religious scholars across a range of theological perspectives—from Walter Brueggemann to Alan Lewis to Cornel West—recognize the dangers in reading death (cross) and life (resurrection) in this particular configuration.[6]

6. See Walter Brueggemann, "Reading from the Day 'In Between,'" in *The Shadow of Glory: Reading the New Testament after the Holocaust*, ed. Tod Linafelt (New York: Routledge, 2002); Alan Lewis, *Between Cross and Resurrection: A Theology of Holy Saturday* (Grand Rapids: Wm. B Eerdmans Publishing Co., 2001); Cornel West, "A Philosophical View of Easter," and "Subversive Joy and Revolutionary Patience in Black Christianity," in *The Cornel West Reader* (New York: Basic Civitas Books, 1999).

This thrust toward life can foster Christian triumphalism and supercessionism. If redemption is depicted as a happy or victorious ending in which life wins out over death, or in which death is somehow concluded/ended, such a depiction runs the risk of glossing over a more mixed experience of death and life.

If resurrection is the event of new life in Christian theology, reconciling these claims with the experience of survival in which life is not experienced as new, or as better, is difficult. Insofar as resurrection is proclaimed as life conquering or life victorious over death, it does not speak to the realities of traumatic suffering. In fact, one must recognize the ways in which resurrection proclamations may gloss over and negate the difficult experience of life in the aftermath of death. Theology, in its narration of death and life, can fuel the "get over it already" statements that Deacon Lee and others hear in the aftermath of Hurricane Katrina. The rush to life can belie the realities of death in life.[7] To what degree is the central narrative of death/life in Christianity able to attest to this complex experience of remaining in the aftermath of violence?

A rereading of these two events—death and resurrection—is timely in light of what we know about trauma. The dynamics of traumatic experience press Christian discourse beyond the site of the cross to think about what it means to live in the aftermath of death. Studies in trauma suggest that trauma has a double structure: the actual occurrence of a violent event(s) and a belated awakening to the event.[8] Trauma is not solely located in the actual event but, instead, encompasses the return of that event, the ways in which the event is not concluded. This phenomenon is described in different ways, but the nature of trauma is such that an inability to fully process an event means that it returns. This return distinguishes trauma and suffering. Suffering is what, in time, can be integrated into one's understanding of the world. Trauma is what is not integrated in time; it is the difference between a closed and an open wound. Trauma is an open wound. For those who survive trauma, the experience of trauma can be likened to a death. But the reality is that death has not ended; instead, it persists. The experience of survival is one in which life, as it once was, cannot be retrieved. However, the promise of life ahead cannot be envisioned.

The structure of trauma introduces what I refer to as the "middle"—the figurative site in which death and life are no longer bounded. Instead, the middle speaks to the perplexing space of survival. It is a largely untheologized site, because the middle is overshadowed by the other two events. Because of its

7. According to Brueggemann, "The church must and will continue its Easter declaration or it ceases to be the church. But the Shoah, so it seems to me, is uncompromising in its insistence that the second day looms larger, deeper, and more seriously than we had noticed in the drama we Christians regularly confess and claim. The rush to the third day must be profoundly slowed" (Brueggemann, "Reading," 111).

8. See Caruth, *Trauma.* As Caruth writes, "The impact of the traumatic event lies precisely in its belatedness, in its refusal to be simply located, in its insistent appearance outside the boundaries of any single place or time" (9). "The pathology consists, rather, solely in the structure of its experience or reception: the event is not assimilated or experienced fully at the time, but only belatedly, in its repeated possession of the one who experiences it" (4).

precarious positioning, the middle can easily be covered over and ignored. It is subject to the elisions of time, body, and language and therefore is difficult to witness. The good news of Christianity for those who experience trauma rests in the capacity to theologize this middle. It does not rest in either the event of the cross or resurrection, but instead in the movements between the two—movements that I identify through the concept of witness. The good news lies in the ability of Christian theology to witness between death and life, in its ability to forge a new discourse between the two.

The work of this book is to uncover this middle discourse—to resist the redemptive gloss that can often be placed, harmfully, over experiences of suffering and to orient us differently to the death-life narrative at the heart of the Christian tradition. Looking from the middle, we are oriented to suffering in a different way—always in its dislocation, its distance, and its fragmentation. This orientation calls for a theology of witness in which we cannot assume presence or straightforward reception of a violent event but, instead, contend with excess of violence and its tenuous reception. Without witnessing to what does not go away, to what remains, theology fails to provide a sufficient account of redemption. The challenge to theology, then, is to account for what exceeds death yet cannot be interpreted as new life. The challenge is to account for what remains—to provide a discourse of remaining that can speak to life in the aftermath and to the shattering of familiar frameworks by which persons and communities have oriented themselves in the world. Theology must navigate uncharted waters in the attempt to witness experiences that "fall outside the range."[9]

METHOD

Standing in the Lower Ninth Ward with Deacon Lee, I am reminded of the way that I learned theology: spatially. The work of theology was presented to me as the work of cartography, the work of theologians mapping the landscape of Christian faith, the work of providing markers and directions for believers attempting to orient themselves in the life of faith.[10] As cartographer, the theologian

9. This is terminology from the *Diagnostic and Statistical Manual III* (Washington, DC: American Psychiatric Association, 1980). For posttraumatic stress disorder in particular, the *DSM-III* states, "The essential feature is the development of characteristic symptoms following a psychologically traumatic event that is generally outside the range of usual human experience" (309.81). One should note that the *DSM-III's* description of PTSD, notwithstanding its unfortunate designation as a "disorder," encompasses the physical and psychological effects of a wide range of traumatic events including, but not limited to, military combat, personal assault, the threat of physical harm, the threat of a loved one's physical harm, natural disasters or disasters of either intentional or accidental human design.

10. The cartographical metaphor comes from Serene Jones, *Feminist Theory and Christian Theology: Cartographies of Grace* (Minneapolis: Augsburg Fortress Press, 2000). "I find the image of mapping to be a useful metaphor in describing this relationship (between feminist theory and feminist theology). Taking up the role of cartographer, in the pages ahead, I lay feminist theory over the terrain or landscape of Christian doctrine to see how the lines of theory might map the contours of

looks out over the expansive landscape of Christian faith. She or he attempts to map this landscape, providing believers with signposts and directions for faithful living. Doctrines, teachings of the faith, are theological markers. Christian doctrines, insofar as they are professed and practiced, shape human identity. They give form to human life, shaping individuals and communities. Theologian Serene Jones refers to doctrines both as "imaginative lenses" for viewing the world and as conceptual spaces that we inhabit.[11]

By probing the relationship between cross and resurrection in connection to the experience of death and life in trauma, I am attempting to find, in Jones's words, a place to inhabit for those persons and communities that have experienced trauma. In this sense, theology is understood to be a healing discourse, a discourse that seeks to transform lived realities. But the reality of trauma is such that it cannot be isolated to particular persons. Marking this space is not simply a way of advocating for persons who are unaccounted for. Instead, attempting to map the experiences of trauma comes from my conviction that our lives are inextricably bound together. Given what we know about the historical dimensions of trauma, no one remains untouched by overwhelming violence.[12] Trauma becomes not simply a detour on the map of faith but, rather, a significant reworking of the entire map.

Twenty-nine months after the floodwaters forged through this neighborhood, the remains are still there. Amid talk about rebuilding and restoring, these particular streets of New Orleans are not restored. The streets and the land bear the marks of an overwhelming storm. Long after persons and communities experience trauma, the storm is still there.[13] The mapping metaphor returns to me. How do I map the razed terrain of the Lower Ninth Ward? There is something in

---

theology" (19). This metaphor also orients the introductory theology textbook *Constructive Theology*. See Serene Jones and Paul Lakeland, eds., *Constructive Theology: A Contemporary Approach to Classical Themes* (Minneapolis: Fortress, 2005). A metaphor used for doctrines therein is "theological landscapes," according to which "doctrines are like maps" and the landscape of beliefs is "a vast and complex terrain holding within its borders all those images, stories, concepts, practices and feelings that make up the sum total of 'what we believe in'" (9).

11. See Jones, *Feminist Theory*, 16–17; also Serene Jones, "Hope Deferred: Theological Reflections on Reproductive Loss," in *Modern Theology* 17, no. 2 (April 2001): 227–45.

12. See Marjorie Suchocki, *Fall to Violence: Original Sin in Relational Theology* (New York: Continuum, 1995). I am not diminishing the experience of those who encounter and survive personal violence. The danger, here, is to universalize trauma—to somehow incorporate it into the human condition. But the study of trauma suggests that there is a fragility of human persons to the widescale violence that has caused us to see that events cannot be isolated to time/space but curiously and insidiously travel. They do not respect borders. In this sense, we inherit/receive the effects of these events in ways that we have not accounted for—especially theologically.

13. See Bessel van der Kolk, "The Body Keeps the Score," in *Harvard Review of Psychiatry* 1, no. 5 (1994). For example, the physical and psychological effects of Katrina are grossly evident, with post-Katrina death and morbidity rates escalating. These findings are available in a report compiled by Dr. Kevin U. Stephens, health director for the City of New Orleans, and staff: Kevin U. Stephens Sr., David Grew, Karen Chin, Paul Kadetz, P. Gregg Greenough, Frederick M. Burkle Jr., Sandra L. Robinson, and Evangeline R. Franklin, "Excess Mortality in the Aftermath of Hurricane Katrina: A Preliminary Report," in *Disaster Medicine and Public Health Preparedness* 1, no. 1 (2007): 15–20. See also Steve Sternberg, "New Orleans Deaths up 47%," *USA Today*, June 22, 2007.

the visible landscape of New Orleans that mirrors the internal processes of persons and communities living on in the aftermath of trauma. Using this tangible image of land and cartography, I want to forge an understanding of redemption that witnesses to the shattering of lives by overwhelming violence. The challenge in writing about trauma is that trauma is the experience that is the most difficult to put into language and to conceptualize; it is the unimaginable territory. The language of theology must, I argue, take the form of witness and testimony.

My readings aim, then, to express the testimonial dimension of Christian discourse.[14] To render in language what is inarticulable and often linguistically elided is the persistent challenge of theological discourse. Theologian Hans Urs von Balthasar reminds us that our theological forms often fall short of attesting to the fullness of God's being; this point was a driving force behind his development of a theological aesthetics. But the same is true, as well, about inarticulable experiences of violence. Keen awareness of what language speaks—and fails to speak—demands that we continually acknowledge that some forms of language are insufficient to account for certain realities, whether the reality of God's beauty or the ineffability of human violence. Continually questioning the relationship between form (of language) and its purpose (representing what is inexpressible) is not an aesthetic luxury but a necessity.[15]

I read the biblical and theological texts with particular attention to their literary and rhetorical dimensions. The language of theology cannot be simply reduced to one logic or one single interpretation. In this case, they cannot yield a simple interpretation of redemption. Reading through the lens of trauma, my readings press the edges of these frameworks, blurring the lines of logic precisely because the phenomenon of trauma draws us to the enigma of what remains. In the end, the handing over and reception of these texts (their interpretation) is more tenuous. If they do not yield what we expect, what do they yield? It is precisely at the edges of comprehension, the places where comprehension fails, that something else emerges and the possibility of something else arises.

Trauma poses deep challenges to theology in terms of the radicality of suffering. It exposes the impossibility of professing Christian claims—of God's presence and of human goodness. In constructive theological work on trauma, it is common to interpret the insights of trauma as the problems posed to theological claims and teachings; theology must answer to these in order to provide an

14. For more on the testimonial dimension of Christian discourse, see Rebecca Chopp, "Theology and the Poetics of Testimony," in *Converging on Culture: Theologians in Dialogue with Cultural Analysis and Criticism*, ed. Delwin Brown, Sheila Greeve Davaney, Kathryn Tanner (New York: Oxford University Press, 2001), 56–70; John Beverly, *Testimonio: On the Politics of Truth* (Minneapolis: University of Minnesota Press, 2004).

15. For recent works that speak to the importance of reviving theological aesthetics in response to violence, see Grace Jantzen, "Beauty for Ashes," *Literature & Theology* 16, no. 4 (December 2002), that initiated her trilogy and posthumous volumes. See also Alejandro Garcia-Rivera, *The Community of the Beautiful* (Collegeville, MN: Liturgical Press, 1999); Roberto Goizueta, *Christ Our Companion* (Maryknoll, NY: Orbis, 2009); and Don Saliers, "Beauty and Terror," in *Minding the Spirit: The Study of Christian Spirituality*, ed. Elizabeth A. Dreyer and Mark S. Burrows (Baltimore: Johns Hopkins University Press, 2005).

adequate account or response to traumatic suffering. Yet the claim that I am making here is slightly different: the insights of trauma actually constitute the hermeneutical lens through which an alternative theological vision of healing and redemption emerges. This lens casts the relationship between death and life in the Christian narrative in a much more complex light. Trauma is the key to articulating a theology of redemption rather than the problem around which theology must navigate. The dynamics of trauma guide my readings, and I refer to them as the "lens of trauma" through which theological claims about healing and redemption must be newly forged. Reading through this shattered lens, we discover things we had not noticed before—things that have been, and continue to be, covered over.

The lens of trauma turns us to these familiar texts in a different way. In *Becoming Divine: Towards a Feminist Philosophy of Religion*, theologian Grace Jantzen articulates a way of reading between the lines of Christian theology.[16] These familiar lines are often scripted according to a binary, oppositional logic that excludes certain truths from being told. Jantzen enacts a process of "double reading" that defamiliarizes and disorients readers from these texts, in an attempt to draw attention to the gaps in reading.[17] This process of reading disrupts the binary logic and makes room for new forms of language. Jantzen identifies it as a new imaginary. Although she is not offering this specifically in relationship to trauma, this way of reading is consistent with the lens of trauma as I employ it here. This way of reading reflects the salient and keenest insights of deconstruction and poststructuralism; these approaches to reading texts aim to disconnect us from familiar logic and patterns of reading while simultaneously displaying a "surplus" emerging within the process of reading.[18] The challenge of reading the middle is that it escapes familiar logic and is always in danger of being consumed or silenced by it. Enacting the double reading proposed by Jantzen becomes a

16. See especially chap. 3 of Grace Jantzen, *Becoming Divine: Towards a Feminist Philosophy of Religion* (Bloomington: Indiana University Press, 1999).

17. "Double reading" involves a careful reading of the initial text, and it looks within that text for the "rupture that opens up the alternative" (Jantzen, *Becoming Divine*, 61–64). Jantzen writes, "In terms of the philosophy of religion, therefore, the work of deconstruction would not only deliver a double gesture which would overturn traditional binaries and open up conceptual space between them. It will also challenge the institutionalized methodology and pedagogy by which binaries are maintained, the social practices by which alternatives—in this case specifically feminist alternatives—are excluded or marginalized" (64).

18. I take Rieger's novel use of the concept of surplus that he draws from Jacques Lacan. For an introduction to the concept of surplus, see Joerg Rieger, *Christ and Empire: From Paul to Postcolonial Times* (Minneapolis: Fortress Press, 2007), 9–11. Rieger speaks of a "christological surplus" as that which cannot be reduced to the status quo, that cannot be fully contained, and that exceeds the boundaries of imperial control. He writes in *Christ and Empire*, "The real of Christ . . . not only holds up a mirror to the reality of the status quo but also creates a christological surplus that cannot be captured by this reality and thus points beyond it" (10). He also speaks about the tradition of Christianity in this way as well, saying, "For our interpretation of the creeds this means that creeds cannot be reduced to purely theological statements, but neither can they be reduced to purely political statements. Reading between the lines of theological statements, we need to identify the connection of theology and life and of theology and empire. Where do we find ambivalence? Is there a surplus? Which theological claims refuse to be dictated by the demands of empire?" (80).

way of witnessing to what often goes unwitnessed. At its best, this practice of reading is consonant with what I understand to be the difficult task of witnessing to what exceeds the boundaries of death.

OUTLINE

I outline this lens of trauma in chapter 1 by situating my work within the field of trauma studies, more specifically trauma theory. In this chapter, I bring an understanding of the term "witness" in trauma to bear on theological concepts of witness. Examining the structure and dynamics of witness outlined in contemporary trauma theory, I begin to forge a theological concept of witness from within the experience of trauma. Locating witness between the Christian narrative of death and life, cross and resurrection, I turn in the next two chapters to explore the middle territory. In chapter 2, I examine Holy Saturday, the theological middle day between death and life. I work with the theology of Hans Urs von Balthasar and Adrienne von Speyr, who develop the middle site in order to attest to the distinctive message of redemption from Holy Saturday. Looking through this lens, what do we see? In chapter 3, I turn to a reading of the Johannine Gospel and its witness to the middle movements of the disciples between cross and resurrection.[19] Looking through this lens, what we do we see? In both cases, I display the difficult movements of witnessing to events that exceed the parameters of death and yet cannot so easily be identified as life. Instead, these readings reveal the complex territory of witnessing to the ongoing traces of death in life. These texts become, if read through this lens, survival texts, witnessing to life in its remaining. As the biblical and theological texts become less familiar, the testimonial aspect of these texts emerges. They trace the ways in which certain aspects of the narrative are elided and smoothed over in service of particular interpretations. The traumatic lens focuses the reader on what remains.

These texts testify to this difficult aftermath, but they do even more. They testify to the unique movements of witnesses between death and life. This witness can often be covered over, skipped over, and rendered theologically insignificant. Yet witness, as I uncover it here, suggests an orientation to suffering that is distinctive and necessary, given the nature of ongoing suffering. Whereas redemption has classically been linked to the event of suffering (cross) or to the miraculous event of life (resurrection), these readings center on the process of witnessing. In chapter 4, I align this movement of witness with the interstitial figure of the Spirit moving between cross and resurrection. As death and life come into a curious relationship in the middle, the figure of the Spirit emerges in

19. I am appealing to a tradition of biblical theology that Catherine Keller describes as a "scriptural-literary hermeneutic" in her *Face of the Deep: A Theology of Becoming* (New York: Routledge, 2003). There she writes, "This theology continues an attempt, necessarily from inside the biblical tradition, to heal that desiccating hope" (xvii).

unanticipated ways. Spirit emerges as witness in both the biblical and theological texts. In the territory where the death on the cross extends beyond the cross and the tenuousness of life is ever palpable, Spirit—both human and divine—takes shape. In the midst of trauma, conceiving of divine presence is impossible. Here, I begin to imagine the form of presence and power arising in the places where life is least discernible. Divine power and presence take the form of witness.

When thinking about the cycles of trauma—individual, historical, and global—it is critical to think in terms of the traces of the events, the marks they leave in their wake. The challenge in addressing trauma is to continually resist the temptation to cover over—to elide—the suffering in an effort to witness it. The challenge is to attend to the ways in which violence continues to mark persons and communities long after the violent event. This work of resisting and attending is the work of the Spirit. The work of the Spirit is often cast in terms of a forward movement—as a drive to life, and as the re-creative and renewing force of God. But a theology of the Spirit, as I develop it here, is less clearly the life principle and more a sustaining power that continually witnesses the ruptures, moving between death and life. The final chapter imagines the form of this witness within contexts of trauma and its aftermath. What would it mean for us to think about these movements as redemptive?

CONCLUSION

Deacon Lee leans out the window of his van as we walk around his property. I ask him what it was like to grow up here. He tells me that the streets were always filled with kids playing after school, biking to the corner store, and playing street ball. His family and neighbors are scattered. They are all "making their way," he says, trying to figure out how to get by. He does not know if they will make it back to the Ninth Ward. They are, like many others, still haggling with insurance companies over the value of their property. I am aware, when listening to him, that even if the corner stores, schools, and homes are rebuilt, there are a million little things they cannot get back.

This is not new and victorious life. It is more uncertain, tentative, and murky. It calls for unique theological recognition and expression. This book attempts to honor the ways in which people move on and envision life where no signs of life can be found. These experiences point to a different way of envisioning life in the Spirit. It is a theology of the Spirit birthed from the middle rather than one birthed from the resurrection event. The presence of the Spirit is more fragile and unrecognizable in the middle space. It is divine presence marked by absence. Forsakenness, abandonment, and alienation are truths of the cross that remain, extending beyond death to transform the landscape of life. The question for Christian theology is this: is this remainder a threat to proclamations of resurrection, or is this remainder the seeds of witness upon which all resurrection claims must be grounded?

Trauma forces us beyond a familiar theological paradigm of life and death, and places us, instead, on the razed terrain of what remains. Trauma presses theologians to seek new language to express God's relationship to the world. This is not a new task. In fact, it is the perennial work of theology. Amid the claims about redemption and new life, there must be theologians who testify to the undertow, to witness the pull of death in the tenuous territory of the aftermath. As death and life are thought to be in a complex relationship to each other, the depiction of redemption begins to shift. By linking redemption so closely to one event or the other, we can run the risk of elevating suffering or of negating it. But what if we began to see the work of witnessing, the work of the Spirit between death and life, as redemptive? The terrain is more perilous, and it will press us to come up against the question of whether redemptive language has run its course. The capacity to think beyond an ending is, I believe, a capacity developed and exercised in the face of traumatic suffering. This hermeneutic not only provides a way of reading between the lines for experiences that are not typically accounted for in Christian discourse; it provides a way of interpreting Christian discourse itself and the continual search for new language and forms to speak about God's movement in the world.

Chapter 1

Witnessing Trauma

Therefore, survival means what? Living over, living through.[1]

Trauma is the suffering that does not go away. The study of trauma is the study of what remains. The phenomenon of trauma's remainder presents challenges to our understanding of what constitutes an experience and, subsequently, what it means to witness an experience. In the aftermath of violence, persons and communities are challenged to orient themselves in the aftermath of events that shatter familiar frameworks of meaning and trust. In turn, people surrounding them struggle to witness the effects of suffering that often cannot be brought into speech and symptoms that persist long after an event is over. Witnessing the suffering that remains involves encountering the ways in which death pervades life; it entails attesting to the temporal distortions and epistemological ruptures of an experience that exceeds a radical ending yet has no pure beginning. Looking through the lens of trauma, the pressing questions for theology are: Can theology witness to this suffering that does not go away, to the storm that is "always here"? If so, how?

---

1. Elie Wiesel, "Matters of Survival: A Conversation," in Elie Wiesel and Timothy K. Beal, *Strange Fire: Reading the Bible after the Holocaust* (New York: New York University Press, 2000), 23.

"Witness" is a term organic to Christian theology. My claim in this chapter is that the study of trauma moves us to rethink witness, particularly as it relates to witnessing the suffering that remains. Current studies in trauma complicate interpretations of witness, by turning us to a "crisis of witness" at the heart of our central narrative of death and life, cross and resurrection. Looking through the lens of trauma, the complex practice of witnessing suffering draws theology back to its most familiar theological claims about death and life. We are confronted with the enigma of suffering at the heart of the Christian narrative of passion and resurrection.[2] What does it mean that life is connected to an event of death? What does it mean to remain in the aftermath of that death? What form of life arises there, if any? Looking through this shattered lens, we approach these questions differently and are attentive to dimensions of these texts that often get covered over. We come to see that the relationship between death and life is a more mixed one. Death is not an event that is concluded. Neither is life a victorious event that stands on the other side of death. Instead, trauma uncovers a middle to this narrative; it reveals a theological territory of remaining.

By listening to the language of theology through the discourse of trauma, I unearth a dimension of theological witness that has the potential to speak to suffering that persists, that remains. To witness is a complex and often indirect task. To account for and recognize suffering in its remaining is to be subject to multiple elisions. In *Martyrdom and Memory*, Elizabeth Castelli suggests that the Christian tradition has this more textured concept of witness inscribed within it. However, it has been overwhelmed by dominant interpretations of witness as martyrdom and self-sacrifice, interpretations rooted in the event of death. She writes, "What if, instead, we retrieved and critically engaged the dimension of the term [martyr] that emphasizes a different range of ethical options: witnessing, truth-telling, testimony? . . . Perhaps the figure of 'the martyr' that we need to mobilize here is not the one who sacrifices him- or herself but the one whose compulsion is to witness and to provide testimony."[3] Castelli gestures toward this eclipsed concept of witness, believing that, if recovered, it could turn us to see suffering differently. This concept, I claim, could turn us to attend to suffering in its remaining.

Revisiting texts at the intersection of death and life, cross and resurrection, I reveal the potential of these texts to speak to the complex process of witnessing to truths that often lie buried and are covered over. I reclaim the testimonial power of these texts, to speak to the realities of death's persistence and also to speak to a different form of life arising in this middle territory, the territory of remaining. Insofar as theology ascribes to a certain governing logic of the passion and resurrection, theology is complicit in covering over suffering, in offering a redemptive gloss over its deep wound. Wedded to particular ways of reading

2. See Cathy Caruth, ed., "Introduction," in *Trauma: Explorations in Memory* (Baltimore: Johns Hopkins University Press, 1995).

3. Elizabeth Castelli, *Martyrdom and Memory: Gender Theory and Religion* (New York: Columbia University Press, 2004), 203.

the narrative of death and life, theology can elide a narrative of remaining that speaks to the complexities of ongoing suffering.

In this chapter, I examine the enigma of suffering as it has come to be known in the twentieth-century term "trauma." These discussions have moved from an analysis of individual suffering to interpreting trauma as a symptom of history. The phenomenon of trauma brings theology to a new ignorance, unsettling familiar categories and placing the discourse of theology in a more tenuous place.[4] But this shifting ground underfoot also unearths a discourse of remaining. If theology can "listen through the radical disruption and gaps of traumatic experience," something new arises from within the discourse itself. Trauma is not the problem presented to theology from outside, but the key to an aspect of witness that has been lost in the interpretive tradition. Theology does not need to turn outside to respond to the challenges of trauma but, rather, turn within to discover a language of remaining. The language of trauma thus resonates with something deep within the discourse of theology.

I develop this internal witness by reading biblical and theological texts, exploring a language of remaining that is often elided. I track this language and the elisions in relationship to literary readings associated with trauma theory, specifically the work of Cathy Caruth. The language of remaining within theology speaks back to trauma theory, offering a distinctive vocabulary to think about the challenges of traumatic survival. In the end, the language of remaining also provides a way, within theology, to reframe and reengage questions about divine presence in suffering. The classic question, "Where is God in the midst of suffering?" comes to new expression if read through a traumatic lens. To interpret theology from the middle, I create theological space for dimensions of experiences that are often unregistered and invisible.

Multiple ways to enter the discussion of trauma are available. Note that I am not engaging trauma in psychiatric terms but in relationship to the concept of trauma as it appears in survivor texts and clinical texts. I am not aiming to do a psychological assessment of trauma or even, more theologically close to home, aiming to provide a theology of pastoral care. My primary aim is to probe the interpretive frameworks of theology and to reexamine the narratives that frame Christian claims about suffering. In the aftermath of trauma, these frameworks often fail to speak to the depth of suffering that persons experience; they shatter. In my readings, I meet these texts in their shattering; I listen for the ways in which language falters and is transformed into the language of testimony and survival. My engagement with trauma is at the site of the literary, a site where psychoanalysis and theology enact a textual witness to suffering. I reexamine the theological "lexicon" for its potential to speak in and beyond its limits, in and beyond the shattering of its own interpretive frameworks.[5]

4. Cathy Caruth describes the interdisciplinary venture of trauma studies as one in which disciplines gather around the enigma of suffering and listen "through the radical disruption and gaps of traumatic experience" (Caruth, "Introduction," 4).

5. Castelli, *Martyrdom*, 203.

THE LENS OF TRAUMA

Trauma begins with an event or series of events that are too much to bear. The experience is beyond the "'edge" of what is possible to perceive and respond to, beyond what we are able to include in our identities, as individuals or communities.[6]

Speaking about his time in Vietnam as a military intelligence officer, Paul says that he remains haunted by his work there—its successes and its failures. Vietnam, Desert Storm, and Iraq presented him with a series of crises—moral, historical, and spiritual—that were never fully resolved; these crises continue to live inside him. The difficulty for Paul, as with many who have experienced situations of overwhelming violence, lies in locating, naming, and identifying the suffering. The roaming character of the suffering haunts him. Aspects of those war experiences remain with him, but they do so in ways that continually escape him. He is always encountering the enigma of his own suffering. As someone who seeks to hear something of his experience, I, too, am drawn into this enigma.

Trauma is distinguished from other experiences of suffering in that a person's capacity to respond to and integrate the experience is severely impaired. Due to the force and the unexpected nature of the precipitating event, the normal pathways by which a person takes in, processes, and interprets an experience shut down, resulting in a range of symptoms. One of the most defining symptoms of trauma is the persistent intrusive and distressing images or recollections of the traumatic event.[7] Fragments of the past return in the present. Given the frequent and unpredictable intrusions of the past into the present, life, for many survivors, is reorganized around the trauma. In all cases of trauma, a person's relationship to herself and to others is fundamentally altered in response to an event.[8] In the aftermath of trauma, the relationship to one's own physical body and to other bodies, as well as one's access to language and the ability to communicate with others, is profoundly affected.

Something of a violent experience remains, and its remaining is a continual encounter with the enigma of suffering. Although a range of symptoms attach to trauma and traumatic experiences, the enigma of suffering speaks to three broad alterations that occur: alterations in time, body, and word. These three are

---

6. Arlene Audergon, "Collective Trauma: The Nightmare of History," *Psychotherapy and Politics International* 2, no. 1 (2004): 19.

7. Although experiences may be designated traumatic in nature, not all persons who experience them are considered to be traumatized. The designation of PTSD (posttraumatic stress disorder) is not assigned to all people who experience insurmountable violence; instead, persons who are designated with the disorder are unable, in time, to regain an adequate level of functioning in the world. The symptoms persist and overtake their daily life.

8. See Kali Tal, *Worlds of Hurt: Reading the Literatures of Trauma* (Cambridge: Cambridge University Press, 1996). "An individual is traumatized by a life-threatening event that displaces his or her preconceived notions about the world. Trauma is enacted in a liminal state, outside the bounds of 'normal' human experience, and the subject is radically ungrounded" (15).

not exhaustive, but they represent distinctive aspects of trauma that constitute what I refer to as the "lens of trauma." When we consider the ways in which we normally function in the world, we understand ourselves to be temporally oriented. We have a past that we relate to through processes of memory; we also experience the present and, in turn, have the capacity to imagine and live into the future. We often think of these as progressive. The past is behind, the future ahead, and the present is the viewpoint from which we relate to both. The central problem of trauma is a temporal one. The past does not stay, so to speak, in the past. Instead, it invades the present, returning in such a way that the present becomes not only an enactment of the past but an enactment about what was not fully known or grasped.

There is a familiar saying: time heals all wounds. Trauma represents an antithesis to this statement. In fact, in trauma, distortions in time constitute the wound. The problem of temporality is at the root of the phenomenon of trauma. Trauma is not a one-time event. Instead, trauma speaks to an event in its excess. The fact that the event was not fully integrated at the time means that something of that event returns at a later time. Its unintegrated nature makes it difficult to locate the suffering in any one place or time.[9] Sigmund Freud first indicated that timing was a—if not the—defining factor distinguishing traumatic experiences from other experiences of pain and suffering. When Freud began to work with soldiers returning home from World War I, he made a simple but profound observation: the past does not stay in the past. Veterans were experiencing vivid war scenes in the form of haunting nightmares or flashbacks. The past was flashing back to them, carrying them psychically and physically back to the scene of the action. Their bodies were braced as if the threat were imminent. The veterans were not simply remembering the past; they were reenacting it in the present. Freud was perplexed by the ways in which time—past and present—was distorted for these veterans. The nightmares were causing a great deal of psychic suffering precisely because they could not be distinguished from present reality.

Up to this point in his thought, Freud had interpreted dreams, whether frightening or pleasurable, as unconscious attempts to fulfill wishes. The dreams reflected the mind's attempt to bring certain desires into being. Traumatic flashbacks defied this theory. What was returning for these veterans was not what was desired but, instead, what was profoundly undesirable and haunting. The flashbacks also seemed to put one into a state of uncontrollable fright, as if the

9. There is also a "too soon" aspect to trauma. See Sigmund Freud, *Beyond the Pleasure Principle*, ed. and trans. James Strachey (New York: Liveright Publishing, 1961); Freud writes, "The study of dreams may be considered the most trustworthy method of investigating deep mental processes. Now dreams occurring in traumatic neuroses have the characteristic of repeatedly bringing the patient back into the situation of his accident, a situation from which he wakes up in another fright. This astonishes people far too little. . . . We may argue that the function of dreaming, like so much else, is upset in this [the traumatized] condition and diverted from its purposes, or we may be driven to reflect on the mysterious masochistic trends of the ego" (7–8). See also Cathy Caruth, *Unclaimed Experience: Trauma, Narrative and History* (Baltimore: Johns Hopkins University Press, 1996), 16–18.

psyche was not just replaying a terrible experience of the past but was encountering something frighteningly new—something it did not know from the past.

Freud's observations of these "returns" became the basis for theorizing a double structure of trauma.[10] In his observations, the veterans were manifesting symptoms of an earlier experience, but these returns were also sites of intense suffering. There is the actual experience on the battlefield, and then there is the flashback, a reliving of that event. Freud began to speculate that the root of traumatic suffering was the confusion in the relationship between the two—in the experience of time. The suffering experienced by veterans, he noted, is a suffering that arises from a missed event, from an event that escaped comprehension. The trauma is not located in the past but instead is located in the gap between the occurrence of the traumatic event and a subsequent awakening to it. The suffering does not solely lie in the violence of trauma's impact (in its happening) but in the ways in which that happening, that occurrence, was not known or grasped at that time. The veterans were suffering, according to Freud, from this belatedness.

The return of the event in the form of fragmentary visions, flashbacks, and symptoms displaced from their context is an intrusion into life. Death returns in an unrecognizable and ungrasped form; life then becomes a perplexing encounter and continual engagement with death. What happens is that the past event—both what is known about it and what is inaccessible to cognition—enters into the present in a way that confuses a trajectory of past, present, and future. In the present, these veterans were *in the past*. The experiences were haunting them, and present life became organized under the threat of the return. We can thus imagine that trauma not only impairs one's ability to reckon with the past but also to imagine the future. Any planning capacity becomes centered on protecting oneself from being triggered by the past.

Freud's exploration of these unwanted returns led him to revamp some of his most fundamental theories.[11] At the heart of combat neuroses is the return of an undesirable and unknown experience. The past event ceases to be contained in the past. Our relationship to the past is often expressed in terms of memories and our ability to access them. But the veterans, according to Freud, were not accessing their memories of what happened. Instead, these fragmented clips of the past were overtaking and possessing the individual. What Freud is probing is the enigma of experience—the fact that an event can be so strong and forceful yet somehow remain unregistered in conscious experience. As a result, the experience returns as something profoundly unexperienced and unknown.

The suffering that remains also alters a relationship with body and word. We are embodied, moving in the world through a complex web of physical processes. We are grounded in the world through our bodies. When someone experiences trauma, the body draws all of its resources together to respond to the threat. Basic functioning processes in the body are unable to sustain the level of impact,

10. Later interpreters of Freud, namely Jacques Lacan and Cathy Caruth, develop this theme. In particular, see Caruth, *Unclaimed Experience*, and Jacques Lacan, *The Four Fundamental Concepts of Psycho-Analysis* (New York: W. W. Norton & Company, 1981).

11. Namely his theory of dreams and his theory of the death drive.

and a person's ability to regulate his body in response to the physical world is severely impaired. With the rise of neurobiological studies of trauma at the turn of the twenty-first century, we can more accurately track the ways in which over-whelming experiences of violence alter a person's fundamental biology. Most significant, however, is the research that suggests the body experiences trauma in ways that escape cognitive functioning and awareness. In cases in which the body is responding to extreme levels of stress, areas of the brain shut down. Typically, sensations are received and registered through coordinating functions of the limbic system and the prefrontal cortex. However, traumatic impact is shown to limit the function of the limbic system, therefore stopping the system from passing along the experience to the prefrontal cortex, the part of the brain that assigns to an experience language and meaning. These studies suggest that the body bears the marks of trauma in ways that escape cognitive knowledge.[12]

The third aspect of trauma is the loss of one's ability to register the event and its effects through the use of language. As humans, through language and speech we can put words to our experiences and can interpret our world in rich and imaginative ways. This ties closely with the insights about the bodily impact of trauma. In trauma, the access to speech is, in many cases, limited, and this loss of speech intensifies the trauma sufferer's sense of isolation. Traumatic suf-fering breaks down one's social world, severing bonds of trust that are essential for establishing a sense of self. Language is a primary means of connection. In most strains of trauma work, the recovery of a narrative is an integral part of trauma healing. Although trauma cannot always be brought into speech, trauma is communicated and expressed even in the absence of words. In her compelling work with adolescents, Annie Rogers makes the case that trauma has its own language—the language of the unsayable.[13] There is a language to trauma; it just takes different form. Also, from studies in the intergenerational transmission of trauma, we know that an event can be transferred between persons without being accessed in speech. Fragments of an unspoken event can take symptomatic form in a family member. This phenomenon tells us that there are ways in which an event can be communicated—transmitted—in the absence of anything spoken.

Each of these aspects speaks to the ways in which persons and communities move and make meaning in a world after, in Paul Celan's words, "the world is gone."[14] Another world emerges beyond this ending. In the aftermath of the known world, what remains?

12. See Bessel van der Kolk, "The Body Keeps the Score: Approaches to the Psychobiology of Posttraumatic Stress Disorder," in *Traumatic Stress: The Effects of Overwhelming Experience on Mind, Body and Society* (New York: Guilford Press, 1996), and Bessel van der Kolk and Otto van der Hart, "The Intrusive Past: The Flexibility of Memory and the Engraving of Trauma," in Caruth, *Trauma*.

13. Annie Rogers, *The Unsayable: The Hidden Language of Trauma* (New York: Random House, 2006).

14. See "Rams" in Jacques Derrida, *Sovereignties in Question: The Poetics of Paul Celan*, ed. Thomas Dutoit and Outi Pasanen (New York: Fordham University Press, 2005). Derrida analyzes a line of Celan's poem, which reads, "The world is gone; I must carry you." This is a fascinating discussion of survival.

WITNESS

How do we witness suffering in its remaining? Describing his clinical work as a psychoanalyst with Holocaust survivors, Dori Laub outlines different witness positions. A survivor himself, Laub says that a survivor witnesses his or her own experience of survival. As one who listens to survivor testimonies, he also witnesses to another's experience of survival. The third position of witness is a process in which, he says, "witnessing is itself being witnessed."[15] He writes, "I observe how the narrator and myself as listener alternate between moving closer and then retreating from the experience—with the sense that there is a truth that we are both trying to reach, and this sense serves as a beacon we both try to follow."[16] Laub identifies a much more entangled process of testimony; there is no simple speaking and listening, no clear outsider or insider to the traumatic testimony. This third notion of witnessing speaks to the ways in which the enigma of suffering challenges our fundamental conceptions of what is involved in witnessing an experience that remains. The experience is in many respects unknown, not just to the person listening to a survivor but to the survivor herself. This third aspect, according to Laub, involves not only a gathering around an enigma but also a process of handing over and receiving an experience that continually refuses straightforward communication, yet bears within it the force of an imperative. It refuses to be fully captured "in thought, memory, and speech," yet it carries within it an imperative to tell and to be heard.[17]

The term "witness" underwent a significant transformation in the last half of the twentieth century in response to the enormity and scale of historical events of that era. The Holocaust embodied the realities of human cruelty and human vulnerability, and questions emerged in the aftermath that challenged and profoundly reshaped the ways in which we represent and relate to historical events. The discourse around suffering was taken to new heights, given the level of human devastation emerging from the Holocaust. The terms "witness" and "testimony" were employed to articulate a new relationship to events of this scale.

With increased attentiveness to the phenomenon of trauma, our understanding of witness has become more textured and multilayered. It is *thick* witness. The often flattened-out concepts of witness have been challenged and expanded by events of mass suffering that reveal the degree to which we fail to recognize suffering—both as it is taking place and in its aftermath. In order to recognize suffering, we need to wrestle in new ways with the impact of suffering on persons and communities and position ourselves differently in relationship to that suffer-

15. See Dori Laub, "Truth and Testimony," in Caruth, *Trauma*, 62.
16. Ibid.
17. Ibid., 63.

ing. Writer and Holocaust survivor Elie Wiesel, more than anyone else, provides a picture of what it means to be a witness to mass atrocities. In his novels and essays, he depicts the experience of the Holocaust survivor. Through this term, he articulated a relationship to radical suffering—a relationship to events that fall outside the sphere of what is ethically imaginable. The term "witness" came to mean something weighty in the hands of Wiesel and other writers of the Holocaust. By using this term, they ushered us, individually and collectively, into a relationship with a death event. They revealed the distinction between witnessing an ordinary event and an event of this nature and magnitude. An event such as the Holocaust makes impossible demands on those who attempt to witness.

By definition, "to witness" means to observe, to stand by, and to look on. A witness is a spectator. Within a juridical context, a witness is also someone who provides testimony about events for, and on behalf of, another party. "Witness," in this case, has to do with getting at the truth. When considered within the context of devastating violence, this definition of "witness" seemed thin and insufficient. In the case of trauma, the object of witness is not only jarring and disorienting in its force; it is often difficult to detect, to recall, and to acknowledge. To be a witness, in relationship to the horror of the Holocaust, is to stand in a place where you cannot see clearly and where the evidence of what took place is not fully available to you.[18] It is an unwitnessable witness.

Wiesel framed the concept of witness in terms of his own experience, but he also extended the term to describe multiple witness positions, from the role of the survivor to the role of those once, twice, and thrice removed from the experiences of World War II and the Holocaust. Although the witness roles are distinctive in respect to the diversity of these experiences, the term itself becomes a way of describing a new relationship to history, both individual and collective. The relationship is complex and multilayered. For Wiesel, witness also describes a new relationship to language. He declared that a new genre of literature was birthed in this century—a literature of testimony: "If the Greeks invented tragedy, the Romans the epistle, and the Renaissance the sonnet, our generation invented a new literature, that of testimony."[19] This genre was distinctive not only in its attempt to speak the truth about the atrocities experienced but also in its struggle to find an appropriate form of language to speak such truths. Wiesel insisted that the imperative to bear witness was at the heart of this new genre. This literature acknowledges that words are employed in a larger moral struggle to bear witness to atrocities, to register them in language so they will not be

18. In her discussion of Claude Lanzmann's film *Shoah*, Shoshana Felman describes the difficulty of seeing, of being a bystander, when there is an intentional erasure of the evidence of an event. This erasure gives way to a different kind of seeing. See Shoshana Felman, "The Return of the Voice: Claude Lanzmann's *Shoah*," in Shoshana Felman and Dori Laub, *Testimony: Crises of Witnessing in Literature, Psychoanalysis, and History* (New York: Routledge, 1992), 206–11.

19. Elie Wiesel, "The Holocaust as a Literary Inspiration," in *Dimensions of the Holocaust* (Evanston, IL: Northwestern University Press, 1977), 9.

repeated.[20] Witness then becomes instrumental in preventing future violence. The shape and the demands of witness come to new expression in the study of trauma. Healing from trauma clearly cannot take place without witness, yet the particular dynamics in trauma constitute a distinctive understanding of witness. Shoshana Felman points to the ways in which our understanding of history is reframed in a post-Holocaust world. She asks, "Can contemporary narrative historically bear witness, not simply to the impact of the Holocaust but to the way in which the impact of *history as holocaust* has modified, affected, shifted the very modes of the relationship between narrative and history?"[21]

With the proliferation of post-Holocaust studies in trauma, the question of how to witness the impact of these unspeakable events on human persons was pressing and complex. Laub has written extensively about the challenges of therapeutic work with persons who survived the Holocaust. He outlines the demands of this work on the one attempting to speak the trauma as well as the one attempting to listen. The complexities of speaking and listening arise from what Laub identifies as a "collapse of witnessing." Testifying in respect to trauma involves a speaking and listening across a gap largely defined by the temporal dilemma of trauma.[22] A new kind of knowledge is birthed when both parties encounter the impossibility of comprehending and accessing the event in a particular way. An analyst, in witnessing the trauma of her client, is drawn into a new process of unknowing, in which each person encounters the profound collapse of epistemological certainty and straightforward communication.

Judith Herman framed the study of trauma in terms of witness. The 1995 publication of *Trauma and Recovery* signaled, in many respects, the birth of modern trauma studies.[23] She names central components of the traumatic experience and maps out a path to recovery. Having a witnessing presence is an essential first step to traumatic recovery, she says. A survivor must reconnect to the world; this reconnection is only possible through some form of witness. Herman also applies the term "witness" to the study of trauma: "To study psychological trauma means bearing witness to horrible events."[24] Tracing the history of

20. See Kali Tal's description of the literature of trauma. "Literature of trauma is written from the need to tell and retell the story of the traumatic experience, to make it 'real' both to the victim and to the community" (Tal, *Worlds of Hurt*, 21). Maurice Blanchot enacts this struggle with words in *The Writing of the Disaster*, trans. Ann Smock (Lincoln: University of Nebraska Press, 1995), in which he demonstrates the new relationship with language in the aftermath of horrific events. To write about certain events demands a different form of writing.

21. Felman and Laub, *Testimony*, 95.

22. See Laub, "Truth and Testimony," 68–69.

23. Judith Herman, *Trauma and Recovery: The Aftermath of Violence—From Domestic Abuse to Political Terror* (New York: Basic Books, 1995). In *Trauma and Recovery*, Herman connects the experience of male combat veterans and women who suffered what came to be known as fits of hysteria, noting that, in both cases, the phenomenon of trauma was not gender specific but was defined by a cluster of symptoms that emerged from a violent event that the person did not fully integrate at the time it occurred.

24. Ibid., 7.

trauma studies, she notes the ways in which trauma rises in public consciousness at certain points and recedes at others. The student of trauma is one who bears witness to a phenomenon that continually escapes comprehension and that, as a result, is continually contested, forgotten, and covered over in public discourse.[25] A student of trauma works to uncover and excavate what does not come into the light.

Wiesel, Laub, and Herman provide brief glimpses into the concept of witnessing to traumatic experience.[26] To witness to trauma is a complex and disorienting process. It is a process of witnessing death and life in a radical reconfiguration. Because trauma shatters so much of what we understand to constitute life, the very definition of life is in question. Given the obstructions of time, body, and word, it is difficult to interpret life apart from what is often understood as an encounter with death. In respect to time, body, and word, the concept of life is significantly altered. Trauma is often spoken about as a dissolution of the death-life boundary. In *The Forever War*, journalist Dexter Filkins describes his experience with American marines during the military ground war in Falluja: "Out there, the boundary between life and death shrank so much that it was little more than a membrane, thin and clear. With hardly a step you could pass from life into death—and sometimes, it seemed, from death back to life."[27] Between explosions, he hears the murmur of prayers from the soldiers. They were the ones who survived, but life now meant something very different than it did before, more indistinguishable and fragile.

In an early essay, "Living On," Jacques Derrida works with the term "survival."[28] It is literally translated as over-living or living on, taken from the French word *survivre*. The term conveys a sense of life exceeding itself. This excess or overflow emerges from the experience of death. Although a person does not experience a literal death, the radical dimensions of the traumatic event are experienced as an end—a death. Surviving is not a state in which one gets beyond death; instead, death remains in the experience of survival and life is reshaped in light of death—not in light of its finality but its persistence. Persons who experience trauma live in the suspended middle territory, between death and life. To imagine and re-create life in the aftermath of this experience is the challenge of traumatic survival, and one that cannot be imagined apart from the encounter

25. This perspective gives Herman's book an added richness. See her chap. 1.

26. The study of trauma has developed in close connection with the history of Judaism and the Jewish people. In *Moses and Monotheism*, Freud connected his understanding of history and trauma to the history of the Jewish people. Studies of the Holocaust, in turn, are inextricably linked to Judaism. I draw from these studies for the wisdom (and the implicit indictment) they offer to Christian theology, but I also recognize the problematic history of anti-Semitism that Christian discourse often fuels. I trust that I do not repeat the dangerous elisions of history in this study. For a helpful study of the relationship between Jewish and Christian studies of sacred Scriptures following the Holocaust, see Tod Linafelt, ed., *A Shadow of Glory: Reading the Bible after the Holocaust* (New York: Routledge, 2002).

27. Dexter Filkins, *The Forever War* (New York: Random House, 2008), 199.

28. Jacques Derrida, "Living On: Border Lines," in *Deconstruction and Criticism*, trans. James Hulbert (New York: Seabury, 1979), 75–176.

with death. The enigma of three aspects in trauma—time, body, and word—constitute the challenge of remaining in the aftermath of trauma, of remaining beyond a death without being able to anticipate life ahead.

The possibility of trauma healing lies in the capacity to witness to this complex relationship between death and life, to the persistence of the storm even after the literal storm has ended. The question facing those who want to assist in trauma healing is this: how can theologians witness to the reality that the "after the storm is 'always here'"? My aim is twofold. First, I want to explore what it means to witness to this aftermath, to witness beyond the shattering of the categories we employ to make sense of the world. When trauma destroys our basic assumptions about the world, what remains? I reframe Derrida's term "living on" by referring to trauma as a crisis of remaining or a crisis of the middle. The crisis is one of living between death and life, of living in the middle. The images of remaining and the remainder speak to what exceeds an experience, to what continues on despite its ending. To remain and to be one who remains is a central challenge in trauma, and the term carries with it existential weight. "Witness" is an accompanying term to "remaining"; it describes a way of being oriented to what remains, to the suffering that does not go away. These terms—remaining and witnessing—resonate with the language and images of the biblical and theological traditions that I examine in this book. These terms are organic to the theological tradition. My second aim, then, is to examine the ways in which theological language, newly conceived through the lens of trauma, witnesses to what remains. Concepts like love, divine presence, and redemption are reshaped through this language of witness.

THEORIZING TRAUMA

The recent reemergence of the language and theories of trauma signals a reassertion of an old question in twentieth-century experience: how do we account for suffering that remains? Judith Herman's watershed text, *Trauma and Recovery*, first outlined the history of trauma studies, beginning with Charcot's and Freud's early studies of hysterical women at the turn of the nineteenth century. The psychoanalytic model became the standard for interpreting traumatic experience, with Freud at the helm of the earliest analysis of trauma. His turn-of-the-century studies of hysterical women and his analysis of World War I veterans shaped our primary vocabulary of trauma. In this historical overview, Herman connects the experience of these women, war veterans, and survivors of sexual abuse in order to identity the phenomenon of trauma.

One of the critical aspects of this history is that the study of trauma moved off the psychoanalytic couch, so to speak, and beyond strictly clinical fields to fields like literature, history, politics, and religion. The study of trauma was no longer the exclusive domain of therapists, psychoanalysts, and workers in the social science or medical fields. Analysis of trauma began to move into multiple disciplines, as each attempted to understand the nature and impact of violence in its social, historical, and political dimensions. The personal and distinctively Western European image of the trauma victim expanded to encompass an analysis of the multiple levels of our experience of violence and its impacts on us: communal, institutional, national, and international. Not only a single entity experiences a violent event; instead, communities, institutions, and nations experience violent events and manifest symptoms of an overwhelming experience.

The central dynamics of trauma—its overwhelming violence, the shutdown of adaptive processes, and its lack of integration—can be interpreted on a larger scale. Our national lives become reorganized around traumatic events. Histories of violence are repeated. Robert Jay Lifton's work with Vietnam veterans moves beyond an analysis of combat trauma to attest to the broader political reality that trauma returns in unending cycles of war and violence. If experiences of violence are not integrated in time, they can, in fact, be unearthed in another time and in another form. According to Lifton, what is unresolved about one war becomes the seeds of the next war; fragments of an unintegrated Vietnam reappear with a new face in Desert Storm. The struggle to reconstitute an individual self is transformed, as well, into the struggle to reconstitute a national self.[29] Studies of slavery and racism in America point to the cycle of traumatic repetition enacted in respect to historical truths that are continually covered over and buried. Analysis of Hurricane Katrina tells us that the trauma of Katrina cannot simply be limited to the violence of a natural disaster, but must be located within the broader and long-standing structures of oppression that existed long before the storm hit.

Theories and interpretive frameworks for trauma sought to take seriously the "collapse of witnessing" at the heart of trauma.[30] If an event is, in some way, missed in its actual occurrence, accessing that event is going to be a significant challenge. Different fields of study began to assess what it means not to have straightforward and simple access to past events. Rhetoric began to shift from one of comprehension and understanding to one of witnessing and testifying; this shift takes into account a more complex relationship to violent events. For example, what does the phenomenon of traumatic repetition—the invasion of past into present—mean for the ways in which we understand and interpret history? Shattering any straightforward access to the past, the question shifts: how do we witness events in the past? This shift in rhetoric reflects the changing

29. "It's not a logical process, and it's not a conscious process primarily. So one is inwardly or unconsciously struggling with how to cohere and how to absorb and in some measure confront what one has had thrust upon one, what one has been exposed to. And that's what trauma is all about" (Cathy Caruth, "An Interview with Robert Jay Lifton," in Caruth, *Trauma*, 137). See also Robert Jay Lifton, *The Broken Connection: On Death and the Continuity of Life* (New York: Simon and Schuster, 1979), and his *Superpower Syndrome: America's Apocalyptic Confrontation with the World* (New York: Thunder's Mouth Press/Nation Books, 2003).

30. More fully, Caruth says, "The traumatic reexperiencing of the event thus *carries with it* what Dori Laub calls the 'collapse of witnessing,' the impossibility of knowing that first constituted it" (Caruth, *Trauma*, 10).

assumptions we have of our relationship to the world given the ongoing realities of violence. Knowledge, truth, and experience of our world are suddenly transformed, placed on much more fragile terrain. "Witness" becomes a term describing the complex relationship we have to persons and events, given the realities of the suffering that remains.

In the mid- to late 1990s, scholars began to work across disciplinary lines to try to make sense of the phenomenon of trauma. Several volumes on the interdisciplinary studies of trauma emerged.[31] Trauma challenged traditional conceptual frameworks upon which many disciplines strongly relied. If scholars are going to take trauma seriously, they have to confront the status of their own discourses and rethink core assumptions about truth, experience, and knowledge. They began listening, in Cathy Caruth's words, "through the radical disruption and gaps of traumatic experience."[32] Scholars rallied to address the question: how can we speak, write, communicate, and teach given the profound shattering of language and meaning in trauma? The speechlessness that survivors experience demonstrates the instability of the word in multiple disciplines. These interdisciplinary volumes gathered around this paradox, and scholars began to move across disciplines to think about trauma, not only for what it tells us about personal suffering, but also the ways in which that term speaks to cycles of history and broad-scale experiences.

The theorizing of trauma was birthed at the intersection of Holocaust studies and literary deconstruction, specifically by the 1992 publication of *Testimony: Crisis of Witnessing in Literature, Psychoanalysis, and History*, cowritten by Dori Laub and Shoshana Felman. Felman, a literature professor at Yale, and Laub, a professor of psychiatry at Yale's School of Medicine, situate their work in relationship to the Holocaust by asking, what does it mean to testify to historical events? Moving between clinical and literary essays, they each reveal the ways in which their fields facilitate a new encounter with history and its traces in the present. Other literary scholars—who, like Felman, were rethinking the relationship between history and literature—began to make their own contributions as well.

The literary work circled around rereadings of Freud, particularly his insights about the temporality of trauma. Referring to Freud's reflections on traumatic temporality, Cathy Caruth identifies the "peculiar paradox": "that in trauma the greatest confrontation with reality may also occur as an absolute numbing to it, that immediacy, paradoxically enough, may take the form of belatedness."[33] In

31. In addition to Caruth, see Bessell A. van der Kolk, Alexander C. McFarlane, and Lars Weisaeth, eds., *Traumatic Stress: The Effects of Overwhelming Experience on Mind, Body and Society* (New York: Guilford Press, 1996); Marion F. Solomon and Daniel J. Siegel, eds., *Healing Trauma: Attachment, Mind, Body and Brain* (New York: W. W. Norton & Company, 2003); and David L. Eng and David Kazanjian, eds., *Loss: The Politics of Mourning* (Los Angeles: University of California Press, 2003).

32. "Such a crisis of truth extends beyond the question of individual cure and asks how we in this era can have access to our own historical experience, to a history that is in its immediacy a crisis to whose truth there is no simple access" (Caruth, *Trauma*, 6).

33. Ibid.

respect to literary theory, the temporal structure of trauma resonated with a crisis of representation in the field, a refusal of a certain straightforward correspondence between representation and language. But it also pointed to a demand for witness emerging from the site of trauma. The phenomenon of trauma speaks to the impossibility of any simple correlation between experience and our expression of it, but it also points to the imperative for a form of witness, a new language of survival.[34]

The work of literary scholars gave expression to an ethical and political trajectory of deconstruction. They address a frequent charge launched against deconstructive thinkers such as Paul de Man and Jacques Derrida that "deconstruction necessarily leads to political and ethical paralysis."[35] In the introduction to *Critical Encounters: Reference and Responsibility in Deconstructive Writing*, Caruth addresses the charges against deconstruction by revealing the ways that deconstruction's troubling of the relationship between text and reality has been misinterpreted. Deconstructive thinkers do not deny reference, Caruth says; instead, they rethink reference apart from "laws of perception and understanding."[36] She writes,

> The analyses by which deconstruction comes to distinguish reference from perceptual or cognitive models thus do not eliminate reference, but rather examine how to recognize it where it does not occur *as knowledge*. It is indeed in this surprising realignment of reference with what is *not fully masterable by cognition* that the impact of deconstructive writing can be said precisely to take place.[37]

Although she does not name trauma directly in the introduction or in the essay, she expands her essay on Paul de Man and places it in her later collection of essays on trauma. Trauma speaks to "what is *not fully masterable by cognition*."[38] Caruth's readings of texts by de Man, Derrida, Freud, and others enact a textual witness to experiences that cannot be cognitively registered. She tracks the ways in which reference continually fails; in that failure, reference becomes something

---

34. This crisis of representation found a natural home with the literary school of deconstruction, an approach to texts within the field of literary criticism that emphasized the inadequacy of words to represent reality. Trauma epitomized this crisis of representation. The birth of trauma theory is usually associated with this group of literary theorists from Yale University. With the presence of Paul de Man and, later, Jacques Derrida in Yale's Department of English in the late 1980s, Yale was considered the flagship for the Americanization of the literary school of deconstruction. Deconstruction's critique of straightforward referentiality in literature provided an avenue for literary theorists to attest to real experiences that escaped representation. This opening corresponded with the rise of Holocaust studies within universities. Yale had also become the site of the Holocaust Video Archives, and Yale Psychiatric Institute a major center for work with Holocaust survivors.

35. Caruth, *Unclaimed Experience*, 181.

36. Cathy Caruth and Deborah Esch, *Critical Encounters: Reference and Responsibility in Deconstructive Writing* (New Brunswick, NJ: Rutgers University Press, 1995), 2.

37. Ibid., 3. Deconstructive theorists explore the ways that texts have been contained within certain cognitive frameworks in which cognitive certainty is preserved at all costs. The cost, as Caruth develops in her essay on Paul de Man in *Critical Encounters*, has direct bearing on the ability, or rather the inability, of certain forms of writing to witness to the phenomenon of trauma.

38. Ibid.

new. She writes, "In thus breaking the tie between *reading* and *certainty* [these essays] permit reference to arise where understanding may not."[39]

This failure of reference around which much deconstructive writing circles suddenly takes new form in the writings of Caruth and others. In their readings of literary texts, they display the ways in which this referential failure is, simultaneously, an awakening of theory to witnessing trauma. The impossibility of direct referentiality does not lead to ethical paralysis; instead, rethinking reference in this way provides an avenue for ethical reflection around the peculiar temporal paradox of trauma. She writes, "What would it mean, on the contrary, to conceive of an experience that is constituted by the very way it escapes or resists comprehension? . . . In what ways could we define a politics or ethics that derives from a position in which full understanding is not possible?"[40] Geoffrey Hartmann, a key figure in the Yale School and a noted Holocaust scholar, says that trauma theory turns the study of literature toward "more *listening*, more *hearing* of words within words, and a greater openness to testimony."[41]

TRAUMATIC WITNESS AND THEOLOGY

Theologians and biblical scholars have turned to trauma theory both to make sense of the accounts of violence, suffering, and catastrophe within these sacred texts and to give theological expression to contemporary contexts of suffering. These explorations have moved in a variety of directions, from post-Shoah explorations of the Hebrew Scriptures to theological reworkings of major conceptions of sin, grace, and the nature of God in light of trauma survival. With the expansion of trauma studies, discussions of trauma within the fields of theology and religion have expanded, moving beyond the designated psychological fields; an intradisciplinary conversation is taking place alongside an interdisciplinary one.

The textual tradition of Christianity gives rise to authoritative truth claims, in and through which people and communities interpret themselves and God's relationship to the world.[42] Trauma theory provides a distinctive lens through which to interpret sacred texts and for rethinking the claims and central beliefs arising from them. I return to texts within the Christian tradition to explore the ways in which they can attest to traumatic experiences. Instead of confirming

39. Ibid., 5.
40. Ibid., 1.
41. Geoffrey Hartmann, "On Traumatic Knowledge and Literary Studies," *New Literary History* 26, no. 3 (1995): 541.
42. Scholars in other fields within religious studies are exploring the phenomenon of trauma in other ways. I'm thinking here about work in counseling and psychology of religion. However, this textual study, given the performative function of sacred texts, is not divorced from lived experience. These texts function within religious spaces. They are preached, taught, and liturgically engaged by communities of faith. In this way, interpretations of these texts powerfully shape human lives and therein foster harm or healing. This lived (performative) aspect of sacred texts distinguishes theology from literary studies and does so in a way that is fruitful for thinking about the phenomenon of trauma in cross-disciplinary conversation.

the truth of the faith, I want to inspect the ways in which these texts testify to uncontainable truths.

One of the difficult things about this trajectory of trauma theory is that these scholars do not present a theory of trauma. In this sense, the term "trauma theory" is a misnomer. They, instead, engage in readings of texts, exposing the ways in which the language of these texts exceeds the claims attributed to them. For example, Cathy Caruth reads Freud's theory of the death drive, pointing to the ways in which his own writings attest to something more than this theory. He moves beyond interpreting trauma as a pathology and, she suggests, offers a language of life arising from the site of trauma. He points to something else. This "something else" is what emerges in Caruth's reading of Freud, as she reads him beyond his own theory. This interpretive process is much more complex, revealing a way in which readings enact a witness to what the writers themselves did not know or grasp. The act of interpretation is an encounter with the collapse or failure of theory but, simultaneously, the birth of something new emerging from this failure.

Trauma theory, like deconstruction, is a way of reading that exposes the gaps and fissures in the texts. In so doing, it unearths dimensions of the texts that otherwise lie buried. These readings reveal the ways in which language exceeds theory, thus exposing the insufficiency of claims that reduce language to frameworks of meaning. The significance of trauma theory is that it tracks this remainder, this excess. This persisting, this remaining, give rise to a unique series of relationships that center around an attempt to give expression to what cannot be fully known. The challenge of trauma is the challenge of witnessing to a phenomenon that exceeds the categories by which we make sense of the world. These literary readings expose the insufficiency of our frameworks for understanding and also point to a different relationship that we have to language, given these traumatic dynamics. Trauma theory shares with deconstruction a common misperception: that it is a theory to be applied. Instead, trauma theory and deconstruction both enact ways of reading that expose certain dimensions of texts. Trauma theory that draws from deconstruction is a practice of unmasking, unearthing, and tracking what escapes interpretation.

Rather than importing insights from trauma into the discourse of theology, I turn to texts within the tradition to listen for the language of remaining that I hear in the witness literature.[43] The relationship between theology and trauma theory does not rest in the degree to which theologians employ insights from trauma into the discipline of theology but in a resonance between two languages.

43. It is easy to cast the relationship between trauma theory and theology in this way: trauma theory presents insights that are then brought to bear on theology. These insights can support or dismantle certain theological claims surrounding these texts. I have resisted this importation or employment of insights from trauma theory into the discourse of theology, because it does not speak to the kind of encounter that I believe takes place when discourses gather at the site of trauma. In this encounter, theology and trauma theory (via psychoanalysis) are gathered around what is not known. The language of theology and the language of trauma theory find resonance around this unknowing. In line with Caruth's vision, they hear themselves anew through the ruptures and gaps of trauma.

Theology hears itself differently in the language of trauma; in turn, trauma theory hears itself differently in the language of theology. This witness from within a discourse is made possible through another, but this meeting point is the site of trauma. At the site of trauma (with its epistemological ruptures, etc.), discourses are pressed to their limits and become something new in this encounter. The language of trauma turns theology to its own language and texts, illuminating aspects that would not otherwise be noted or recognized. How are the disorientations of time, body, and word evidenced in texts? What truths might emerge through these disorientations, through this shattering? This lens of trauma involves, to some degree, defamiliarizing these texts, pointing to the enigma of time, body, and word in the language of theology. It requires unmasking certain epistemological assumptions that govern familiar interpretations of these biblical and theological texts.

I want to emphasize two particular meeting points between the languages of trauma and theology. First, trauma theory highlights a mixed relationship between death and life and, in so doing, unearths a middle territory in the Christian narrative of death and life. There, we encounter a territory of remaining, a term organic to the theological tradition. Situated alongside the discourse of trauma theory, theology speaks something new from the middle. Cathy Caruth returns to Freud's speculations about trauma and opens up a conceptual middle space for thinking about the experience of trauma and traumatic survival. Death and life are no longer clearly delineated and opposed; they can no longer be interpreted in oppositional terms. Instead, in trauma, death and life come to new expression. Caruth points to this perplexing relationship between death and life. Death is not an ending as we normally conceive of it; neither is life a new beginning. Instead, Freud's writings point to trauma as a crisis of survival that exceeds our previous conceptions and claims about death and life. We meet death in its excess and life in its impossible emergence.

At the beginning of *Beyond the Pleasure Principle*, Freud employs a literary reference to the medieval epic *Jerusalem Liberated* to make an analogy to his analysis of what is taking place in soldiers after they return from war.[44] Freud likens his observations of war veterans to the story of Tancred and Clorinda in Tasso's sixteenth-century epic. In that story, Tancred, the hero of the epic, slays his lover Clorinda when she is disguised in battle. But he does not slay her once, Freud notes; he slays her a second time. "Unwittingly," he writes, Tancred slashes a tree in which the soul of his departed lover is imprisoned. When he slashes the tree with his sword, Clorinda's voice cries out from the wounded trunk. Combat neurosis is patterned similarly, according to Freud. Something about the first event of wounding gives way to a repetition of the wound. The fate of the war veteran is likened to that of the tragic lovers. The past is vividly enacted in the present in the form of flashbacks. The traumatic structure of the war experience is a literal reenactment of a past that was not fully grasped at the point when it

44. See Freud, *Beyond the Pleasure Principle*.

occurred. The original death event—the first slaying of Clorinda—is the unbearable context of combat. Yet the return, in traumatic nightmares and flashbacks, is what perplexes Freud. As Tancred's experience suggests, the unwitting return reveals the puzzling enigma of trauma—that this return is a return of what was fundamentally unknown or missed.

In *Unclaimed Experience: Trauma, Narrative and History*, Caruth expands on Freud's literary reference, pointing to ungrasped dimensions of this traumatic parable. She writes, "Just as Tancred does not hear the voice of Clorinda until the second wounding, so trauma is not locatable in the simple violent or original event in an individual's past, but rather in the way that its very unassimilable nature—the way it was precisely *not known* in the first instance—returns to haunt the survivor later on."[45]

Caruth, in her reading of Freud's *Beyond the Pleasure Principle*, points to the double structure of trauma toward which Freud gestured. She suggests that Freud's observations of trauma move him beyond his initial theories, challenging his basic articulations of life and death—the life drive and the death drive. In this parable, Freud reworks his theories in order to attest to the excess of death that he is observing, to the curious puzzle of the nature of traumatic survival. Freud is pointing beyond trauma as pure pathology to something more.

One central insight of Caruth's interpretation of Freud is that trauma is an encounter, a crisis, involving both death and life. Trauma is typically understood as an encounter with death. But this encounter is not fully integrated and known; because of this, it returns in an unrecognizable form. Death, thus, returns. But the crisis of death lies in the fact that it returns not as something known but as the force of something that was unknown. Its return makes life impossible to be conceived in any way as life was before the traumatic event. Instead, life takes a different form as it is forged in continual engagement with death. Thus, the narrative of death and life cannot be read in any straightforward way if one is looking through the lens of trauma. Death is not concluded; instead, it continues on in forms of life that may not be recognized as such. Life is reconfigured as the excess of death, as what remains.

Caruth claims that Freud's insights about trauma move him beyond his theory of the death drive. In her rereading of Freud, she claims that Freud's insights do not confirm but disrupt his theory of the death drive, unearthing a new and distinctive language of life emerging from the site of trauma. The parable of trauma is a parable about a death-life encounter. The story it tells is that trauma is not merely an encounter with death—and thus something to be solely pathologized—but trauma is also a rewriting of life. She writes,

> The crisis at the core of many trauma narratives . . . often emerges, indeed, as an urgent question: Is the trauma the encounter with death, or the ongoing experience of having survived it? At the core of these stories, I would

---

45. Caruth, *Unclaimed Experience*, 4.

suggest, is thus a kind of double telling, the oscillation between *a crisis of death* and the correlative *crisis of life:* between the story of the unbearable nature of an event and the story of the unbearable nature of its survival.[46]

This oscillation between death and life opens up a distinctive middle in which neither can be read apart from each other. Instead, the experience of survival is a death-life experience.

Caruth, by way of Freud, positions readers in this middle between death and life. She does this most powerfully through her reading of Clorinda's voice in the Tasso parable. Clorinda's voice becomes the site of ethics for Caruth, revealing a truth emerging from the site of trauma. She writes, "It is in the moving quality of this literary story, I would suggest—its striking juxtaposition of the unknowing, injurious repetition and the witness of the crying voice—that best represents Freud's intuition of, and his passionate fascination with, traumatic encounters."[47] Caruth's attention turns to the enigma of Clorinda's cry that seems to speak a truth about trauma from the site of its wounding. The voice from the wound makes a demand: witness death and witness the possibility of life arising from it. The voice prompts a different kind of relationship constituted around the missing and the epistemological shatterings in trauma. Neither a figure of death or life exclusively, the cry from the wound is the hinge that links the two. It is a cry of witness from the middle.

The figures of death, life, and the wound are familiar figures in the Christian narrative of cross and resurrection.[48] Situated alongside Caruth, the language of death and life come to different expression. Christian claims about the significance of these events and the truths that they express may be met and reshaped through the language of trauma. The oozing wound in the Johannine text meets the crying wound in trauma theory. The events between the death of Jesus and his resurrection, often thought of as incidental to the featured events of death and life, take new expression. In both discourses, a sign of life is emerging from the site of death, the site of death's excess. The truth that it speaks is a truth from the middle. Theologian Hans Urs von Balthasar asks, "What persists between death and life?" This question leads him to a study of Holy Saturday, a middle day between death and life in the Christian liturgical calendar. As trauma theory turns to this middle site of witness between death and life, so, too, theology turns to find a witness to what remains. The language of witnessing in trauma theory illuminates a vocabulary of remaining within the biblical texts of cross and resurrection.

Second, trauma theory points to a different constitution of relationships at the site of trauma. The truths emerging from the middle orient persons differently to each other at the limits of understanding. The form of communication

46. Ibid., 7.
47. Ibid., 3.
48. Exploring the Tasso story in more depth, it is interesting to note the religious dimensions of this parable; Tancred is the Christian warrior prince, and Clorinda is the pagan warrior goddess.

in trauma speaks to a transmission of what cannot be fully known, to truths handed over in the context of death. Multiple iterations of people and messages handed over occur in the Johannine text. Situated alongside the discourse of trauma, these biblical exchanges come to new expression.

Trauma is an encounter with death and with life. At the intersection of death and life, a cry emerges. Clorinda's cry is a voice of witness to uncontainable suffering. Caruth writes, "For what seems to be particularly striking in the example of Tasso . . . is the moving and sorrowing voice that cries out, a voice that is paradoxically released through the wound. . . . The voice of his beloved addresses him and, in this address, bears witness to the past he has unwittingly repeated."[49] The cry from the wound of death is not simply a death cry but, according to Caruth, a wound that speaks something beyond the death. The analysis of Clorinda's voice reveals Caruth's ethical contributions to theorizing trauma. Beyond the pathology of trauma, there is, Caruth claims, a truth emerging from trauma. Its truth is figured in Clorinda, whose voice reveals an ethical and relational dimension to trauma. The cry of trauma is not simply the suffering of Tancred confronting his past; instead, Clorinda's cry from within the event of trauma is also the possibility of witness to trauma. She writes, "But we can also read the address of the voice here, not as the story of the individual in relation to the events of the past, but as the story of the way in which one's own trauma may lead, therefore, to the encounter with another, through the very possibility and surprise of listening to another's wound."[50] Dori Laub's work with survivors also reveals that the work of witnessing is not a simple task of listening *to* trauma but, instead, a process of listening *through* it. The testimonial process is not simply a retrieval of past knowledge, but a process of confronting the impossibilities of simple retrieval.

Relationships are newly constituted around trauma. Caruth develops this point most extensively in "Literature and the Enactment of Memory," her analysis of Alain Renais' and Marguerite Duras' 1959 film *Hiroshima mon amour*. Caruth explores the relationship between two persons whose present experiences are locked up in their past traumas. They do not speak the same language, and they do not know the other's history. The tangle of translations, bodies, and unstated histories create a picture of traumatic relationality. The theme that keeps surfacing is the epistemological uncertainty around which and through which they encounter each other. The communication taking place between them seems, at every point, fragmented and failed. Literally, the two lovers do not speak the same language. But what looks like failed communication and a continual missed encounter between them is, in fact, what constitutes speaking and hearing in the wake of trauma. Caruth insists that we are implicated in each others' traumas: "The film dramatizes something that happens when two different experiences, absolutely alien to one another, are brought together."[51] In other words, we are tied to what we do not comprehend about each other's pasts. The

49. Caruth, *Unclaimed Experience*, 3.
50. Ibid., 8.
51. Ibid., 34.

problem of translation between the two lovers represents the impossible knowledge of the traumatic past. "Their ability to speak and to listen in their passionate encounter," she writes, "does not rely, that is, on what they simply know of one another, but on what they do not fully know in their own traumatic pasts."[52]

Instead of simple knowledge between persons, there is a transmission of what is unknown and what could not be contained in the past. The transmission or handing over that Caruth describes replaces what we typically refer to as communication. If, as she in her reading of Freud suggests, trauma involves a gap between an event and the experience of that event, then the communication in trauma will reflect that gap as well. Trauma is not only a fragmenting of a self (an inability to speak and physically integrate the past experience); in its aftermath, trauma poses a fundamental challenge to the constitution of human relationships.

As a literary theorist, Caruth describes the impact of traumatic relationality on the process of writing, reading, and interpreting literary texts. Clorinda's voice represents an address within literary texts that can only be read through attention to the gaps and disruptions of language. Caruth's task becomes, then, to track the ways in which what is unknown returns in the texts that she reads. She tracks what remains. These returns indicate more than traumatic repetition; instead, they are attempts to speak something true from the site of trauma. She describes the aim of her readings in *Unclaimed Experience* in this way:

> It is this plea by an other who is asking to be seen and heard, this call by which the other commands us to awaken (to awaken, indeed, to a burning), that resonates in different ways throughout the texts this book attempts to read, and which, in this book's understanding, constitutes the new mode of reading and of listening that both the language of trauma, and the silence of its mute repetition of suffering, profoundly and imperatively demand.[53]

The relationship between writer, reader, and text is described as a witness to what is unknown and what cannot be contained. She reenvisions the role of literary texts. The transmission of trauma is understood as a textual transmission, in which texts enact dimensions of trauma and, simultaneously, reveal a potential witness to trauma. The speaking and listening that Dori Laub outlines in the therapeutic relationship is now enacted between the writer and reader, the author and the translator.

Caruth probes the ways in which histories are traumatically structured and the ways in which persons bear these histories. This bearing, or carrying, is not based on any straightforward knowledge or on any straight line from past to present to future. Instead, her readings point to a handing over and a reception of what cannot be known. As the Johannine texts refer to truths and persons handed over within the context of death, the language of trauma sheds new light

---

52. Ibid., 56.
53. Ibid., 9. The reference to burning occurs in Lacan's reading of Freud. She analyzes this "traumatic awakening" in the last chapter of the book.

on what is taking place there. Looking from the middle, something of death is handed over into the territory of survival. But, like the cry of Clorinda, there is also a witness in the aftermath. Bodies and breath remain, speaking to a fragile and tenuous relationality in the biblical territory of survival. But the handing over also speaks to the ways in which texts are handed over, speaking to the heart of the concept of tradition(ing) within Christianity. What if the truths handed over were not truths of what is known but truths about what is not known and not fully grasped? To receive these truths is always, in some way, to be turned back to the event of death, not as something known but as something that calls for a witness to its remainder. These are the questions that the biblical and theological texts posed from within. When we turn to the final statements in the Gospel of John, we also encounter peculiar statements about the inexhaustibility of texts and the truths they contain. The question of the reception of truth is central to religious faith, not just to Christianity but other traditions as well. But, looking through the lens of trauma, this questionable reception may transform our conception of truth. Perhaps the truth referenced in this Gospel text functions to orient us to what is not easily or fully accessed, shaping the recipients to witness what emerges through the shattering of knowable worlds.

This discussion briefly points to a resonance between the discourse of theology and trauma. The readings in the following chapters extend these initial insights, showing how the lens of trauma invests theological discourse with new depth. As we turn to the death-life events in the Christian texts, the question of what it means to witness the death and resurrection of Jesus is a question resonant with the language of trauma. For those who stand in the aftermath of that death, the nature of life is bound to that death, not in terms of what is known of that death but the ways in which that death continually escapes comprehension. For those who stand in the aftermath of that death, they are bound together in that unknowing. They stand as witnesses, not to a truth easily or simply communicated, but to indirect truths that bind them to each other. Their lives are constituted as witnesses.

THEOLOGICAL MODELS OF WITNESS

I opened the chapter by stating that "witness" is a term organic to Christian theology. How has that term functioned? How is it different from the witness that I have presented here? In developing an alternative theology of witness, I want to briefly sketch two familiar interpretations of the term "witness" as it is employed within the Christian tradition. The first is what I call the proclamation model of witness; the second is the imitation model. Although there may be other uses of the term, these two models engage two aspects of the concept of witness that I am reworking here—namely the relationship of witness to word and body. The proclamation model is word-centered; the imitation, or sacrifice, model is body-centered. I identify these two models as reflecting a more straightforward relationship to word and body than what can be assumed, given what we know about trauma. These models are also primarily identified with the figure of Jesus—with communicating a truth about his words and his body. This communication of word and body is much less stable, if it is understood through a particular conception of what it means to witness between cross and resurrection, death and life.

By definition, a witness is an observer, an onlooker, a bystander, or a spectator of a particular event or events. The juridical use of the term adds another dimension to this; the observer is also called upon to speak about the events—to testify or bear witness on behalf of someone or something. The juridical image of the courtroom places the witness in a position in which his verbal testimony supports a particular case being contested. This legal understanding of witness was prevalent in the context of the origins of Christianity, and early models of Christian witness drew upon this juridical understanding. A witness provides verbal testimony for the sake of shedding light on a situation, therein exposing an aspect of the truth in question.

This definition translated easily into the context of those who came to identify themselves in connection with Jesus and his ministry. They professed faith in Jesus as the Christ. As witnesses, they were understood to provide a testimony to the things that he had said and done; they were witnesses on his behalf. In the proclamation model, a witness is someone who conveys, through words, a testimony to what one saw, heard, experienced, and had come to believe about Jesus. In the Gospel narratives, and especially in the Johannine writings, witness had an evangelistic dimension. The profession was also a proclamation, aimed at bringing about belief in others. In acknowledging the nature and significance of the person of Jesus and his mission, the witness in turn conveyed that message to others. Witness was linked not only to a belief in Jesus but also involved telling or sharing that belief with others.

The witness, then, links the message of Jesus to prospective recipients of that message. The witness becomes the vehicle by which the message is conveyed. It is the model drawn from the picture of the early disciples spreading the news about the life, death, and resurrection of Jesus. There is an urgent message to be conveyed, and witness refers to the communication of that message to a particular audience. This proclamation model is rooted in the arenas of preaching and in the development of Christian missions. In both cases, the witness speaks on behalf of someone for the sake of someone else. To bear witness in word is to convey a message in a way that it can be received. The aim of the proclamation is to bring about conversion in the heart of the recipient. The focus is on speaking and word. Witness, then, is about what we profess or proclaim about Jesus.

Elizabeth Castelli, in her observations about the self-sacrificial model of martyrdom, speaks to the second model of witness.[54] While the emphasis on the

54. See Elizabeth A. Castelli, *Imitating Paul: A Discourse of Power* (Louisville, KY: Westminster/ John Knox Press, 1991).

proclamation model is on word, the imitation model focuses instead on the body. The imitation model entails patterning one's life after the movements of Jesus. This model, in its extreme form, involves one's willingness to sacrifice one's life in witness to Christ. The imitation model of witness grew out of the early centuries of Christianity in which the good news of Jesus as the Christ had to be defended. As Christians came under increased threat of religious persecution, the term "witness" evolved and became increasingly tied to persons who would risk their lives for the sake of their faith.[55] The logic of this model is as follows: Jesus suffers, therefore I suffer. Their testimonies to belief in Jesus required physical risk, even to the point of death. A faithful witness is not only one who professes belief in Jesus; the faithful witness demonstrates belief by imitating Jesus in his life and death. To witness to the gospel was not merely a matter of spreading the good news about what Jesus had taught and done; it was about taking on the life and cross of Jesus in imitation of the one they professed to be the Son of God. One was no longer the vehicle of the gospel message; a witness literally became, in body, that message. The model of imitation cannot, however, simply be reduced to self-sacrifice and martyrdom. Imitative witness also involves a faithful demonstration of the life of Christ, as it is interpreted through the Gospels. To imitate Jesus is also to imitate his life—his works of love and service.

Both models of witness—proclamation and imitation—are drawn from biblical texts and are expressed throughout the historical tradition of Christianity. They constitute, in their most basic structure, the way that many Christians interpret what it means to witness to the life, death, and resurrection of Jesus. Note that these models primarily interpret witness in relationship to the figure of Jesus. They rely on the assumption that witnesses are able to clearly discern the message and movements that they proclaim or imitate. These models assume that the witnesses can identify the substance or subject that they witness.

Looking through the lens of trauma, I challenge the centrality and stability of both the figure of Jesus and the clear identification of the message that the disciples are receiving. By taking into account the middle, this centrality and stability can no longer be assumed. The displacement of the figure of Jesus and the lack of clarity surrounding the events pushes against familiar conceptions of what it means to witness these events. At stake in these readings is the nature of redemption, as narrated through the events of the passion and resurrection.

The language of trauma directs us to a different theological territory—the territory between death and life—to what Caruth identifies as the crisis of witness between them. The term "witness" takes on new meaning in this between

---

55. "In the 2nd century the impulses found in the NT, especially in the Johannine writings, are carried a stage further. Like the beginnings, the development was due to the persecutions which fell on the Christian community. . . . It now referred to as a witness under threat" (ibid., 505). Tracing this history, Castelli writes: "In the end, however, the scripts of persecution and martyrdom that were written and enacted in the early Christian centuries . . . produced versions of Christian identity that would be formative even in the current moment" (*Martyrdom and Memory*, 200).

territory and provides a means by which experiences that "fall outside the ordinary order of things" are brought to light. It takes into account the depth to which human persons can be shattered—in Elaine Scarry's word, "undone"—and it equally takes into account the important work of remaking the world.[56] Witness is the hinge linking the shattering and remaking, the undoing and the regeneration. Witness is the hinge between death and life, as it is experienced through trauma and traumatic survival.

Looking at witness through the lens of trauma, these theological models of witness shatter. While I do not dismiss the fact that there is something to profess or imitate in relationship to the death and resurrection, I suggest that looking through the lens of trauma yields something more than these interpretations of witness. In my readings of the biblical and theological texts, the distortions of time, body, and word that they expose call into question what is being witnessed. What is the truth there? The continual elisions of the object of witness turn our attention away from some pure presence or true message. Instead, we gaze into a territory of remaining.

As Elizabeth Castelli points out, the understanding of a martyr as one who testifies to human suffering is subsumed under the model of the martyr as one who gives up her life for the sake of her religious beliefs. This self-sacrificial model, according to Castelli, "won the day" in the history of Christianity. But this "witness" dimension of the term, even if frequently subsumed, remains there as well. What is it about witness and truth telling that makes it susceptible to the dangerous eclipsing to which Castelli refers?[57] Witnessing occurs at the tenuous intersection of death and life; it is a middle activity. Witnessing, as I explore it here, is largely defined by its positioning. This tenuous middle placement allows the witness to see, but never directly; to hear, but never directly; and to touch, but never directly. This indirectness allows the witness to acknowledge and attend to that which rarely emerges into speech. Different forms of life are imagined in and through this witness.

When I refer to witnessing from the middle, I understand this to mean two things. First, a person is positioned in respect to suffering in such a way that she can see truths that often escape articulation, that emerge through cracks in the dominant logic. Second, this tenuous placement also means that the witness is subject to the continual elisions that make it impossible to see, hear, or touch clearly. In order to witness, one must enter into the elisions at the heart of suffering. This twofold witness constitutes the middle that I develop throughout the

56. See Elaine Scarry, *The Body in Pain: The Making and Unmaking of the World* (New York: Oxford University Press, 1985), and Veena Das, Arthur Kleinman, Margaret Lock, Mamphela Ramphele, and Pamela Reynolds, *Remaking a World: Violence, Social Suffering, and Recovery* (Los Angeles: University of California Press, 2001).

57. Castelli says, "What I want to suggest is that the overprivileging of the self-sacrificial dimensions of the 'martyr' results in a flattening out, the dangerous eclipsing of the possibility of recognizing the suffering of others" (*Martyrdom and Memory*, 203).

book. By marking out a distinctive middle space, I am making room for a particular configuration of theological witness that speaks to the realities of trauma. It is a space in which the disorientations of time, word, and body are seriously engaged, even amid the multiple elisions that constitute them. This engagement is critical to the possibility that Castelli imagines—the possibility of recognizing the suffering of others.

This eclipsing, as Castelli names it, is not only what happens as a result of being a witness; the experience of witnessing itself is a position that is defined by such eclipses. It is not just that one's witness will be deemed incredible or unbelievable, though this is nonetheless true and problematic. We can recognize this as true, for example, in the witness of Mary Magdalene, which I examine in chapter 3. She runs to tell the other disciples about her experience at the tomb, and they question her witness. But I am referring, as well, to the eclipse within her witness. As I have displayed through these three aspects of trauma, the experience of trauma involves a profound disorientation in one's way of being in the world in relationship to each of the three—time, body, and word. To witness this disorientation is to be in a space where the content of witness is continually eclipsed, where the source of suffering cannot be clearly identified, and where clear boundaries are shattered. Trauma, and witnessing to it, is marked by these multiple elisions. Witnessing places persons in this tenuous middle position, in which clear and stark oppositions no longer hold—between death and life, absence and presence.

Judith Herman refers to this eclipsing as the "forgetting" that constitutes the phenomenon of trauma and the study of it.[58] Distortions in memory are central to trauma. A great deal of suffering stems from the fact that the past cannot be recovered. But suffering also comes because fragments of the past invade the present. The study of trauma also, she says, has bouts of recall and forgetting; attention to trauma rises and falls in public consciousness, and this cycle is reflective of the phenomenon itself. Herman's introduction has a prophetic quality to it. Just as she is writing the study of trauma, she is forecasting its eclipse, its recession from public memory. I am suggesting that this remembering and eclipsing, uncovering and eliding, distinguish witnessing and make it so difficult in respect to radical suffering.

This aspect of forgetting (Herman) and eclipsing (Castelli) is akin to what I am referring to as eliding—instances in which certain truths are suppressed, omitted, ignored, or passed over. I choose the word "eliding/elision" for two reasons. First, the word "elision" captures the intentionality that is often at play in trauma. It takes into account the fact that, in many cases, certain parties are invested in suppressing the truth of certain events. The effects of trauma may quickly be passed over in order to keep certain persons in positions of power.

58. See chap. 1 of Herman, *Trauma and Recovery.*

Second, the word "elision" is a linguistic term referring to the omission of a final or initial sound in pronunciation as well as an omission of an unstressed vowel or syllable in order to keep or achieve a metrical pattern. This latter reference is particularly interesting, because it gives expression to what often takes place in trauma. Although the suffering is present, it is often not given voice in order to keep a certain understanding of the world in place. Though it is marked in the text, it is not vocalized, because the pattern of things is smoother when it is not spoken.

As I have presented it here initially, witness is not a straightforward access to an event, an account of something seen or heard in any traditional form. But it is also not captured in the etymological reference of "martyr" and the ways in which it has been interpreted, particularly within Christian contexts. Instead, witness is neither a straightforward proclamation of something that has taken place nor a straightforward imitation of what has taken place. It is a tenuous orientation to suffering that presses central theological claims about death and life in and against themselves.

In discussion of the biblical and theological texts, I highlight the enigma of suffering—distortions in time, body, and word—that expose and argue the importance of a middle space of witness in the Christian narrative of death and life, passion and resurrection. Instead of mapping out what witness looks like in trauma, I turn to the biblical and theological texts to see how witness is depicted there. The Johannine figures are identified as witnesses to the passion and resurrection. Christian interpretations of witness are drawn from these accounts. In turn, theologians exploring the more mixed narrative of death and life on Holy Saturday uncover a territory of witness. Balthasar and Speyr claim that the logic of death and life is shattered, and, in so doing, a unique theological testimony to suffering and its aftermath is exposed. What do they tell us about witness? In the following chapters, I unearth a testimony to the fracturing of time, body, and word operative within these texts. What grows from these is a witnessing presence that rewrites conceptions of redemption through death and suspends claims about resurrection life. The enigmatic truth arising at the site of trauma is this: love remains.

My aim is to mark out a conceptual territory that acknowledges the difficult movement of life in the wake of a death. This movement actually comprises a series of difficult movements, of attempts to witness to what is easily elided. By difficult movements, I am acknowledging that the relationship between death and life can no longer be structured along the lines of a forward and progressive time line. In this sense, I am honoring the difficult temporality in the experience of trauma. The movements also have to be figured bodily in order to take seriously the deep cognitive limitations in traumatic experience. These movements witness to both the insufficiency and the imaginative force of language as it is reconfigured in and through experiences of death. To revisit claims from this conceptual middle territory is the task of this book.

I am interested in speaking about the potential of human persons to witness violence that we may not directly experience but in which we nonetheless participate. We are affected or, as Catherine Keller says, implicated.[59] I am thinking theologically here about the ways in which biblical and theological texts, through their rhetoric, aim at shaping a way of being in the world. How do they situate us, as readers, in relationship to the world? The life, death, and resurrection narrative of Jesus ideally functions in such a way as to shape and empower persons toward a certain way of life. The nature of witness and what it means in the biblical and theological texts is significant in that the term "witness" has been a primary way of describing Christian life in the world, of describing the ways in which we are connected to the narrative of Jesus' death and life and the ways in which we translate that narrative in the world. Witness as it is articulated in respect to trauma challenges us to rethink the concept. Have these familiar interpretations of "witness" hindered us from reading another aspect of witness in these texts—namely the difficult witness to radical suffering?

The framework that I develop is not intended as a new template to be placed on the theological and biblical texts. Instead, it serves as a means of highlighting dimensions of the texts that familiar interpretations often deem insignificant or smooth over. Looking at these texts through the insights of what we have come to know about trauma and its impact on human persons is a way of reclaiming their testimonial power. I am calling us to rethink our working lexicon, reviving it for its potential to heal. In *Spirit and the Politics of Disablement*, Sharon Betcher describes her constructive work as gathering intuitions.[60] The intuitions that I gather here are these: The insights of trauma cast new light on a redemptive narrative indebted to a progressive reading of the relationship between death and life. In doing so, they also displace the figure of Jesus, pointing to a different configuration of the Spirit, one that is shaped by practices of witness. These other models fail to capture the ways in which witness is shaped by the absence of Jesus, by his departing. They fail to register a critical shift—a witness of and to Spirit. What would it mean to recast witness primarily in pneumatological terms, in terms of the witness of the Spirit? In many cases, the witness that we see in the biblical texts is much less straightforward than these interpretations suggest. What if conceptions of Christian witness acknowledged the incommunicability, the indirectness, the questionable reception of witness? What if the content of what is being witnessed is continually elided, shifting the focus from the content to the practice of witnessing? Instead of a straightforward truth to be proclaimed, the lens of trauma turns us to uncontainable truths to be witnessed.

In the chapters that follow, I explore how the biblical and theological texts contain an alternative understanding of what it means to witness. Although

59. Catherine Keller, *Face of the Deep: A Theology of Becoming* (New York: Routledge, 2003), 232. See her discussion of the Deleuzian *implicatio*.
60. Sharon Betcher, *Spirit and the Politics of Disablement* (Minneapolis: Augsburg Fortress Press, 2007), 22.

the two sets of texts that I engage can support the proclamation and imitation models of witness, they also testify to another dimension of witnessing. This dimension is linked to the figure of the Spirit. At the intersection of death and life, a new orientation to the fractured word and body emerges. *This* orientation at *this* point displaces our attention from the figure of Jesus and his presence to a deep engagement with the experience of his absence. "What remains in the aftermath of death?" is the central question of witness. Acknowledging the fractured nature of both word and body in witness moves us into distinctively pneumatological territory, in which the Spirit is not a life-giver but is, instead, witness to the emergence of life out of death. We have, through the Spirit, a theological picture of what it means to remain.

Chapter 2

Witnessing Holy Saturday

There is a total end and there is a total beginning, but
... what comes in between them?[1]
                                        Hans Urs von Balthasar

Hans Urs von Balthasar posed this question to radio listeners on Easter Saturday, March 31, 1956.[2] He asks them to take a step back and to think about the day between the account of the passion and the resurrection: Holy Saturday. Positioned between Good Friday and Easter Sunday in the Christian liturgical calendar, Holy Saturday is often overshadowed by the two days and remains, in many traditions, a day that merely marks a turn between the events of Jesus' death and resurrection. Admittedly, Balthasar says, there is a biblical silence in the aftermath of the crucifixion; the Gospel accounts do not reveal much about the activities between cross and resurrection; the events are limited to burial negotiations and preparations. Yet the middle develops in the Christian tradition into a rich literary and liturgical landscape of the underworld, filled with images of Christ's postdeath travels to hell. Christ's descent and presence in hell

---

1. Hans Urs von Balthasar, "We Walked Where There Was No Path," in *You Crown the Year with Your Goodness: Sermons through the Liturgical Year*, trans. Graham Harrison (San Francisco: Ignatius Press, 1989), 90.
2. Although the heading "Easter" is listed above the title of the sermon—"We Walked Where There Was No Path"—it was, in fact, delivered on Holy Saturday.

is inserted into the Apostles' Creed, and it becomes a component of Christian belief—"he descended into hell."

Despite its presence in the Christian creedal tradition, Balthasar believed that Holy Saturday had not yet been fully theologically articulated. He examines its tradition, believing that Holy Saturday, if attended to theologically, provides the key to interpreting Christian redemption. He writes, "The danger is very real that we, as spectators of a drama beyond our comprehension, will simply wait until the scene changes."[3] He breaks theological silence surrounding the day and provides a theology that resists the smooth progression from death to life as it is often narrated in accounts of the passion and resurrection. According to him, the ease or even neglect of Holy Saturday in the tradition means that we have a limited vision of the Christian message of redemption. If we look from the site of Holy Saturday, what do we see?

In this chapter, I identify Holy Saturday, the middle day, as the site of witness to a more complex relationship between death and life. There is no clear seeing in the aftermath of death. As Balthasar insists, there is no simple waiting until the scene changes. Instead, Holy Saturday narrates a more indecipherable time and place in which death and life are brought into a unique relationship. In the next chapter, I explore the Johannine figures of witness, revealing the middle territory of remaining and the centrality of witness to what cannot be fully known or contained of the death event. In both chapters, I show that there is not finality to the event of the cross but rather a confrontation with something of death remaining and extending into the territory of life. Both resist a picture of triumphant life arising out of death. A different concept of witness arises from the middle.

What would it mean to read this narrative of death and life from the middle? I explore this question by engaging the theology of Holy Saturday in the writings of Hans Urs von Balthasar and Adrienne von Speyr. Together, they provide an account of redemption beyond the death on the cross and before resurrection. They examine the middle territory that finds expression in the account of Jesus' descent into hell. Holy Saturday reveals a distinct landscape of suffering that cannot be understood exclusively in terms of the passion; neither can it be interpreted in relationship to resurrection. Instead, the experience of God in hell is an experience of death extending beyond its conceivable boundaries; it is, in Balthasar's words, "a drama beyond our powers of comprehension."[4] Their multifaceted entrance into this day exceeds the boundaries of theological inquiry.

My attempt in this chapter is to read Balthasar and Speyr's theology of Holy Saturday for what it contributes to a concept of witness unfolding in the after-

3. Hans Urs von Balthasar, *Mysterium Paschale*, trans. Aidan Nichols (Grand Rapids: Eerdmans, 1993), 50.
4. Ibid.

math of death.[5] The relationship between passion and resurrection, death and life, comes to new expression in their writings on Holy Saturday, as they attempt to reconcile the biblical and liturgical tradition with Speyr's mystical participation in Christ's descent into hell. Their theological inquiry into Holy Saturday is instigated by Speyr's unusual entrance into the territory of hell. Her repeated visions of the descent open up a complex landscape of witness, in which they attempt to give expression to her physical participation in the postcrucifixion forsakenness of Christ as well as the wordlessness of the territory of hell. Balthasar's earliest work, *Heart of the World*, reflects his struggles to render the events of Holy Saturday in words. On a day when the "Word falls silent," he must seek out a unique form of expression; Holy Saturday becomes for him a literary struggle of words against wordlessness.[6] The complexities of witnessing bodies and wordlessness between passion and resurrection are enacted on Holy Saturday. Through this, they offer a powerful testimony to what remains.[7]

Yet this testimony is, in turn, elided in their work. I argue that their increasing drive to develop a logic of redemption from the site of Holy Saturday leads them away from a vital testimony to the middle, as expressed in the embodied and aesthetic aspects of Holy Saturday. In the course of developing a theology of Holy Saturday, their testimony to the tensions of this day are increasingly occluded by a particular polemic and a desire to establish theological legitimacy (both of Speyr and Holy Saturday). The quest to find appropriate form and expression for this middle day is sidelined in service of these other factors. Speyr's physical experience of Holy Saturday and the literary expression of Holy Saturday recede, in favor of a logic that enacts certain elisions of body and word.

Looking through the lens of trauma, the concept of witness speaks to, rather than elides, the more difficult expressions of death and life, past and present, and absence and presence. Because the complexities of death's aftermath can easily be covered over, this witness tracks the effects of an event whose impact is not immediately known or recognizable. This witness acknowledges what has been

5. For a concise summary of a theology of Holy Saturday in Balthasar's thought, see David Lauber, "Hans Urs von Balthasar and a Theology of Holy Saturday," in *Barth on the Descent into Hell: God, Atonement, and the Christian Life* (Aldershot, UK: Ashgate, 2004), 42–75. This current chapter is not so much a summary of Balthasar's thought. Instead, it highlights dimensions of the development of Holy Saturday that are often conceived of as incidental and, therefore, unimportant. It aims to expose the narrative of Holy Saturday that runs alongside the authorized account and, in fact, disrupts its logic at particular points.

6. See Balthasar, "The Death of God as Wellspring of Salvation," in *Mysterium Paschale*. For Balthasar, the love of God cannot be fully translated into a lucid logic, especially if the climax of love's revelation is Holy Saturday. Love, as he often presents it, surpasses knowledge and renders one silent. Theology must be conceived of differently "at the moment when the word of God falls silent in the hiatus," taking away human logic and, as he depicts it, taking our breath away (83).

7. The next chapter also develops this concept of remaining in relationship to the Johannine texts; in both, I claim that remaining has a distinctively pneumatological character. In my own analysis, I turn Balthasar and Speyr back to the Johannine texts in which they are so firmly rooted. Between death and life, the figure of the Spirit takes particular shape in their stated theologies. It fails, however, to have the kind of texture that the Johannine texts present or even that is enacted within the broader dynamics of their thought.

lost and what remains. It is in and through this witness that life, in its reconfig-ured form—as remaining—can be discerned. As a theologically undercharted site, Holy Saturday provides the landscape in which to develop this alternative concept of witness. These interpretive struggles, as I unearth them here, tell us something about the nature of Holy Saturday and its theological significance. If redemption is narrated there, as Balthasar and Speyr profess, then an under-standing of redemption must take into account the layered witness of Holy Sat-urday. I argue that this witness is constitutive of the theology of the middle day and not incidental to it. The tensions between the enacted and written, the embodied and the authorized, the aesthetic and the systematic theologies of Balthasar and Speyr reflect the interpretive challenges of witnessing between death and life. The middle day becomes the site of witness to the truths that are in danger of being covered over and buried.

Balthasar's and Speyr's account of Holy Saturday displays both the seeds of this alternative witness and the elision of this witness. It does not emerge in their overall account of Holy Saturday. Their interpretations, instead, perpetu-ate an understanding of witness much like the one that I referenced in chapter 1—what Elizabeth Castelli describes as a theology of martyrdom and sacrifice. They interpret the significance of redemption through a christological model of imitation and self-sacrifice that cannot, I claim, bear the tensions of death and life as they exist on Holy Saturday. In Balthasar and Speyr, Holy Saturday iterates a logic of redemption that repeats, albeit in a different form, the logic of the cross. They increasingly link Holy Saturday to a christocentric logic that secures rather than testifies. The subtext of witness in their thought—attested to in Speyr's bodily experiences and in Balthasar's more literary works—is elided in favor of an imitative model of martyrdom that replicates while expanding a certain logic of the passion. Their struggle to interpret the physical realities of Speyr's experience and their struggle to find fitting language for the day are, thus, subsumed under this martyrdom model and become mere contextual side notes to their theology of Holy Saturday.[8]

Highlighting two key aspects of their theology of Holy Saturday, I look through the lens of trauma at their theological testimony to what persists between death and resurrection. On one level, they enact a witness to what remains. On another level, they elide it. Reading their theology of Holy Satur-day involves a process of unearthing the witness that gets covered over; in this unearthing process, a vision of redemption is reshaped, and familiar terms such as truth, spirit, and love are infused with new meaning.

8. The result is that scholars no longer contend with the bodily experience of Speyr or the more literary writings of Balthasar. For an interpretation of Holy Saturday, they can move directly to the systematic works. Balthasar and Speyr pave this way for their subsequent scholarship, but I am concerned here with what is lost in that process. The context is frequently noted but not seriously incorporated into accounts and assessments of Balthasar's Holy Saturday.

DISCOVERING HOLY SATURDAY

*Every year the passion ended on Good Friday, at about three
o'clock in the afternoon, with a death-like trance into which
flashed the thrust of the lance. Then, shortly thereafter, began the
"descent into hell" (which lasted into the early morning hours
of Easter Sunday) about which Adrienne gave detailed accounts
year after year.*[9]

Balthasar reported that one form of suffering came to an end on Friday. After
that, something completely different came. The "something" was Adrienne von
Speyr's entrance into the mystical territory of Holy Saturday. Flooded with
supernatural experiences, she entered into a form of suffering unrecognizable to
either of them. In 1941 and for the next twenty-five years, Speyr began to give
an account, both verbally and physically, of Christ's descent into the territory
of hell following his crucifixion.[10] She spoke of and enacted rich descriptive
accounts of her visions of hell where the mysteries of redemption were disclosed
to her. Each passion week, she prepared herself to enter into periods of intense
suffering. These travels to hell began Friday afternoon and lasted until early
Sunday morning. Speyr would often receive intense migraine headaches, as if
the crown of thorns was being pressed into her temples. Drops of blood would
sometimes spot her linens, as if the wounded heart of Christ was her own. She
would be transported to multiple places, encountering the saints of the tradition
or encountering Christ himself on his path to and beyond the cross.

But on Holy Saturday, all active suffering would cease. Another more inex-
plicable form of suffering began. It was a suffering that extended beyond death.
She reports, "I didn't feel anything physically on Holy Saturday. . . . I felt only
a great weariness . . . a soul-condition."[11] She describes the suffering as more
psychological than physical, the anguish stemming from what was absent rather
than from what was present. There was extreme loneliness, forsakenness, and
abandonment in hell. The experiences were marked by what was absent and
unavailable to her in hell. The pain of hell meant that she was completely cut
off from all forms of relationship. Just as the Son is cut off from the love of the
Father, Speyr believed that she had entered into what she called the "internal
condition" of suffering.[12] The uniqueness of the suffering on Holy Saturday lies

9. Hans Urs von Balthasar, *First Glance at Adrienne von Speyr*, trans. Antje Lawry and Sr. Sergia
Englund (San Francisco: Ignatius Press, 1981), 65. See also Adrienne von Speyr, *Kreuz und Hölle* I,
vol. 3: *Die Passionen* (Einseideln, Switzerland: Johannes Verlags, 1966), 27.

10. Balthasar compiled these visions and organized them into a multivolume set. For accounts
of the visions and missions to hell, see Speyr, *Kreuz und Hölle* I, vol. 3: *Die Passionen*, and *Kreuz und
Hölle* II, vol. 4: *Die Auftragshollen* (Einsiedeln, Switzerland: Johannes Verlags, 1966). For Balthasar's
initial account of Speyr's first visions in 1941, see vol. 3, 17ff.

11. Speyr, *Kreuz und Hölle* I, vol. 3: *Die Passionen*, 36. Author's translation.

12. In his observations of Speyr's 1941 visions, Balthasar notes a distinction between her visions
on Friday and those on Saturday: "Now the visions from hell begin. . . . She is inside, really, but
somehow not participating. She feels admittedly a type of compassion for this condition in hell and

in the finality of its disconnection. One does not take on sufferings in hell; one endures what it is to be abandoned.[13]

Balthasar's theology of Holy Saturday is not simply the product of studying the Christian tradition's account of the descent. His articulation of the descent was precipitated by these unusual events. His exploration was initially sparked, and continually fed, by these living expressions of Holy Saturday in the mystical experiences of Adrienne von Speyr, his lifelong theological partner and companion.[14] Her visions moved him to search for the meaning of Holy Saturday. Speyr understood that she was receiving visions of the Trinity in its unique and perilous configuration. In these visions and in the subsequent accounts of them, the descent narrates a divine love story that is deeply troubling. It is, at first glance, an anti–love story, a story of abandonment and separation, a story of God-forsakenness. The Son's cry of dereliction from the cross was not a plea but an implicit declaration; the Son *is* forsaken by the Father. The Father is no longer recognizable to him.

According to Balthasar, Speyr provided "whole maps of suffering" that were previously unnarrated in the tradition.[15] In her 1945 vision, she saw the cross and, on it, the dead Lord. On the cusp of Saturday, everything grew dark again. "He is in the condition of the dead, not yet resurrected."[16] The visions were of the Son making "trackless tracks" through hell.[17] What is clear is that the space she entered defied conceptual boundaries. She described falling into the gap, the

---

its terror, but in the sense of an inner participation in this condition. . . . In the passion one was allowed to suffer. One participated in the monstrous pains. . . . By contrast, here, it is from the very beginning hopeless to take on anything. She remains a non-participant" (*Kreuz und Hölle* I, vol. 3, 28). She claims, "You know that I enjoy praying. On Holy Saturday, I couldn't pray, it seemed to me that every approach to God was missing there. . . . I remained alone and unheard" (37).

13. Balthasar writes, "While bereft of any spiritual light emanating from the Father, in sheer obedience, he [the Son] must seek the Father where he cannot find him under any circumstances. And yet, this hell is a final mystery of the Father as the creator (who made allowances for the freedom of man). And so, in this darkness, the Incarnate Son learns 'experientially' this darkness, what until then was 'reserved' for the Father" (*First Glance*, 66).

14. See Johann Roten, "The Two Halves of the Moon: Marian Anthropological Dimensions in the Common Mission of Adrienne von Speyr and Hans Urs von Balthasar," in *Hans Urs von Balthasar: His Life and Work* (San Francisco: Ignatius Press, 1991), 70. Roten refers to a "psycho-spiritual symbiosis" between them.

15. Balthasar writes, "Whole maps of suffering were filled in precisely there where no more than a blank space or a vague idea seemed to exist. Adrienne was able to describe in her own clear and penetrating words what she was experiencing—during the suffering itself, in intervening pauses and also afterwards. I have taken these passions out of the stream of the diaries and grouped them together to form a separate book, *Cross and Hell*" (Balthasar, *First Glance*, 35). It is interesting to note that Balthasar describes Holy Saturday as timeless. Although Holy Saturday refers to a day—temporal—it becomes, in Balthasar and Speyr's analysis, a space, a landscape.

16. See *Kreuz und Hölle* I, vol. 3, 1945 vision, 86–115. The 1945 vision provides a full account of the relationship between the Father and Son in hell.

17. See Hans Urs von Balthasar, *Science, Religion and Christianity*, trans. Hilda Graef (London: Burns and Oates, 1958). He claims, "This track through the trackless way makes an opening where before all had been completely closed" (134).

hiatus, and the abyss. Hell's landscape is likened to a wilderness.[18] There is no sign of life. No possibility, no agency. It was a passive place in which the Son is not able to do anything. Instead, the Son receives a vision of his complete separation from the Father and a vision of the separation of all things from God.

What did they make of this? The construction of Holy Saturday began with these visions. From 1941 to 1965, Balthasar was present with her, witnessing these visions, writing them down, and later using them as a primary source for his written theology of Holy Saturday.[19] He interpreted her share in Christ's sufferings as a gift—"the greatest theological gift"—that she offered to the church as a whole.[20] The profession of belief in "Christ's descent into hell" in the Apostles' Creed was given bodily expression and theological depth through Speyr. She provided physical and contemplative commentary on the work of redemption enacted by Christ in hell. In the introduction to the collection of her visions— *Kreuz und Hölle*—Balthasar writes, "Holy Saturday stands as the mysterious middle between cross and resurrection, and thus between all of revelation and theology. . . . Perhaps our time is ripe for this blessing (Adrienne's visions)."[21]

This mystical partnership on Holy Saturday was part of a broader partnership between them. It began in 1940 and continued until her death in 1967.[22] In

---

18. Hans Urs von Balthasar, *Heart of the World* (San Francisco: Ignatius Press, 1979). In the closing chapter of *Heart of the World*, he provides a picture of Christian discipleship by employing a vocabulary similar to that of the descent into hell. Thus, he not only conveys the centrality of Holy Saturday in the Triduum but also implies that Holy Saturday is the landscape for all life that follows. Just as Jesus did not have a clearly discernible, but rather chaotic, journey through hell, so, too, Balthasar presents the path of following Jesus in similar terms. In this final chapter, he describes love as a wilderness and the journey of faith as a hike in which "regional maps and measuring devices" are thrown aside (205); "But you yourself, Lord: how are you a way? . . . the Way that you are—and you ARE a way—should remove every solid road from beneath our feet. . . . Where is there a way here? Where any kind of indication? Is this not the wilderness?" (207–8).

19. See John W. Coakley, *Women, Men, and Spiritual Powers: Female Saints and Their Male Collaborators* (New York: Columbia University Press, 2006). It is difficult to find a fitting description of their relationship. It defies the clear delineations of colleague, friend, or partner. They demonstrate, in many ways, a modern expression of the medieval relationship between male monastics and female mystics. Also, Balthasar writes, "And so began the first of those 'Passions,' ending with the remarkable experience of Holy Saturday which was to become so characteristic of Adrienne. They were repeated from then on, year after year, revealing in ever new ways a variety of theological relationships" (Balthasar, *First Glance*, 35). "From 1941 on, year after year—in the interior experience which she has described—she was allowed to share in the suffering of Christ. This occurred during the days of Holy Week (and often the whole of Lent was an intensive preparation for it). A landscape of pain of undreamt-of variety was disclosed to me, who was permitted to assist her: how many and diverse were the kinds of fear, at the Mount of Olives and at the Cross, how many kinds of shame, outrage and humiliation, how many forms of Godforsakenness . . . ; but numerous mystics through the centuries have been allowed to experience a great deal of it in ever-varying aspects—if only by drops, as it were, compared with the Son of God. In Adrienne's passions it was the vagueness of the relation of her own suffering to those of the Lord which was purely impressive" (64–65).

20. Balthasar, *First Glance*, 64.

21. Hans Urs von Balthasar, "Einleitung," in *Kreuz und Hölle* I, vol. 3, 10.

22. Much of what we know about Adrienne von Speyr is through Balthasar's *First Glance*. It is not my intention here to provide a full character study or a psychological portrait of Speyr. Instead, I am examining her biography in order to better understand her role in the development of Holy Saturday and her significance in shaping the interpretation of redemption that arises from their joint exploration of the Paschal Triduum.

October 1940, just months prior to her reception of these passion week visions, Speyr converted to Catholicism, a decision that she credits to the influence and guidance of Balthasar.[23] Her conversion was foreshadowed, she said, by a childhood flesh wound that flared up in response to her visions of Mary, the Mother of God, and in response to her first meeting with Balthasar. She interpreted this "living" wound as a sign of deep spiritual connection, which unfolded in a common task between them, of lives lived out in obedience to God, as patterned in Christ's mission in the Johannine Gospel. Balthasar was a novitiate in the Jesuit order at the time. A medical doctor, Speyr maintained her medical profession throughout her life, yet she understood her central mission to be the development of a lay community centered on the Johannine Gospel and the practice of the Ignatian exercises. Their joint call to start a lay community initiated his departure from the Jesuit order. The long and painful process of authorizing Speyr and her visions would eventually put him at odds with the Society of Jesus. This mission was to be shared with Balthasar, and as he grew convinced of this joint calling, his participation in the Jesuit order was threatened. The continual denial of her charisms by the church pained Balthasar, and his struggle to verify her mystical visions in the eyes of ecclesial authorities came to a head in 1948. He left the Jesuits in order to found the Community of St. John with Speyr.[24]

Speyr's entrance into Balthasar's life was considered by many not only puzzling but to be what limited Balthasar from realizing his calling as a Jesuit brother and his potential as a Catholic theologian. He, however, believed the opposite. Many published pages of his work argue her critical influence on his theology and make a case for her to be recognized as a theologian in her own right. In 1975 he claimed, "The greater part of so much of what I have written is a translation of what is present in more immediate, less technical fashion in the powerful work of Adrienne von Speyr, only part of which has been published."[25] He argued, continually, the inseparability of their theology. He further affirmed, "Her work and mine are neither psychologically nor philologically to be separated: two halves of a single whole, which has as its center a unique foundation."[26] Balthasar established Johannes Verlag, a private publishing house, with the intention of publishing her works. This was just one of several moves that he made to make sure that she would be taken seriously, both as a visionary and as a theologian.

23. This is not a conversion to Christianity, but instead a conversion from Lutheranism to Catholicism. See Hans Urs von Balthasar, *Our Task*, trans. John Saward (San Francisco: Ignatius Press, 1994), 119, 151–52, and 213. Balthasar writes, "During her first Holy Week as a Catholic she was given a share in Christ's Passion" (77).

24. Ibid., 77–82. In discussing Adrienne's experiences with others, Balthasar was often met with great resistance and skepticism. He insisted on speaking about her. "In most cases, though (for example, with my superiors), I just could not avoid it. So began the long and painful story of my departure from the Jesuits" (79).

25. Hans Urs von Balthasar, *My Work: In Retrospect* (San Francisco: Ignatius Press, 1993), 105.

26. Ibid., 89.

Their partnership was most pronounced and yet most unusual on Holy Saturday. Balthasar attributed his development of Holy Saturday wholly to Speyr.[27] Writing about Holy Saturday became a process of reconciling ancient sources with what he understood as a special revelation taking place in her. Both believed that her visions were not only consistent with these sources but that they offered new insight to, and illumination of, Christ's work of redemption in hell. She witnessed the drama of Father, Son, and Spirit at its most threatened point. Entering into the forsakenness of Christ's experience in hell, Speyr was able to convey the deepest mystery of faith—the paradox of divine love evidenced not in victory but in its seeming opposite.

Holy Saturday first appears in their theological writings in 1943, two years after she first received her visions.[28] Over the next several decades they attempted to convey the significance of Holy Saturday to a theological audience. The private experience of hell must become public. In Sheol, he writes, the Son is dead with the dead in the depths of hell.[29] "The Son cannot be introduced into Hell save as a dead man, on Holy Saturday."[30] From this statement, a series of mysteries unfold. God's love is demonstrated in the place devoid of love. They affirmed that God reveals God's love for humanity on the cross, but the descent into hell reveals another dimension of that love. Their narration of the events of hell is a testimony to the persistence of love in utter forsakenness and abandonment.

It is beyond the scope of this project to give a full account of the status of Adrienne von Speyr in the scholarship on Balthasar. Prominent interpretations of his theology of Holy Saturday mention the influence of Speyr and her visions, but they do not explore her influence in any depth. It is as if the context of the exploration of the descent bears little on the interpretation of it. This bracketing of Speyr is commonplace. In *Light in Darkness*, Alyssa Pitstick writes, "I have deliberately eschewed the question of the *origin* of Balthasar's doctrine of the Descent, focusing instead on examining its *doctrinal content* in comparison with the traditional doctrine. Hence I do not draw conclusions about the nature of his personal rejection of that doctrine."[31] Pitstick indicates in a footnote that further discussion of Speyr is "outside the present scope" of her project.[32] Similarly, Edward T. Oakes writes, "I have, however, decided to postpone

27. "The implications of Adrienne's Holy Saturday and other 'hellish' experiences—for theology, mysticism, and ordinary Christian life—are incalculable and will have to be studied slowly and carefully. In so doing, we must not forget that, for Adrienne, despite all attempts at clarification, this experience remained an absolute mystery, resisting resolution into the formulas of any 'dialectic'" (Balthasar, *Our Task*, 65–66).

28. Balthasar described these visions as "missions of hell" in which Adrienne was transported to places of intense suffering. Her early visions transported her to contemporary contexts of suffering, one of which was the German concentration camps. See Balthasar, *First Glance*, 67, and *Our Task*, 70.

29. Balthasar, *Mysterium Paschale*, 161.

30. Ibid., 175.

31. Alyssa Lyra Pitstick, *Light in Darkness: Hans Urs von Balthasar and the Catholic Doctrine of Christ's Descent into Hell* (Grand Rapids: William B. Eerdmans Publishing Company, 2007), 346 (italics added). When pressed to speak about Speyr, Pitstick acknowledges that Speyr's descent experiences did heavily shape his theology at key points (389n50).

32. Ibid., 412n186.

a consideration of the greatest influence on his life, Adrienne von Speyr, to the end of the book. . . . I must admit that such a stance might not have met with approval of the master of the house [Balthasar]."[33] Speyr remains, in many works on Balthasar, incidental to his scholarship despite his assertions of his profound indebtedness to her as a theologian.[34]

WRITING HOLY SATURDAY

Balthasar's first attempt to present Holy Saturday to a theological audience is in *Heart of the World*. He claims, "*Das Herz der Welt* [*Heart of the World*] (written in 1943) is the first direct echo of my involvement with Adrienne's paschal experiences—the Eastertide and Eucharistic experiences as well as those of Good Friday and Holy Saturday."[35] He writes it, he says, in a flurry of passion and identifies it later in his life as his thirteen hymns to Christ.[36] Described by the translator, Erasmo Leiva, as a work of christological poetry, the text is a dramatic reading of the Gospel of John, and it is centered on the image of the divine heart.[37] The divine incarnation is described using the image of the heart. The incarnation is the descent of God's heart into the world, and the events of Jesus' life, death, and resurrection are all described as the process by which the divine heart seeks to transform the human heart. Balthasar's commentary on the Johannine text weaves images of vineyards and wilderness, bloodstreams and rivers, to narrate what he believed to be the central thrust of the Gospel: divine love. Love descends into the world, and the path of love is a mixture of suffering and

33. Edward T. Oakes, *Pattern of Redemption: The Theology of Hans Urs von Balthasar* (New York: Continuum, 1994), 10.

34. A notable exception to this postponement of Speyr is in the work of John Saward, *The Mysteries of March: Hans Urs von Balthasar on the Incarnation and Easter* (Washington, DC: Catholic University of America Press, 1990). Saward refers to the "Adrienne-Balthasar theology of the Descent" and speaks about Balthasar and Speyr equally when describing their analysis of the descent into hell (112). Saward also acknowledges the bizarre and puzzling nature of this coauthored theology. "Magnificent and inspiring though it is, Balthasar's theology of the Descent in many ways bewilders me. . . . Despite my puzzles, I am convinced that this account of the Descent into Hell is of enormous importance, not only theologically but apologetically" (129, 132).

35. He continues, "The lyrical hymn-like style of the book is not appropriate to her own, which was always very plain and down-to-earth. It is a sign of my enthusiasm and sense of wonder at these privileged insights into the mystery of Christ in all its fullness. Much seen here is repeated later in more objective form. The chapter on the descent into hell is directly dependent on Adrienne's Holy Saturday experiences, as are all the later references to this mystery" (Balthasar, *Our Task*, 96).

36. Balthasar writes, "What Paul calls the great 'mystery' is that action of God with the world that through creation, revelation and redemption always remains history, action, drama and event and has its center in the fullness of time, in the Incarnation. The aphorisms *Das Weizenkorn* (The grain of wheat) already had the intention of experiencing the world and life in this way; still more clearly is this true of the thirteen hymns to Christ of *Das Herz der Welt* (Heart of the World), in which I wished to give back to the idea of the Heart of Jesus (which has so often degenerated into sentimentality) its cosmic dimension and, even more than this, the incalculable and ultimately Trinitarian inner sphere of the hypostatic union" (Balthasar, *My Work*, 22).

37. Hans Urs von Balthasar, *Heart of the World*, trans. Erasmo Leiva (San Francisco: Ignatius, 1979), 8.

victory, death and life.[38] Holy Saturday is a pivotal part of this divine love story. It narrates divine love at its least discernible point—between death and resurrection, in the recesses of hell.

The Johannine account is rendered dramatically in *Heart of the World*. In chapter 9, "A Wound Has Blossomed," Balthasar describes the experience of a single witness standing at the foot of the cross following the crucifixion. Imagining the thoughts and movements of this witness, Balthasar names Holy Saturday as the site of witness between death and life. In the aftermath of death, something unusual takes place. It is, however, difficult to discern exactly what it is. This witness attempts to articulate the strange postdeath events. Just as *Heart of the World* is somewhat genre defying, so, too, my reading of Balthasar's text attempts to preserve the language of his text in my telling. I attempt to preserve the power of Balthasar's rhetoric in the narration that follows below. Note, also, that I employ the feminine pronoun here. The gender of the witness, in Balthasar's text, is ambiguous; there is no pronoun referenced throughout this narrative. This is also consistent with the attention that Balthasar gives to the women surrounding the cross and to women mystics in the tradition whose visions of the cross strongly inform his work.

A witness stands in the space of death, surrounded by darkness thicker than she has ever known. The stench of death lingers, but the wails, shouts, and mocking have all stopped. It is over. She watched for hours as the body of her leader hung in the space of criminals. Just moments before, Jesus hung his head—defeated. "Suddenly all of them standing around the gallows know it: he is gone. Immeasurable emptiness (not solitude) streams forth from the hanging body. Nothing but this fantastic emptiness is any longer at work here."[39] Now she is alone with the penetrating silence. She stares up at the cross; Jesus has been swallowed up by the dark sky. She can no longer feel her feet. Is she standing? What is she standing on? The sky is as dark as the earth. Nothing separates them.

But wait! Something is happening to the sky. What is it? She does not know. "Was it lightning?"[40] she asks. She cannot decipher what she is seeing. It is something. It is not flashing anymore. It is something so small; it is moving. Yes, it is a tiny moving light. Standing in the space of darkness, she stammers her questions, her eyes following a spark of light coming from the site of Jesus' death. Her inability to discern what is taking place throws her into a maddening whirl of speculation. She thinks she sees a light, but the darkness at the foot of the cross has disoriented her. A glimmer of light is coming from the space where Jesus' body is hanging. But she cannot determine the exact location or nature of the light. She begins to speculate:

38. Ibid., 27.
39. Ibid., 150.
40. Ibid., 149.

What is this light glimmer that wavers and begins to take form in the endless void? It has neither content nor contour. A nameless thing, more solitary than God, it emerges out of pure emptiness. It is no one. It is anterior to everything. Is it the beginning? It is small and undefined as a drop. Perhaps it is water. But it does not flow. It is not water. It is thicker, more opaque, more viscous than water. It is also not blood, for blood is red, blood is alive, blood has a loud human speech. This is neither water nor blood. It is older than both, a chaotic drop.[41]

Something is emerging from the cross, but it is not something definable. The text indicates that this tiny flicker lacks origin and shape, making it difficult to name. It is neither new nor old, blood nor water, light nor dark. But it is moving out of the space of death toward the disciple.

"Is that death? . . . Is it the end? . . . Is it the beginning? The beginning of what?"[42] she asks. The response begins in the negative. It is not the beginning of God or of creation. It is some kind of beginning coming out of the space of death. Yet a beginning out of death seems to defy the very concept of a beginning. This understanding of a different kind of beginning dominates her reflections:

It is a beginning without parallel, as if Life were arising from Death, as if weariness (already such weariness as no amount of sleep could ever dispel) and the uttermost decay of power were melting at creation's outer edge, were beginning to flow, because flowing is perhaps a sign and a likeness of weariness which can no longer contain itself, because everything that is strong and solid must in the end dissolve into water. But hadn't it—in the beginning—also been born from water? And is this wellspring in the chaos, this trickling weariness, not the beginning of a new creation?[43]

Death is producing something, but it is not something new; it is weary and puzzlingly old. Amid chaos and misrecognition, a drop moves through the darkness, gains force, and becomes a rushing stream. Is this death or life? It seems to be both. It is old and new, laden with death but moving toward life, turning nothing into something.

The tone shifts, introducing the voice of the narrator-theologian. A powerful word follows: *Karsamstagzauber*.[44] It is translated from German to English as "the magic of Holy Saturday," but is more properly translated as "the *mystery* of Holy Saturday." The events are suddenly placed within the time of the liturgical Christian calendar, between Good Friday and Easter Sunday. The element of mystery is tied to the startling emergence of something lifelike from the void of the crucifixion. The day between Friday and Sunday is a period of chaos, mis-

41. Ibid., 151.
42. Ibid.
43. Ibid., 152.
44. Hans Urs von Balthasar, *Das Herz der Welt* (Zurich: J. Stemmle & Co., 1945), 112.

recognition, and strange reversals. The questions that follow this declaration of the day have more interpretive force than the previous ones. Rather than asking whether this is death or a beginning, the narrator queries the events:

> Could this be the residue of the Son's love which, poured out to the last when every vessel cracked and the old world perished, is now making a path for itself to the Father through the glooms of nought? Or, in spite of it all, is this love trickling on in impotence, unconsciously, laboriously, towards a new creation that does not yet even exist, a creation which is still to be lifted up and given shape?[45]

The text identifies this tiny and chaotic drop as a drop of love. It is love left over from the love poured out on the cross. Although love was killed on the cross, as the disciple declared, it was not fully extinguished.[46] This residue of love is not powerful but weary and impotent. Its movement suggests that death does not fully govern it. But is this life? It is not life as we know it. Though the witness declared all dead, she witnesses in these postcrucifixion moments something that survives death.

Although the origin of the drop appears to come from the darkness of the cross, the disciple later identifies its origin as the wound of Christ. This strange substance is emerging from the wound: "To be sure, it flows out of a wound and is like the blossom and fruit of a wound."[47] The site of violence and suffering is productive. The wound becomes the site of growth—creative, generative, and alive. This new origin, this new beginning, is a beginning that comes out of death. At the end of the chapter, the narrator declares that this will be the beginning of everything in the future. This second world must be birthed out of death: "Just as the first creation arose ever anew out of sheer nothingness, so, too, this second world—still unborn, still caught up in its first rising—will have its sole origin in this wound, which is never to close again."[48] The disciple witnesses a different kind of beginning in the events of Holy Saturday. Chaos and nothingness mark the events of Holy Saturday, but the events are equally marked by the unidentifiable "fruit" coming out of this wound.

Heart of the World was poorly received by Balthasar's peers; the rhetoric was estimated to be unwieldy, and the style pompous.[49] Yet in writing the text, Balthasar

---

45. Balthasar, *Heart of the World*, 152.

46. "Men wounded your Heart . . . but I have done something very different. I have dealt a sharp blow at the heart of love. I have killed love. . . . It has collapsed into ruin; it is no longer. A corpse hangs on the Cross. I sit at a distance and brood in my lost infamy. I am the son of ruination" (ibid., 147).

47. Ibid., 152.

48. Ibid., 153.

49. See Peter Henrici, "Hans Urs von Balthasar: A Sketch of His Life," in *Hans Urs von Balthasar: His Life and Work*, ed. David L. Schindler (San Francisco: Ignatius, 1991), 7–43. Henrici writes, "Von Balthasar's style was not everyone's cup of tea. For many it seemed too aesthetic, too demanding. He was successful with students of literature and history, with architects, a few lawyers, and some medical students. With scientists and science he never found the right approach. So it was inevitable that the dedication of his 1945 book, *Das Herz der Welt-Electis dilectis*, was seen as utterly elitist, and

believed that he had touched the pulse of the gospel message that was unquestionably evident to him in the testimony of Speyr. It captured, he thought, the importance of her visions.[50] At the time he wrote the text, he had witnessed two years of her unusual experiences, and it was clear that he understood *Heart of the World* as a breakthrough in presenting these experiences in written form. Despite the critiques, Balthasar defended this text and returned to it throughout his career.

Heart of the World reflects the deeply literary character of Balthasar's theology. With respect to formal training, Balthasar occupied a liminal space in the field of theology. Trained in Germanic languages and literature, he never received a degree in theology. His canon is more literary than theological.[51] Because of this, he continually presses the questions of form that were often treated as incidental by his theological peers. This treatment is evidenced in his later development of a theological aesthetics. This early "poetic" work reflects his attempt to find theological language consonant with the mystery of redemption taking place in the paschal Triduum. This mystery presses the limits of literary form. He writes, "What I am trying to do is to express this [the drama of redemption] in a form in which all the dimensions and tensions of life remain present instead of being sublimated in the abstractions of a 'systematic' theology."[52]

Approaching theology as a literary scholar, he conceived himself as out of step with most traditionally trained theologians. Never apologetic about his literary training, he instead often disparaged the field of systematic theology for its shabby rhetoric and its disregard for aligning form and content.[53] Although

---

that von Balthasar himself should be regarded by many people as inaccessible and arrogant" (17). Even Speyr was critical of the text. "You know, there are certain passages at the beginning that I find a little tepid. In other words, your enjoyment of word play, the sound of words, their analysis, their 'cognates,' seems here and there to leave the spiritual aspect in the shade. I'll . . . gladly show you the passages if it will help" (31–32, noted in Hans Urs von Balthasar, *Unser Auftrag: Bericht und Entwurf* (Einsiedeln, Switzerland: Johannes Verlag, 1984), 80).

50. As much was accomplished by, in fact, giving her the status of a biblical disciple.

51. This split between theology and poetics is precisely what Balthasar presses against in the development of his theological aesthetics. Theology, insofar at it seeks to attest to God's revelation, must not be relegated to one particular form of writing. This kind of distinction, however, persists within theology. Another false dichotomy is between spiritual/mystical and theological writings. Julian of Norwich is a good example of this.

52. Balthasar writes, "Only when God appears on the world stage (and at the same time remains behind the scenes) can one work out what the *persons of the drama* stand for, what 'laws' this dramatic action follows, a dramatic action ultimately without parallel, because it constitutes the ultimate drama. All this is what every Christian knows in a spontaneous and unselfconscious way and what he strives to live out. What I am trying to do is to express this in a form in which all the dimensions and tensions of life remain present instead of being sublimated in the abstractions of a 'systematic' theology" (Balthasar, *My Work*, 98–99).

53. This quote reveals, I believe, a familiar tone in assessing Balthasar's work—both a certain awe for his literary talents yet a corresponding need to argue the strength of his logic. Louis Dupré writes, "Von Balthasar writes with the flair of an artist, a very learned one, but an artist nonetheless. In his essays he practices what his theory preaches. They are brilliant exercises in theological aesthetics. Rather than abiding by the rational structures of dissertational writing, they obey the more adventurous order of the creative imagination, shaping each intellectual profile into an aesthetic construction

many of these insights are identified and discussed in his volumes on theological aesthetics, the negative reviews of *Heart of the World* foreshadowed the reception of the literary into the realm of theology. The aesthetic demands on theological writing were very clear to Balthasar; the revelation of the divine could not be exhausted in theo-logic. A good theologian testifies to this journey of love, gleaning from the literary and theological masters in order to attest to the beauty of God's revelation. But despite his confidence in the literary dimension of revelation, he was often, as in the case of *Heart of the World*, unable to convince theologians of the necessity of writing theology with serious attention given to its written form. But it was Holy Saturday, in particular, that he believed demanded a keener attention to language. The view of redemption from the depths of hell, he says, "must necessarily express itself in images, since it apprehends something that lies beyond death."[54]

In these brief pages, he begins his theological speculation about the descent to hell and its significance in Christian theology. *Heart of the World* reveals the seeds of his theology of Holy Saturday. We see in this brief narrative both the problem and the promise of the day. The problem is that the events of the day are profoundly difficult, if not impossible, to articulate. The promise is that they are not overlooked but witnessed. A puzzling birthing process is taking place in the wake of the death, and someone is there to witness it. This witness marks a more difficult passage between death and resurrection that is not often interpreted theologically. Balthasar inserts the liturgical day into this text, delineating between the events of the passion and resurrection. In *Heart of the World*, a chaotic, weary drop moves out of the space of death. It picks up speed, and it becomes a gushing fountain, a wellspring. This movement from death to life defines the place of Holy Saturday. Something is taking place between death and life, and the disciple at the foot of the cross is there to witness it.

There is, however, another crucial element to consider. The witness in the text is never named. The presentation of the text in the first person makes it difficult to discern who occupies this space. Leading up to this point, we assume it is the voice of Peter reflecting on his betrayal of Jesus. Now positioned at the site of Jesus' death, he is flooded with guilt and remorse. He positions himself as one of the criminals crucified alongside Jesus: "To the one on your right up there you promised Paradise. . . . I'll always be the one on your left. And stop torturing me too with your torture. Try to forget me."[55] Then there appears to be a shift in voice. The German text, unlike the English translation, breaks after this,

---

in its own right, fiercely independent of established norms of opinions and free to follow the meandering course of its subjective inspiration. This approach yields marvelous results. Often an idea displays itself more advantageously in the half-light of poetic metaphor than in the full glare of rational conceptualization. To be sure, the method also creates a logical elusiveness potentially discomforting to the philosophically exacting reader. Von Balthasar has repeatedly proven (for instance, in his study of truth) his ability of sustaining a rigorous argument" (Schindler, *His Life and Work*, 205–6).

54. Balthasar, *Science*, 132.
55. Balthasar, *Heart of the World*, 149.

inserting a line division in the narrative. The text picks up with the question: "Was it lightning?"[56] Given the context of the Johannine text, the voice featured on Holy Saturday is that of the beloved disciple, the witness to the blood and water coming from Jesus' side. But, again, there is no clear identification of the beloved disciple in Balthasar's text. In the brief narration, this indeterminate figure assumes the role of a theologian. With the mention of Holy Saturday and the Father, this witness assumes a greater interpretive role, extending beyond the biblical postcrucifixion space into the theological tradition that follows.

The textual ambiguity is significant.[57] The biblical drama transforms into theo-drama, and the characters standing in the middle territory are not exclusively biblical figures. Because this text is so highly connected to Speyr's bodily participation in the mysteries of the passion, she could occupy the space of the disciple, attempting to make sense of the events beyond the cross. She *becomes* Mary Magdalene or Mary, the mother of Jesus, or the unnamed disciple. In this sense, Balthasar attributes to her the biblical status of a witness. Balthasar could also be the witness, standing in the space of death, witnessing to the chaos between heaven and hell, to the weary trickle of love making its way out of death. To consider Balthasar as the main character in the text is to recognize a doubleness operating in his interpretation of Saturday. Balthasar is writing a theology of Saturday, trying to discern its theological significance, but this discernment involves being drawn into the peculiar territory of Adrienne von Speyr's visions. Could this be his testimony to what is taking place in her as well? If we read Balthasar into this narrative space, we see him testifying not only to the peculiar postdeath events, but to these events enacted in and through Speyr. We are reading, in these four pages, his struggle to articulate theologically the inarticulable mystery of Christ's passion evidenced in her.

The anonymity of the witness opens up a variety of shifting witness positions and persons. I am imagining one possible position and its implications: Balthasar is the witness. In this account of Holy Saturday, he is testifying on two levels. He offers a theological description of the descent to hell as witnessed by those standing at the foot of the cross. He simultaneously offers his own testimony to Speyr's experience of Holy Saturday. Struggling to interpret her visions in light of both the biblical and theological testimony to the paschal mystery, he is the unnamed disciple questioning the meaning of what is taking place. The unnamed witness tracks the mysterious descent on Holy Saturday, and Balthasar, each passion week, attends to Speyr while she receives visions of the passion and the descent. If we place Balthasar in the position of witness, we also can read this text equally as his own testimony to what he does not understand and

---

56. The literal English translation is "Was that lightning?" (ibid.).

57. *Heart of the World* features several shifting voices throughout the text, and it is often difficult to discern where one stops and another starts. This is particularly true in chap. 9, the account of Holy Saturday. The most prominent voices are the voice of Christ and the voice of the narrator. In chap. 9, Peter's voice is heard and then an unnamed witness at the foot of the cross.

struggles to receive—to what is transmitted at the site of death.[58] As Speyr is drawn into the events of hell, Balthasar is also drawn in, witnessing to the divine drama of death coming alive in her flesh. *Heart of the World* marks an important aspect of witness: the struggle to discern what exceeds conceptual limits.

In this early account of Holy Saturday, Balthasar provides much more than a commentary on the Johannine drama; he testifies to the events of Holy Saturday and to the difficulty and necessity of witnessing between death and life. He witnesses the descent into hell indirectly through her and, consequently, attempts to write a theology of Holy Saturday that both honors her visions and interprets them for a wider community. Balthasar's theology of Holy Saturday has particularly complex dimensions, one of which is the attempt to witness to events that exceed the boundaries of comprehension and resist articulation. How does he write a theology about a day that defies straightforward expression? How does he testify to the peculiarity of Speyr's participation in this divine drama? In the descriptions that follow, I insist that the answers to these questions are not only inseparable from, but central to, an understanding of Holy Saturday.

In the mystical experiences of Speyr and in the literary expression of Holy Saturday, the witness to the middle events is pivotal. Because what is taking place is not easily discernible, there is increasing importance placed on the role of the witness. The question of "what" shifts to the question of "who." Who will be able to witness such events? For Balthasar, this is a Johannine question, emerging from the Gospel text, but it is also a question posed to theologians, especially at the site of Holy Saturday. In a 1956 radio address, Balthasar inquires, "What is it that takes place on Holy Saturday? . . . What *is* it that persists between death and Resurrection?"[59] He follows these questions with a challenge to theologians. He says, "This [the between] is a problem of theological logic; perhaps it is *the* problem that the theologians have never attended to and that, if it were taken seriously, would threaten to throw into confusion all our beautiful Archimedean drawings on paper."[60] He is urging theologians to occupy this middle space. A theological articulation of Holy Saturday, as he understood it, makes demands on theologians that few will accept. Who will be able to witness such events? It is clear that Balthasar believed that the message of Holy Saturday could not be attained apart from interpreting the unusual witness of Speyr and from exploring this pathless and silent terrain.[61] But he was less convinced that theologians were up to the task of theologically attesting to redemption from the middle.

---

58. This language of transmission resonates with the trauma literature and comes to new expression in the Johannine vocabulary of "handing over" in the next chapter.

59. Balthasar, "We Walked Where There Was No Path," 89–90.

60. Ibid., 91.

61. Balthasar, *My Work*. He indicates that Barbara Albrecht was compiling an anthology of representative works from Speyr: "The richness contained there will only be recognized in more mature times. Then it will be seen how strongly the intuition of this woman has influenced my books—*Herz der Welt* (*Heart of the World*), *Gottesgrage* (*The God Question*), *Theologie der drei Tage* (*Mysterium Paschale*)—and various other works, which essentially are only a theological transcription of so much learned directly from her" (105–6).

Heart of the World is his first, but certainly not his last, writing on Holy Saturday. However, the history of the development of Holy Saturday is telling—from its origins to its contemporary retrievals. It is a history rife with elisions. The history itself speaks to the complex process of witnessing to death curiously extended—"seconded."[62] From the middle, a new language arises to speak to a different form of life that emerges from death but also maintains death within it. It disrupts a straightforward trajectory from death to life and introduces a new vocabulary of the between: residue, chaos, weary love, and trickling impotence. Theological logic is pressed to, and beyond, its limits. And Adrienne von Speyr's body comes to life in the space of death, pressing the limits of religious experience.

Their early witness to Holy Saturday testifies to a unique truth of the middle day: death remains. These two aspects—the mystical visions and the literary expression—witness to this remainder, in all of its chaotic expressions. These aspects recede as Balthasar and Speyr attempt to express a theology of Holy Saturday in more systematic form. With this recession, the witness enacted on Holy Saturday is expressed in terms of Trinitarian orthodoxy and a noticeable christological pattern of witness.[63] The difficult process of witnessing enacted between Balthasar and Speyr and depicted in the testimony of the disciple at the foot of the cross all but disappears. Holy Saturday, as it is developed in their thought, loses the traces of a more textured and entangled witness to the "hiatus" of Holy Saturday.[64]

Balthasar and Speyr, in fact, testify to this hiatus, opening up a unique site of witness in the Christian tradition. Early on, they mark the space of Holy Saturday in a significant way, testifying to a form of presence that is not solely defined by the Christ-form as by its pneumatological forms. Their later articulation of Holy Saturday, however, belies the fullness of this testimony. Insofar as this truth of what remains is enfolded into a familiar logic associated with passion and resurrection, they stop short of this witness. This later theology—what is rendered almost exclusively as Balthasar's theology of Holy Saturday—takes a particular form that repeats the logic of the passion. What gets elided, I argue, is a distinctively pneumatological dimension of Holy Saturday.

I trace here the later—authorized and official—theology of Holy Saturday and its corresponding model of witness. The concept of witness that develops in relationship to Holy Saturday is expressed christologically and in the language of imitation, obedience, and sacrifice that is central to their overall christology. This model of witness as imitation and self-sacrifice does not sufficiently capture what is taking place on this day. Witness, when exclusively tied to the figure of the Son, takes on a specific form for them: the form of martyrdom.

---

62. Balthasar, *Mysterium Paschale*, 168.

63. I am not referring to the Eastern Orthodox church, but rather to a creedal formulation of the Trinity that is dominant in the Western Christian tradition.

64. Balthasar, *Mysterium Paschale*, 49.

THEOLOGIZING HOLY SATURDAY

It was shown again in the descent into hell, when, on Holy Saturday, Nietzsche is right for just one day and God is dead. The Word has ceased to sound in the world, the body is buried and sealed, and the soul descends into the abyss of Sheol, where death rules in all reality and is not defeated beforehand by faith, hope, and love, where the poena damni *[pain of loss] includes all, that is the impossibility of seeing God, looking for him, raising the eyes to him.*[65]

Between passion and resurrection, there is no light, no life, and no words. Between passion and resurrection, there is the event of Christ's descent into hell. Christ, Balthasar insists, does not descend into hell as one victorious over death. He does not go down to the realm of the dead and collect all the sinners and unbelievers; he does not break the chains of the captives. There is no victory there and no activity. Instead, the Son is a dead man in hell. Balthasar holds onto this stark picture of the finality and darkness of death in hell in order to develop his unique conception of its redemptive significance.

I have already noted the contextual backdrop for the development of Holy Saturday—Speyr's visions of hell. The theological backdrop of Balthasar's retrieval and reinterpretation of Holy Saturday is what is referred to as the harrowing of hell.[66] This harrowing is most commonly conveyed through visual representations of the Christ figure in hell. The "harrowing" narrative reads the events in this way: The Son dies on the cross and descends into hell. There he claims victory over the imprisoned souls of the unbelievers. He breaks the hold of sin, death, and unbelief, unlocking the chains of those who dwell there. Harrowing, he ascends victoriously; in this interim between cross and resurrection, he claims the victory of life over death.[67] According to Balthasar, one of the consequences of this "harrowing" reading is that Easter comes too early, before its time. Holy Saturday is completely eclipsed and becomes merely a forerunner to Easter. This activity in hell already anticipates the resurrection. He writes, "We must, in the first place, guard against that theological busyness and religious impatience which insist on anticipating the moment of fruiting of the eternal redemption through the temporal passion—on dragging forward that moment from Easter to Holy Saturday."[68] Balthasar rejects this harrowing, claiming that

65. Balthasar, *Science*, 117.

66. See J. A. MacCulloch, *The Harrowing of Hell: A Comparative Study of an Early Christian Doctrine* (Edinburgh: T. & T. Clark, 1930). For an overview of the development of the descent and its contemporary implications, see Martin F. Connell, "*Descensus Christi Ad Inferos*: Christ's Descent to the Dead," *Theological Studies* 62, no. 2 (2001): 262–82, and Alice Turner, *The History of Hell* (New York: Harcourt Brace, 1993).

67. See Balthasar's discussion in *Mysterium Paschale*, 179–80. See also his "Descent into Hell," in *Spirit and Institution*, vol. 4 of *Explorations in Theology* (San Francisco: Ignatius Press, 1995), 401–14.

68. Balthasar, *Mysterium Paschale*, 179.

the rush to Easter, this anticipatory trajectory, removes the distinctive witness of Holy Saturday.

By contrast, he insists that there is no active victory in hell. "Jesus does not descend into Hell as Risen but as Dead,"[69] John Saward writes of Balthasar's account. The experience of death on the cross is extended into hell, revealing both a different face of the Son's mission and a different understanding of divine redemption. "Dead with the dead in hell," the Son is neither active nor victorious in the interim. He is *really* dead. And it is this insistence on the seconding and the passivity of this death that provides the groundwork for Balthasar's distinctive development of a theology of Holy Saturday. Contrary to the depictions of hell in which there is abundant activity, Balthasar, informed by Speyr's visions, interprets the descent as a place of absence, emptiness, and profound loneliness.

How does he narrate Holy Saturday? Balthasar develops Holy Saturday most extensively and systematically in three places: *Mysterium Paschale* and *Theo-Drama* volumes 4 and 5.[70] In these works, we see a clearer and tighter articulation of the theological significance of the day. In *Mysterium Paschale*, Balthasar identifies the three critical elements that underlie the descriptions of Holy Saturday in all their works. First, the events of hell are interpreted within the broader context of the Triduum.[71] They cannot be read in isolation from what precedes and follows. Second, the drama is fully Trinitarian. The descent to hell is a narrative moment in the triune life of God. Father, Son, and Spirit are all operating in the descent. Third, it is soteriological. The divine drama narrates the process of human redemption. If we are to understand redemption, we need to examine the drama enacted between Father, Son, and Spirit in hell.

In the overall drama of redemption, the descent to hell narrates a critical scene. On Holy Saturday, the Son descends as a dead man into the abyss of hell. It is neither a stunning picture of victory, nor can it simply be folded into the burial accounts in the Gospels. Between passion and resurrection lies the descent. On the cross, the Son takes on the sins of the world. In his suffering and death, he fulfills the mission of the Father by displaying his obedience, even

69. Saward, *Mysteries of March*, 113.

70. His descriptions are continually infused with Adrienne's insights and physical participation in the paschal events, and she increasingly assumes a primary authorial position, evidenced most clearly in his *The Last Act*, vol. 5 of *Theo-Drama: Theological Dramatic Theory* (San Francisco: Ignatius, 1998). In the Introduction, he indicates that he draws extensively from her writings: "Here many passages from the works of Adrienne von Speyr are reproduced and referred to in footnotes. . . . These quotations are not intended to give a full picture of her theology: that would require far more space." He writes, "I quote her to show the fundamental consonance between her views and mine on many of the eschatological topics discussed here" (13). The consonance is inarguable, especially in this final volume of *Theo-Drama*. Her Johannine commentaries overtake the "Final Act" of the divine drama, and Balthasar's voice recedes as she narrates the account of the descent to hell.

71. The Triduum is the liturgical term for the three-day feast in the Christian calendar. Beginning with Maundy Thursday and ending on Easter Sunday, the Triduum attests to the final moments of Jesus' life, his crucifixion, his burial, his descent into hell, and his resurrection. Several high liturgical traditions have recovered a celebration of the Triduum, broadening the paschal drama beyond Friday and Sunday. One of the consequences of this is increased attention to both Maundy Thursday and Holy Saturday.

to the point of death. Balthasar emphasizes the Johannine term *paradidonai*, in which the Son is handed over to death. The cross is a self-surrender of the Son and a delivering up of the Son by the Father. In the resurrection, the Son appears as the Living One.[72] Balthasar describes Holy Saturday as the day of the "second death," in which the Son experienced death in a different way.[73] The Son does not just take on death. The Son *is* dead. The first death is the death on the cross. Balthasar describes this as an active death. The second death (depicted in the descent) is the experience of the Son as a dead man. Whereas the event of the cross narrates the active suffering of the Son, the descent into hell features the landscape of death and a vision of sin in its rawest form. It is the utmost darkness, forsakenness, and alienation. Balthasar provides a passive picture of suffering following the event of the passion. Death takes on different form on Holy Saturday, and Balthasar indicates that hell is the site of a distinctive theological message. This moment is extremely important according to Balthasar, and it becomes increasingly so as his vision of the landscape of hell expands.

Over several decades of writing, Balthasar and Speyr develop a picture of what takes place between death and life. Holy Saturday is the site of divine abandonment, in which the Son not only takes on the forsakenness and sins of the world but, in hell, experiences that abandonment. By insisting on the descent as a Trinitarian event, they provide the picture of the Father and Son at the furthest reaches from each other in hell. Balthasar's emphasis on the kenotic nature of God is expressed, at this point, as the completion of this process of divine self-emptying. The descent is not simply one event in the redemption narrative of Christianity; it becomes, in his estimation, the climax of the narrative.[74] The liturgical proclamation and practice of Holy Saturday must not simply be revived; it must be the focal event of the Triduum.

The importance of a nonharrowing Holy Saturday lies in its depiction of God's love. Anne Hunt expresses it in this way: "The paschal mystery means that God, in love, has entered into the hiatus of death—physical and spiritual—and has taken the full measure of our situation not from the outside, as it were, but from the inside, sharing our desolation, bearing our sin, as Son experiencing God-forsakenness."[75] This is narrated primarily as a drama of the Father and Son. The key source for this drama is Adrienne von Speyr's visions and mystical commentaries on the Gospel of John. The Son glimpses something of the Father that had previously been kept from him: the darkness of the Father. The

---

72. Balthasar, *Mysterium Paschale*, 190.

73. Ibid., 172–73.

74. In the introduction to *Mysterium Paschale*, Aidan Nichols writes, "His principal interest—nowhere more eloquently expressed than in the present work—is located very firmly in an unusual place. This place is the mystery of Christ's Descent into Hell, which Balthasar explicitly calls the center of all Christology. . . . While not relegating the Crucifixion to a mere prelude—far from it!—Balthasar sees the One who was raised at Easter as not primarily the Crucified, but rather the One who for us went down to Hell" (Balthasar, *Mysterium Paschale*, 7).

75. Anne Hunt, *The Trinity and the Paschal Mystery: A Development in Recent Catholic Theology* (Collegeville, MN: Liturgical Press, 1997), 80.

Son shares the secret of the Father, experiencing, so to speak, the mystery of the Father's darkness. On Saturday, the Father turns away from the Son. The mystery of wrath is transformed into the mystery of love by this communion of Father and Son.[76]

This is a sketch of Balthasar's theology of Holy Saturday in its most familiar and recognized expression. I want to reveal briefly here a key factor that shapes this later articulation of Holy Saturday. In the wake of World War II, Christian theologians were revisiting theological interpretations of God and human suffering in response to the bleak realities of the Holocaust. Several turned to the cross, the site of divine suffering, for theological explanation. Nietzsche's Zarathustrian cry that "God is dead" was reclaimed by philosophers and theologians and became, for many, a new starting point for thought in the second half of the twentieth century. Within theological circles, theologians such as Jürgen Moltmann and Kazoh Kitamori were claiming that the traditional understandings of divine omnipotence could not be supported in light of mass violence and genocide. The site of their examination was the cross. Instead of the cross enacting a sacrificial exchange in which God wills, but is removed from suffering, these theologies of the cross narrate the story of God taking the pain of the world into Godself. God becomes subject to the pain of the world.

For Balthasar, a theology of Holy Saturday becomes linked to these discussions about divine suffering. Balthasar's articulation of the descent, as noted in the opening quote of this section, addresses Nietzsche's claim that "God is dead."[77] The descent is, in many respects, Balthasar's theological answer to Nietzsche, and Balthasar's extension of death into this middle space resonates with an existential dimension of the Christian narrative of redemption. The language of Holy Saturday reflects the existential mood of the times. But Holy Saturday also becomes a site from which Balthasar launches a polemic against theological interpretations of the claim that "God is dead" and their narrations of divine suffering. For Balthasar, a certain reading of Holy Saturday becomes instrumental in preserving a concept of God in the face of perceived theological dangers.[78] Balthasar insists that there is no tragedy in the God of Christians.[79]

---

76. Adrienne von Speyr, *The Birth of the Church: Meditations on John 18–21* (San Francisco: Ignatius Press, 1991). Speyr writes, "Now the two encounter each other. This encounter is no demonic mystery but a Christian one, a mystery of love. For it has its origin in the Father's love: out of love, he gives his mystery over to the Son, and his Son over to death. Everything remains a mystery of communion between Father and Son. But also a mystery of darkness, since, in the netherworld, the Son experiences the estrangement of sin. Yet the darkness of sin remains enclasped in the darkness of love" (157).

77. See Balthasar, "The Death of God as Wellspring of Salvation, Revelation and Theology," in *Mysterium Paschale*. "It now becomes extraordinarily difficult to keep together in our sights the 'absolute paradox' which lies in the hiatus, and the continuity of the Risen One with the One who died, having previously lived" (52).

78. See Balthasar, *Theo-Drama 5: The Last Act*, 227–34.

79. Aidan Nichols, *No Bloodless Myth: A Guide through Balthasar's Dramatics* (Washington, DC: Catholic University Press, 2000), 213.

We see this development in *Mysterium Paschale*, the text that outlines a theology of the Triduum and features a chapter on Holy Saturday. The history of this text exposes this developing polemic. It was first included as a section in a multivolume series titled *Mysterium Salutis*, which was intended as a comprehensive treatment of the mystery of salvation in Catholic theology.[80] Balthasar wrote several sections for the series, but it is interesting to note that he was not initially asked to author this section on the paschal mystery. When one contributor declined, Balthasar stepped in to take his place. A few years later, Balthasar decided to publish the text separately, and it appears, with very few modifications, as *Theologie der Drei Tage*.[81] What motivates him to pull this from the series and publish it elsewhere? The introduction to *Mysterium Paschale* is telling. The paschal mystery, as he presents it, wards against certain misunderstandings about the nature of God that he sees taking place around him. Although the first German edition has little by way of introduction, at the time of the second edition (the English translation in 1993) his theological descriptions of the Triduum increasingly circle around this polemic.

He targets several theological interpreters: Kazoh Kitamori, American process theologians, and Jürgen Moltmann. Each theologian, or set of theologians, develops an understanding of divine suffering in a direction that Balthasar finds deeply problematic. Balthasar's fear is that these theologians compromise something of the divine nature in their attempts to dismantle the concept of God as apathetic. These current theologians debate a long-standing issue in the Christian tradition: in what sense can and does God suffer? These authors are mentioned in the preface to *Mysterium Paschale*, but longer discussions of them can be found in *Theo-Drama*. The mention of their names here indicates that his discussion of Holy Saturday is increasingly employed as what he perceives to be a necessary corrective to the theological descriptions of his contemporaries. Balthasar believes that the way to address the issue of divine suffering is to return to the divine Trinitarian drama narrated in the Gospels and, more specifically, to the account of the descent. Contrary to other theologians who narrate this death, he believes that this death is not a divine tragedy but, in fact, a divine love story that reveals the fullness of the divine Being. The divine life, according to Balthasar, is not extinguished. He walks a very fine line in his claims about divine suffering. Balthasar writes, "We cannot say that the Father is involved in 'risk' by allowing his Son to go to the Cross. . . . However, if we ask whether there is suffering in God, the answer is this: there is something in God that can develop into suffering."[82]

---

80. Hans Urs von Balthasar, "Kapitel: Der Zugang zur Wirklichkeit Gottes," in *Mysterium Salutis: Grundriss Heilsgeschichtlicher Dogmatik*, ed. Johannes Feiner and Magnus Löhrer (Einsiedeln, Switzerland: Benziger Verlag, 1978).

81. Hans Urs von Balthasar, *Theologie der Drei Tage* (Einsiedeln, Switzerland: Johannes Verlag, 1990).

82. Balthasar, *Theo-Drama* 4: *The Action*, 327–28.

As Holy Saturday becomes increasingly employed in this polemic, the embodied and aesthetic dimensions of Holy Saturday recede. It is possible to read this later theology without any knowledge of Speyr or her visions. Her insights are prominent in the footnotes of these later texts and are drawn from her special revelations and visions. It seems, as well, that Balthasar and Speyr are intentional about downplaying these visions, in service of conveying certain truths of Holy Saturday. In short, there is an authorizing process that comes to play in and around their development of Holy Saturday. In an attempt to authorize Holy Saturday and to protect particular theological claims about God, the witness of Holy Saturday is in Castelli's terms "flattened out."[83] The body of Speyr must be theologically erased. Also, the form of their written theology becomes increasingly uniform. Evidence shows that Balthasar and Speyr deliberated about the form this theology should take. These deliberations increasingly reflect their desire to legitimate Holy Saturday within theological circles. As the polemic around divine suffering intensifies, the writing of Holy Saturday is increasingly prescribed in form, and, in turn, wedded to the Christ-form. In turn, the model of witness that grows out of this later and more formally developed theology of Holy Saturday follows a similar logic to Good Friday, and it is decidedly christological in form. I present here the model of witness that unfolds in their thought and then query its form, claiming that the distinctive message of Holy Saturday does not reside in a repetition of the Christ-form but, instead, in a pneumatological witness that emerges between death and life.

CRUCIFORM WITNESS

Both Balthasar and Speyr believed that Holy Saturday offers an unparalleled picture of divine love. The picture of divine forsakenness that the Son experiences in hell is interpreted redemptively as the complete solidarity of God with humanity.[84] Divine love is revealed at the point at which it is most threatened. God experiences, within God's inner life, the forsakenness of those in hell. Instead of heroically rescuing the forsaken in hell, the Son identifies with them. Becoming one of the forsaken, he is without the Father. This translates into a picture of love traveling to the place where there is no love, and this is the central force of Holy Saturday. There is no place that God does not go. The impact of this point is existentially powerful. We receive, in the drama of hell, assurance that there is no place that God has not been. God has traveled even to the regions of godforsakenness.

83. See Elizabeth A. Castelli, *Martyrdom and Memory: Early Christian Culture Making* (New York: Columbia University Press, 2004), 203.
84. Balthasar writes, "A first vantage point to be taken up is that of the solidarity of the Crucified with all the human dead" (*Mysterium Paschale*, 160).

Yet Balthasar and Speyr struggled to translate this godforsakenness and its significance for Christian believers. For those who want to follow the example of Christ, where does Holy Saturday take them? John Saward asks of their thought, "Can Christians in this life be said to share in any way in the Holy Saturday mystery?"[85] What model of Christian witness emerges out of Holy Saturday? The message of Christian witness from Good Friday is often translated into the call to take up one's cross and follow. Christian witness is expressed through identification with, and imitation of, the suffering Christ. But how, then, does one take up the mystery of Holy Saturday? In response, both Balthasar and Speyr hesitate:

> On Holy Saturday the Church is invited rather to follow at a distance. . . .
> It remains to ask how such an accompanying is theologically possible—
> granted that the Redeemer placed himself, by substation, in the supreme
> solitude—and how, moreover, that accompanying can be characterized if
> not by way of a genuine, that is a Christianly imposed, sharing in such
> solitude: being dead with the dead God.[86]

This quote concludes the chapter on Holy Saturday in *Mysterium Paschale*. The question of how one follows is not resolved.

Interpreters hesitate on that same question as well. John Saward speculates as to the possibility of participation in the descent. He offers two practical applications of the theology. First, one can regularly meditate on hell. Second, one can offer prayers with the aim of assisting souls in purgatory. But he suggests that Balthasar and Speyr offer more than this: "They envisage the possibility of certain souls in this life being given the taste of something of the Lord's experience in Sheol, not as an end in itself, but in order, in and through Christ the Conqueror of Hades, to assist their brethren in the Church, to aid those who find themselves plunged into the black hole of depression, doubt, confusion, despair."[87] The model of Christian witness on Holy Saturday does not, thus, extend to all. Instead, it is the privileged calling of those who are asked to bear the supreme solitude of Christ. They bear this solitude, like Christ, on behalf of others.

The mystic, in the end, is the one who is able to share in the solitude. Speyr entered into the passive death of Christ on Holy Saturday. She experienced this difference not as an active suffering but as a passive entrance into the internal condition of hell. It becomes increasingly difficult, given Speyr's intense experiences of Holy Saturday, to translate Christian witness more broadly. It not only becomes a privileged mystical space into which few are called and few enter; it becomes an experience that defies much of what we understand to constitute an experience. Instead, hell is better likened to the absence of experience. The paradox of absence and presence, intimacy and separation, nearness and distance,

---

85. Saward, *Mysteries of March*, 126.
86. Balthasar, *Mysterium Paschale*, 181.
87. Saward, *Mysteries of March*, 127.

alienation and consummation in hell are the mysteries engaged by those who are given a share in the descent. It makes sense, then, that drawing a theology of Christian witness from the site of Holy Saturday is difficult. As Speyr's insights into hell come to define the landscape of Holy Saturday, articulating a model of Christian witness more generally becomes increasingly difficult. Saward remarks, "Many holy people have been given a mystical share in the Lord's Descent into Hell."[88]

In the end, their understanding of Christian witness to the cross and to the descent is expressed in terms of a theology of martyrdom. This theology permeates their works, and it is the outgrowth of much of their theology of the Triduum. A clear articulation of Christian witness as martyrdom is evident in the short text, "Cordula," that appears as the final section of The Moment of Christian Witness.[89] The theology of the cross is transposed into life in this way:

> Martyrdom means bearing witness. It is not so very important what form this finally takes—the physical sacrifice of one's life by a bodily death, the surrender of one's whole existence to Christ by vowing to live according to his commands, or by dying to the world in baptism together with Jesus in such a way that this death and resurrection may truly enable one to live one's life for the sake of that other, immortal life (cf. Rom 6:12ff).[90]

The model for Christian witness is the crucified Christ, whose love is best demonstrated in his willing obedience to die on behalf of others. This becomes, as well, the model of life for the Christian believer. Martyrdom entails obedience unto death. Christ's death becomes the ideal model of Christian love and faithful witness.

The connection between martyrdom and the cross is not altered or significantly affected by the development of the descent into hell. With a strong christocentrism undergirding their Trinitarian reading of hell, imitating the Son's condition becomes the basis by which they interpret the faithfulness of Christian life. In hell their gaze remains on the figure of the Son who, after dying on the cross, is now dead in the depths of hell. The call to witness is a call to enter into the sufferings of Christ, but given the nature of the descent, it is an intensified call. It requires being called to enter into the sufferings of Christ in an extreme way. Some receive a share in these sufferings, but it is increasingly clear that few can really enter in. The church, then, follows at a distance, receiving the charisms of holy people, like Speyr, who glimpse for us the mysteries of God's redemption in hell.

---

88. Ibid., 128.

89. See Hans Urs von Balthasar, The Moment of Christian Witness (New York: Newman Press, 1969). This is an interesting piece in that Balthasar begins his reflection on Christian life ("What then should a Christian be?") with reference to "The Legend of the Eleven Thousand Virgins" and the story of Cordula, the lone virgin who hides and nearly escapes being ravaged by the Huns. "The following morning however she offered herself up to the fury of the Huns, and thus received the crown of martyrdom" (81).

90. Ibid., 86.

They shift attention from Good Friday to Holy Saturday, claiming that redemption is uniquely narrated there. Yet in their presentation of the descent into hell, they repeat, albeit in an intensified form, a cross-centered model of witness, as obedience and self-sacrifice. In this sense, Christian witness is patterned no differently on Holy Saturday than it is on Good Friday.[91] But something else happens in this later development as well. In their depiction of the Trinitarian drama of hell, the Spirit is cast in a certain role in this drama. The Holy Spirit, mentioned very little in their descriptions of Holy Saturday, is the figure that secures the love between Father and Son at the point at which the connection is most fragile. In the hiatus between death and life, the Spirit ensures that the Godhead does not sever. The Spirit secures and ensures a conception of the divine Being that Balthasar believes is compromised by his theological contemporaries. This role is critical to warding off the theological dangers that surround current theologies of the cross. The Spirit makes the godforsakenness possible without compromising God's nature. The Spirit's function is here expressed in classically Augustinian terms: the Spirit is the bond of love between Father and Son. Though there is little mention of the Spirit, the Spirit's presence is not only assumed but in fact is extremely critical to Balthasar's argument against his interlocutors. The presence of the Spirit allows Balthasar to maintain the assertion that "God is dead," without rendering the descent as a divine tragedy.

Employing the image of a chasm between Father and Son in the abyss of hell, he refers to the Spirit as the bridge between the two. The function of the Spirit, then, is to hold together what is in danger of separating. The Spirit secures the divine relation at its most threatened point. He maintains an Augustinian formulation here, depicting the Spirit as the bond of love between Father and Son. Yet the Spirit operates in other ways in Balthasar's work; he often notes that the Spirit is the "ever-greater," the "fruit," of the Father-Son relation, implying that the Spirit has a more independent function, as the love that doesn't merely bind together, but extends beyond that relation. This extension over the abyss, however, is not triumphant love, but rather what Balthasar presents in *Heart of the World* as weary love making its way through the chaos of hell. Since he does little to develop his pneumatology of Holy Saturday, it is difficult to discern exactly how Balthasar reconciles the securing Spirit with the fruit that emerges from the wound of death. I make sense of it by suggesting that, given the theological polemic, Balthasar presents the Spirit in a form consistent with Trinitarian orthodoxy. This securing Spirit ensures that the Godhead does not sever, that the divine Being can die but not die a tragic death. In a sense, the Spirit *is* the necessary hinge between tragedy and triumph. His theology of the Spirit moves

91. In fact, participation is restricted, by and large, to those who are called into uniquely mystical participation. Despite Balthasar's insistence that the charisms are shared and are in service of the broader church, the narrowing of Christian witness is still evident in his interpretation. The more that Adrienne is the model of witness on Holy Saturday, the less able they are to translate this witness more generally.

in unique and rather unorthodox directions, but not here.[92] In service of this securing function, a more distinctive and dynamic concept of the Spirit of Holy Saturday does not emerge.

I want to revisit the image of the bridge that Balthasar employs when speaking about the Spirit in hell.[93] I do so in order to suggest that the bridge of the Spirit may not be as secure, or securing, as rendered in the more formal account of the descent. I query the image of the bridge by turning to his Holy Saturday sermon, "We Walked Where There Was No Path," featured at the beginning of the chapter.[94] In this sermon, he directly confronts the question of what persists between death and resurrection. Spirit is the secure bridge that keeps this love story from being a tragic one. But could Spirit, drawing on images from *Heart of the World*, be the weary love that forges a path through the pathless dark of hell?

TOWARD A MIDDLE SPIRIT

At the beginning of this sermon, Balthasar invokes the imagination of his listeners, asking us to imagine the miraculous reappearance of a friend after he has died. We watch him die, hear his final gasps, and lower his coffin into the ground. Then, he writes, "We go home and crawl around like disoriented, half-dead flies, like beings whose present is submerged in the past and to whom the future blows as down a drafty pipe."[95] The next day, suddenly, the friend appears before us, and the boundaries of human reason are exploded. The fantastic element of this reappearance spurs on questions about the power of death, its finality, and the meaning of life's persistence past the point of death. The friend appears before us, speaks to us, and shows us the marks on his flesh. This, we begin to see, is not the death and reappearance of any friend. This reality, this friend, this dead man, is Jesus. The Logos faces us. In Jesus, we are strangely confronted with more than the reality of looking at life *after* death. With his unique reappearance we are forced to see life *through* the wounds of death. "From this realm, therefore, he returns and shows his wounds. The open wounds allow us to see through, as it were, to what *was*—a part that, as such, is past; they also allow us to see what was—what, evidently, now is—and what will be."[96]

92. For more on unorthodox trajectories in Balthasar, see John Sachs, "The Pneumatology and Christian Spirituality of Hans Urs von Balthasar" (PhD diss., Eberhard Karls Universitaet Tuebingen, 1984).

93. Pitstick notes this bridge as a dominant metaphor. "Balthasar is generally not clear about the procession and role of the Holy Spirit in his soteriological discussions, which form the basis for the present work. He usually just asserts the Holy Spirit's existence as 'bridge' of the 'distance' between Father and Son, or 'bond' and 'seal' of their love, or their 'We' without integrating these metaphors in relation to the terms he uses for the Father and Son" (Pitstick, *Light in Darkness*, 218).

94. Although the collection of sermons *You Crown the Year with Your Goodness* classifies this as an Easter sermon, the focus of the sermon is Holy Saturday.

95. Balthasar, *You Crown the Year*, 87.

96. Ibid., 89.

The wound of death becomes a lens for interpreting our lives. We are confronted, in Jesus, with the revelation of our ultimate destiny. The history of humankind, he says, is "really and symbolically in the historical destiny of the man Jesus Christ."[97] Balthasar confronts his listeners with this new reality. Here is the mysterious experience of the Christian faith. We live in the wake of such a miracle, and, most peculiarly, this life after death becomes the beginning of our life. He writes, "But with the Resurrection *from* the dead, of whom the man Jesus Christ is the firstfruits, man comes forth from God, new, eternal. On the other side of death he begins his immortal life."[98] Death is a beginning. The Christian faith is about living in the mystery of this strange beginning.

Midway through, the sermon comes to a halt. "This brings us to the decisive question," he writes: "What is it that takes place on Holy Saturday?" He continues, "What kind of a day is this on which, as the old hymn says (and it is followed here by Hegel and Nietzsche), 'God is dead'?"[99] The question of Holy Saturday is tied up in an understanding of the relationship between death and life. What does life mean in the moments when one leaves the graveyard, walks home, and crawls around and cannot see her way forward? Meaning is dead. Hope is dead. Love is dead. This resonates with the Holy Saturday picture in *Heart of the World*. Death is final. It is not experienced as some segue into life or as a temporary pause in a master plan. The puzzle of Holy Saturday is the emergence of a form of life from death. He pursues the question of the meaning of this day through a series of negations. It is "not merely a day" when life's meaning has faded, when a few strands of the world's reason are ineffectual, or when certain components of rational thought are not clear. "No," he declares. "On this day the world's meaning died and was buried without any hope of the resulting hiatus ever being bridged: there was no hope of ever closing the rift opened up by this death."[100]

Holy Saturday has something to do with the confrontation with this radical ending and what remains in its wake. Preaching Holy Saturday, Balthasar demonstrates, means preaching the powerful reality of death as human beings experience it. It is a closing with no hope of reopening. This is a total end, displayed in the descent as Jesus dead with the dead. But, he says, there is also a total beginning. Through a series of declarations about what Holy Saturday is not, Balthasar emphasizes the profound disruption of what takes place in the abyss of hell. All is plundered. Nothing can be imagined beyond it. Theological logic, he goes on to say, does not negotiate this radical end; it always tries to maneuver around it rather than through it. "What *is* it that persists between death and Resurrection?"[101] he asks. A certain kind of theological logic can never get at this

97. Ibid.
98. Ibid.
99. Ibid., 90.
100. Ibid.
101. Ibid.

question. What persists in the middle of these two powerful realities—a radical end and a mysterious beginning? Balthasar moves rhetorically between the two.

The "*Logos tou staurou*—Jesus Christ and him crucified,"[102] Balthasar declares. He presents the figure of the crucified walking through hell. The crucified one, the one who shows us the world through his wounds, persists in the space following death. Read one way, this follows a very traditional trajectory in Christian apologetics: Jesus is the mediator, the middleman between sinful humanity and God. Jesus bridges the chasm of hell and heaven. Given Balthasar's christocentrism, it could be read in this direction. Jesus is the salvific bridge between eternal ruin and eternal life. But the crucified in hell, as Balthasar depicts him elsewhere, is not going to be the victorious link between death and life. What links the dying and rising is the figure of Christ in the timeless and unmarked territory of hell: "He it is who walks along paths that are no paths, leaving no trace behind, through hell, hell which has no exit, no time, no being."[103] If Jesus is the way, the truth, and the life, Balthasar transforms the meaning of each of these three realities by his picture of Jesus in hell. The way, the truth, the life. No path, no speech, no way out. It is a fragile picture of God.

At this point Balthasar turns to the concluding image in the sermon. "And now," he says, "there *is* something like a bridge over this rift."[104] Over the abyss of hell, there is "a lightly built bridge"[105] that can carry followers across. We are inserted into this narrative. We have watched this friend die. We have experienced the end. But we do not walk the paths of hell, nor are we locked in the abyss with no way out. We, the remaining witnesses, make our way across a bridge that dangles over the abyss of hell. His use of the word "rift" is significant here. Holy Saturday is a rupture, a break, a split; the events in hell confirm that there is no way that death and life can be reconciled. The stark reality of the middle day is that we cannot conceive of life after death. On the one side, there is death in godforsakenness; on the other, there is eternal life. To get from one side to the other, we need a means of crossing. But Holy Saturday declares the impossibility of bridging the two. No human logic can postulate or even construct such a bridge. The descent into hell enacts a fracture that cannot be easily repaired. Balthasar hesitates when describing a means of crossing the divide: it is *something like* a bridge; it is *lightly built*; it is a connective *thread*. His language reflects the fragility of this path above and across the chasm of hell. But what can withstand the rift between devastating death and eternal life? What kind of path can survive the powers of death and hell? What remains in this space? Balthasar indicates that the way through this impossibility can only be conceptualized

102. He writes, "And yet it is what is called the *Logos tou staurou*, the word and the message of the Cross, by Paul, who, in Corinth, renounces all worldly and divine wisdom because God himself 'will destroy the wisdom of the wise, and the cleverness of the clever. . . . Where is the wise man? Where is the scribe? Where is the debater of this age? . . . I decided to know nothing among you except Jesus Christ and him crucified'" (ibid., 91).

103. Ibid.
104. Ibid.
105. Ibid.

through the figure of Spirit. Balthasar presents us with a paradox: the Spirit bridges this rift, but the Spirit is not the bridge.

He indicates that the bridge is sustained by the church's faith, by Mary's faith, and by the watchful prayers of those at the grave. Although part of the support, these pillars do not build the bridge. *He* builds it. Balthasar does not indicate exactly who "he" is in the text, but it is fairly safe to assume that God provides the way across the abyss. And this way across is the Son. He has just declared that Jesus is the "connecting thread linking ruin and rising."[106] He presents us with this image: it is as if the path marked by the footprints of Jesus through hell is elevated to become the fabric of the bridge that reaches from Friday to Sunday. But it is important to read the sentence in its entirety: "Yes, he [the Son] is the continuity for which we have been looking, the connecting thread linking ruin and rising, which does not break even in death and hell."[107] Jesus walks the path of hell and, as a result, becomes the path on which we tread. But Balthasar does not describe a sturdy bridge. It is a thread that links two things, but it is inconceivable that it is strong enough to hold passengers making their way across. The thread is fragile, easily broken. But this thread is distinctive in that it can withstand the incredible forces of death (Friday) and hell (Saturday). There is more operating here than Balthasar offers in the text. We can imagine that grace, faith, and prayers weave around this thread, strengthening it to hold the weight of those crossing.

But the unmentioned partner in this is the figure of the Spirit. The figure of Spirit also links ruin and rising in the Godhead; as the bridge of love in the Godhead, the Spirit is implicit in Balthasar's discussion of the bridge here. The thread does not break in hell because the Spirit maintains the bridge of love at its most fragile point. Something can make its way across the ruptured territory of hell because, Balthasar says, the "Spirit of them both bridges it."[108] It is not the Son alone who is the bridge. Linking this text to his account of soteriology in *Theo-Drama*, we see that the bridge is neither fully Son nor Spirit, but some strange combination of both—a dead man and a fragile trickle of love from his wound.

As the sermon continues, the status of the bridge is called into question altogether. Do people actually walk across it? Is this journey successful? Do believers make it to the other side? Just as enigmatic a picture as Balthasar gives of Jesus walking along "paths that are not paths,"[109] he presents a similarly enigmatic path of believers across the bridge. He envisions a bridge and a journey, but both of these are radically dissolved toward the end of his sermon. Not only has he called into question the reality of the bridge ("now there *is* something like a bridge over this rift"[110]), he seems to imply that something radically disrupts the journey.

106. Ibid.
107. Ibid.
108. Balthasar, *Theo-Drama* 4: *The Action*, 324.
109. Balthasar, *You Crown the Year*, 91.
110. Ibid.

Not surprisingly, he reintroduces the issue of logic's inadequacy to speak about the journey itself. He writes, "Now can we compare the two sides as if from some higher vantage point; we cannot bring the two together in some rational, logical context by using some method, some process of thought, some logic. . . ."[111] Human logic is suspended in this space. After all, Balthasar presents us with an absurdity: we are supposed to walk across the chasm of hell on a thread. We must trust that the thread can support our feet, an image that explodes any system of logic. But this brief disclaimer about the inadequacy of logic serves to prepare the reader for the breakdown of Balthasar's own metaphor.

The followers step onto the bridge and trust that they can make their way across. But Balthasar does not describe a smooth passage from godforsakenness to eternal life. The journey becomes something very different than we would imagine.

> We have no alternative but to trust in him, knowing, as we walk across the bridge, that he built it. Because of his grace we have been spared the absolute abyss, and yet, as we proceed across the bridge, we are actually walking alongside it, this most momentous of all transformations; we do not observe it, but can only be seized and pulled into it, to be transformed from dead people into resurrected people.[112]

The bridge is built for us, but, surprisingly, we do not walk across it. As we proceed across, he says, a transformation takes place and we suddenly realize that we are walking alongside it. The bridge no longer supports us; we walk next to it. One obvious question confronts us here: what are we walking on? With no support under our feet, it appears that we are miraculously walking over the abyss of hell. The transformation from death to life cannot be explained simply by the metaphor of the bridge. He offers a picture of the journey from Friday to Sunday, but he heeds his own warnings about the sufficiency of logic to describe what is taking place on Holy Saturday. This transformation explodes the metaphor of the bridge. The journey is actually a journey that takes place alongside the bridge. The transformation taking place pulls us off the bridge; our feet are no longer supported, and whether we make it to the other side is unclear. The reality and effectiveness of the bridge seem irrelevant. The transformation is not a simple journey from point A to point B.

Holy Saturday is an untraceable journey through hell. We are spared the abyss, he says. But the path keeping us from falling into the abyss is a carpet pulled out from under us. We do not drop into the abyss. Or do we? Is there a transformation of the abyss itself? Can the kind of connection made between Father and Son, God and humanity be contained within the metaphor of bridge? My reading suggests that Spirit *exceeds* this metaphor. What is the transformation from death to life taking place in the middle day? The metaphor of the

111. Ibid.
112. Ibid.

bridge provides a picture of what this transformation is. Calling this metaphor into question invites other pictures. What Balthasar presents through the bridge metaphor is a visual landscape in which we imagine a horizontal bridge linking two things. But, if pressed beyond this bridge metaphor, his language suggests something else. Although the image of a bridge marks a whole conceptual terrain, he actually challenges it in his thicker description.

Although Balthasar offers the image of a suspension bridge across the gorge, his dismantling of the bridge metaphor points to a different image. A fragile thread emerges out of the crevasse. The thread is making its way out of the depths of death and hell; out of this rupture, a path is forged. A vertical image replaces a horizontal one. Balthasar's focus on Holy Saturday shifts our picture of resurrection; our "new life"—our beginning—is not the victorious ascent out of hell, but the experience of absolute death and alienation in hell. The picture of resurrection is a beginning out of death. Is Balthasar altering our picture of salvation without intentionally doing so? In the end, is the picture of salvation as us travelling over the chasm of hell an inaccurate one? Perhaps we plunge into the abyss instead of being spared it. We therefore need to be carried out of the fractured and disoriented space of death's end—to be resurrected out of the space. Our beginning is the radically disorienting space of death and hell.

Balthasar does not explain this transformation in his sermon; it remains, always for him, mysterious. But we are pulled into it and marked by it, he says. Balthasar's next and final comments are offered in the form of a benediction:

> May the sign of this transformation be found on our Janus destiny. May its mark be branded on each of our works, those that come to an end inexplicably and those that, inexplicably, are resurrected through grace. Their two faces can never meet; they can never behold each other, and we can never link up the two ends because the rope across the chasm is too short. So we must put it into God's hand: only his fingers can join our broken parts into a whole.[113]

The mystery of death and resurrection and how they are linked persists in Balthasar's final comments. Death and resurrection are two faces of human experience. We cannot understand how the two are connected. The death and sudden reappearance of our friend (Balthasar's opening example) faces us with the radical divide between the two. Such a loss—a death—is experienced as a complete end. But the resurrection of this friend, while not erasing the reality of that death, is startlingly new. We cannot figure out the link between the two (and the metaphor of bridge also begs the question of linkage), but our existence and works are marked by it. We have two faces of experience, Balthasar writes. One is the face of death, the other the face of resurrection. The image of Janus suggests that these two realities are bound together. Despite the fact that they face different directions, they are connected in some way.

113. Ibid, 92.

There *is* and *is not* a connection. Is this another version of the fragile thread? When talking about the miraculous transformation of Friday to Sunday, Balthasar appeals to images that point to the enigma of the middle space: something is forging its way between two extremes, consequently exploding any conception of either extreme. There is no simple passage in Balthasar from god-forsakenness to eternal life; instead, one must travel through the middle space. The transformation, for him, is the mysterious connection of the two by the figure of Spirit.[114] But the connection is more than mysterious as it is revealed in the middle day. Is there a connection between death and life? Yes, Balthasar answers. But the kind of connection that he envisions throughout the sermon defies familiar understandings of how things are connected. Something emerges and persists through the impossibility of two extreme realities. Spirit is not simply a unifying bond; his images speak otherwise.

Instead of the image of a thread successfully connecting two extremes, Balthasar introduces the image of a short rope that fails to bridge the chasm. The chasm is too big, the rope too short. The impossibility of connection is clear. There is no bridge that can reach across. We could ask Balthasar, "How is this not tragic?" After he has offered the miraculous picture of Christ's rescue from the abyss and the salvation of all humanity, after he has declared Christ the continuity that we have longed for,[115] he calls them into question. There is no rescue or continuity. There is only brokenness, discontinuity, and impossible connection. From this starting point, he says, "We must put it [the rope] into God's hand."[116] We place the short rope in God's hand. This is the image of resurrection. It is not the victorious image of new life. It is a desperate image, in which the impossibility of a beginning becomes its starting point.

The first picture is of a thread crossing from death to life, on which travelers walk. The second picture is of a rope that is too short to span the distance from death to life. We are disoriented and broken travelers, unable to cross the chasm. In this picture, there is no continuity. There is only an impossible meeting out of the chasm: the end of the rope and the finger of God. A thread, a rope emerges out of the alienation of the abyss (the alienation within God, and the alienation of the world's sin), and God reaches down, clasps the end of the thread, and pulls upward.

The transformation that we are pulled into demands the fragility of Balthasar's bridge metaphor. Although he does not explain what happens in the transformation, any straightforward description of the passage from death to life is clearly rendered impossible. We do not know how we get across the chasm; in fact, Balthasar alters altogether this image of a journey *across*. Instead, what he offers

---

114. Balthasar, *Theo-Drama* 5: *The Last Act*, 261–64.
115. "He it is who walks along paths that are no paths, leaving no trace behind, through hell, hell which has no exit, no time, no being; and by the miracle from above he is rescued from the abyss, the profound depths, to save his brothers in Adam along with him" (Balthasar, *You Crown the Year*, 91).
116. Ibid., 92.

is the story of a beginning at the crossroads between two extremes. Out of the chasm of hell—the middle space—we are pulled. We are pulled into the mystery of this miraculous rescue, whereby our new life will not be divorced from the death of godforsakenness. Instead, it will bear the marks of death. In *Heart of the World*, Balthasar describes this new life: "All of your past is like a dream which one can no longer recall precisely, and the entire old world hangs within the new space like a picture in its frame. Only a while ago you still knelt at the empty grace, a sea of tears. And all you knew was that the Lord was dead, that the life of quiet joy you shared was dead."[117] This passage recalls the disorienting condition at the beginning of Balthasar's Holy Saturday sermon. In the aftermath of death we are like "disoriented, half-dead flies."[118] The rescue from the abyss is not being spared from the death; it is not escaping the experience of death's finality but emerging out of it, knowing that this death is pulled into life as we now know it.

Looking through the lens of trauma, it is important to revisit the Spirit not as a figure who secures love between death and life but rather as one who witnesses to what remains—what persists—between them. This is the ever-greater Spirit of the middle, the fruit of love forged through death. This middle Spirit rewrites an understanding of love in significant ways, attesting to a form of divine presence that is difficult to see, to feel, and to touch. The Spirit provides a distinctive way of orienting oneself between death and life, a way of witnessing the fractured dimensions of word and body between death and life. For Balthasar and Speyr, the answer to what persists becomes so christologically tied that this testimony of and to the Spirit is elided. This Spirit can, in fact, be traced in their early movements of witness, in their attempts to decipher and enact the forsaken territory of hell. The secured and securing Spirit of their later theology fails to testify to the rich theological landscape that they open up.

The visionary and literary dimensions of their early theologies point to a pneumatology surrounding what remains. At the critical intersection of death and life, body and word take different form, and a witness arises to a form of life surviving death. They testify to a story of love surviving rather than triumphing. The entangled witness of their earlier testimony to Holy Saturday conveys a more enigmatic terrain of body and word, in which Spirit—both human and divine—comes to unique expression. They witness to a pneumatological residue, drawing on the image that Balthasar provides in *Heart of the World*. There, the disciple attempts to witness to what is moving in the postcrucifixion territory and asks, "Could it be the residue of the Son's love which, poured out to the last when every vessel cracked and the old world perished, is now making a path for itself to the Father through the glooms of nought?"[119] As far as the disciple can ascertain, Balthasar tells us, the movement out of death is a weary residue of love that "trickles on in impotence, unconsciously, laboriously, towards a

117. Balthasar, *Heart of the World*, 158.
118. Balthasar, *You Crown the Year*, 87.
119. Balthasar, *Heart of the World*, 152.

new creation that does not yet even exist."[120] Balthasar provides a vocabulary for Spirit here that expands beyond his stated pneumatology in the descent to hell. Between death and life, there is a testimony to Spirit, to a love that survives and remains not in victory but in weariness.

The figure of the disciple remains in *Heart of the World*, performing a different kind of witness, of tracking what moves out of death, of testifying to a form of life that is not discernible within any conceivable frameworks. The weary love of Holy Saturday seeks theological expression. For this, I turn to the Johannine texts.

120. Ibid.

Chapter 3

Biblical Witness in the Gospel of John

But when they came to Jesus and saw that he was already dead, they did not break his legs. Instead, one of the soldiers pierced his side with a spear, and at once blood and water came out.

John 19:33–34

In the Johannine text, there is something strangely alive about the dead body of Jesus. The other Gospels include accounts of the preparation of Jesus' body for burial, but this is the only one that features this curious scene of the soldier inserting his sword into the posthumous body of Jesus. That a sword wound would produce blood, the fluid of death, is not unusual, but the presence of water suggests that something else is taking place here. Water is associated throughout the Johannine text with life and, in turn, with the Holy Spirit. They are linked at Jesus' baptism in John 1 and then in John 3 when Jesus is talking to Nicodemus: "Very truly, I tell you, no one can enter the kingdom of God without being born of water and Spirit" (John 3:5). Yet water appears here in the territory of death. The fluid of death and life are mixed together, and they mark a space in the text out of which a distinctive witness arises. The wound prompts a testimony: "He who saw this has testified so that you also may believe. His testimony is true, and he knows that he tells the truth" (John 19:35).[1]

1. The reasons for my choice of the Gospel of John are threefold. First, its rich rhetoric and imagery lend itself to the kind of readings that I engage in here. It is ripe for literary interpretation. Second, biblical scholars generally regard the Gospel of John as distinctive in respect to the other Gospel accounts. This difference is often designated by references to it as the more spiritual Gospel. Forging

81

This living wound and the testimony to it provide a guiding image for exploring what it means to witness between passion and resurrection, death and life.[2] This wound signals that something of death cannot be contained in the passion wounds and that some form of life, though difficult to identify, emerges from it. The Johannine Gospel presents us with a testimonial landscape in which witnesses struggle to make sense of life in the aftermath of death. The Gospel links this witness to the figure of the Spirit. The testimonial form of life that I develop is not sufficiently captured in theological interpretations of either the passion or resurrection. The living wound births an alternative understanding of what it means to witness and to remain in the aftermath of death. It also births a distinctive understanding of the Spirit. It is not the Spirit of Pentecost that appears here; it is, instead, a Spirit persisting between death and life that is witnessed in and through the words and movements of those who remain.

In this chapter, I engage in a series of readings of the Johannine text in an attempt to unearth a pneumatology of witness that is present but often unaccounted for in theological interpretations of passion and resurrection. I do this by first examining the witness of Mary Magdalene and the beloved disciple. They are presented, in the Johannine text, as primary witnesses to the passion and resurrection. Drawing on the concept of witness in chapter 1, I show how they cannot be seen as those who simply receive and pass on the news of Jesus' death. I ask, in what way and with what degree of clarity do they receive and convey the death event? The reception of the event is neither straightforward nor direct, as evidenced in the accounts of Mary and the beloved disciple. Consequently, their witness is not defined by a clear and deliverable message, but instead by an encounter with what they do not—and cannot—fully know of the event. Thus, I read them through the lens of trauma and its enigmatic double structure.[3]

---

a pneumatology from the Gospel of John is significant in that it contests our primary understandings of spirituality as something separate from material realities. But the third reason for focusing on this Gospel is the harm that has been perpetuated in its name. Recasting the dynamics of witness as a "handing over," I suggest that the theological claims that have been supported and perpetuated in the name of this Gospel can be called into question by the text itself. The handing over of this Gospel has been rife with elisions, exemplified in the anti-Semitism that hovers in and over the Gospel in its history of interpretation. The Gospel itself has a traumatic history. My reading, then, is to some degree a testimony to the ways in which simplistic readings of witness (proclamation and imitation) have flattened the enigmatic dimensions of the biblical language ("christological repetitions"/interpretive violence). For insights into the kind of reading that I am doing here, see Stephen D. Moore, *Literary Criticism and the Gospels: The Theoretical Challenge* (New Haven, CT: Yale University Press, 1989), 159–70. He writes, "My own reading of the opposition between figural and literal water in John . . . is offered as a dim illustration of what a more thorough reading of Johannine figurality—one that would feel for fault lines through a wide range of oppositions—might reveal" (167). My reading of the death-life opposition could also be understood, similarly, as feeling for fault lines.

2. Balthasar's *Heart of the World* reads as a poetic commentary on the Gospel of John. The living wound in John 19:34 is the site of an exploration of Holy Saturday, opening up an investigation into the underworld (the depths of hell) and an upperworld (the world of the disciples witnessing the events of his depths). Also, the Greek root of the word "trauma" is wound, and we can think about trauma in terms of a wound that remains open.

3. See chap. 1 for a description of the lens of trauma and its double structure; Cathy Caruth, *Trauma: Explorations in Memory* (Baltimore: Johns Hopkins University Press, 1995). "This speaking

I focus on the witness narratives of Mary Magdalene and the beloved disciple and move to the broader Johannine context of passion and resurrection. Their testimonies reveal to us the difficult practice of witness in the aftermath of death. The blurring of the line between death and life presses us to reassess a central and familiar Christian claim: that new life follows from death. By examining their witness, we capture a critical moment in this narrative in which the effects of death are not contained in the event of death but are carried forward in the witnesses themselves. The passage from death to life, if viewed through the lens of their witness, is not so smooth. The difficulties in their witness testify to a more difficult relationship between death and life and displace familiar theological interpretations of redemption. Their witness, framed in the context of the surrounding passages, reveals a deeply pneumatological dimension to the events taking place.

MARY MAGDALENE

Much has been written on Jesus' postresurrection appearances to Mary Magdalene.[4] I focus here on two episodes in the extended scene in John 20—the early and later encounters at the tomb. I aim to show that Mary's witness is bound up in her inability to see, locate, and identify the body of Jesus. The problems that she confronts in the process of witnessing in the aftermath of the crucifixion are constitutive of what it means to witness. The text forces us to confront a very unfamiliar conception of witness. If Mary is witness to the death and resurrection (and indeed a first witness), these texts indicate that much of what she is witnessing is inaccessible to her. Her witness reflects the complexities of seeing in the aftermath of death.

At the tomb, Mary experiences a series of obstructions to her sight. First, the text tells us that it is still dark outside. Second, she is weeping throughout, indicating that she sees through a film of tears. Third, her look into the tomb is partial. The encounters that she has are encounters in which her sight is limited. In terms of being an *eye*witness to the events following the passion, Mary appears to be a rather unsuccessful one. Instead, something is taking place through her

---

and listening—a speaking and a listening *from the site of trauma*—does not rely, I would suggest, on what we simply know of each other, but on what we don't yet know of our own traumatic pasts" (11).

4. See Amy-Jill Levine with Marianne Blickenstaff, eds., "A Feminist Companion to John," in *Feminist Companion to the New Testament and Early Christian Writings*, vols. 1 and 2 (London: Sheffield Academic Press, 2003); Ann Brock, *Mary Magdalene, the First Apostle: The Struggle for Authority* (Cambridge, MA: Harvard University Press, 2003); Susan Haskins, *Mary Magdalen: Myth and Metaphor* (London: Harper Collins, 1993); Richard Atwood, *Mary Magdalene in the New Testament Gospels and Early Tradition* (Bern: P. Lang, 1993); Jane Schaberg, *The Resurrection of Mary Magdalene: Legends, Apocrypha, and the New Testament* (New York: Continuum Press, 2002); Karen L. King, *The Gospel of Mary of Magdala: Jesus and the First Woman Apostle* (Santa Rosa, CA: Polebridge Press, 2003). For an excellent overview essay, see Jane Schaberg, "Thinking Back through Mary Magdalene," in Levine and Blickenstaff, *Feminist Companion*, 2:167–89.

unseeing. If we pay attention to these obstructions, the following questions are raised: What, exactly, is she encountering? What constitutes her witness?

> Early on the first day of the week, while it was still dark, Mary Magdalene
> came to the tomb and saw that the stone had been removed from the tomb.
> (John 20:1)

It is just before morning; it is still dark outside. Mary stands at the tomb weeping. Immediately, the text conveys that Mary has limited vision. The morning light has not yet broken. She cannot see much, because it is still dark at the tomb. From the start, Mary's vision is unclear. Verse 1 opens with the problem of the day and the darkness. The text tells us that Mary arrives at the tomb when it is still dark. She sees that the stone is rolled away, but the preceding statement suggests that she is discerning what is taking place in the dark. Mary runs to the disciples, tells them that the body of Jesus is missing, and then drops out of the account. The two male disciples—the beloved and Simon Peter—take over the text.

Nine verses later, she returns to the tomb and experiences another instance of unseeing. She stands weeping at the tomb. How long she has been standing outside is unclear. We do not know if she returned to the tomb with the disciples when they came to investigate it. We do not know whether she was informed about what they saw in the tomb. We do know that the tomb is, again, a place where her vision is impaired. The text provides us with a picture of a weeping woman, who is present but somehow always on the outskirts of the central scene. Even though Peter and the beloved have entered the tomb, the text implies that Mary remains outside. Her tears reveal not only that she is overwhelmed with grief but they also indicate an obstruction to her sight. Her weeping is featured here, mentioned not only once, but three times in the chapter.[5]

In the interpretive tradition of Christianity, Mary Magdalene's tears come to represent something other than her experience of grief. Her grief at the tomb, over the centuries of the Christian tradition, is transposed into a vision of sorrowful repentance in which Mary is presented as guilty. She is the desired and desiring body. Given this construction of Mary in the tradition, her grief is elided in service of another depiction of her—her depiction as the penitent.[6]

---

5. Gail O'Day notes, "John is the only Gospel in which Mary 'weeps' (κλαίω *klaio*) at the tomb." See her entry in *The New Interpreter's Bible*, vol. 9: *Luke-John* (Nashville: Abingdon Press, 1995), 841. O'Day links this reference to her weeping in 20:11, 13, and 15, and to Jesus' words in 16:20a, when he tells the disciples that they "will weep and mourn, but the world will rejoice," indicating a time of hardship and pain for those who remain as witnesses.

6. See Susan Haskins, "The Weeper," in *Mary Magdalen: Myth and Metaphor* (New York: Harcourt Brace & Co., 1994), 229–96. This essay is compelling in that it traces the history of Mary Magdalene's tears, primarily through her depictions in art. Traditionally, her tears are closely aligned with repentance. "In de Sales' treatise *Of the Love of God* (1616), [Mary] is again a model of conversion: 'Remember the sorrowing Magdalene: "They have taken away my Lord, and I know not where they have laid Him"; but when she had found Him amid her tears she held Him fast in love. Imperfect love longs for Him; penitence seeks and finds Him; perfect love clasps Him tight'" (255; origi-

While she is weeping, she takes her first look into the tomb. The text tells us, "As she wept, she bent over to look into the tomb . . ." (John 20:11). This is the third obstruction to her sight. When she does look into the tomb, her sight is also questionable. The text tells us that she peers into the tomb, but this look is not a full one. The word *parakupto* suggests that she does not have the full scope of vision. The verb used for her seeing—*parakupto*—is unusual. As emphasized by the prefix *para*, it implies a quick, fleeting, or stolen look. Certain writers believe that this translation does not hold for the Johannine text; instead, *parakupto* means to look from the outside through a low entrance.[7] Whether it denotes an awkward position of looking or the brevity of the look, her sight is impaired in some way. So why doesn't she take a longer look? Why doesn't her positioning and the position of the tomb cause her to look longer and harder? She does not enter the tomb; instead she bends down to peer in from the outside.

Her vision is not simply obstructed by her tears and by her positioning; her vision is obstructed by what she does see there. When she finally does see something, she sees beings who are not clearly or fully present. They are disembodied beings, highlighted by their presence in the absence of Jesus' body. Instead of encountering his body or even the traces of the burial cloths, she sees two angels marking the space of Jesus' absence. One is sitting where his head would have been, and the other is sitting at his feet. She sees them, however, still through the film of her tears. In fact, they address her by inquiring about her tears. The tears return here, this time in the form of an address. Her weeping becomes the means by which she is identified.

Mary repeats, in response, the same words that she said to the earlier disciples. "They have taken away my Lord, and I do not know where they have laid him" (John 20:13). She is in search of his body, and he is not there. Repeatedly, she encounters his absence. Although she continues to look for him, she never seems to be in the right place at the right time. She never, though first to the scene, enters the tomb.

> Jesus said to her, "Mary!" She turned and said to him in Hebrew, "Rabbouni!".
> . . Mary Magdalene went and announced to the disciples, "I have seen the Lord." (John 20:16, 18)

Mary's second scene in the postpassion narrative in John is initially one of mistaken identity. In this resurrection appearance, Mary mistakes Jesus for the gardener. She comes to recognize him only through a series of turnings, a

---

nally from Francis de Sales, *On the Love of God*, trans. H. L. Sidney Lear [London, 1888], 83–84); "Mary Magdalen's tears flowed into the great literary cult of penitential poetry, the 'cycle of remorse,' which sprang up in Italy during the Counter-Reformation, flooding across Catholic Europe. . . . George Herbert's poem Marie Magdalene: In Herbert's poem, she weeps not for Christ's death but as Luke's sinner. A series of hyperbole, incongruous and extended metaphors, and violent transitions, forges a narrative which moves decisively to its quiet end" (Haskins, "Weeper," 270, 273–74).

 7. *Theological Dictionary of the New Testament*, ed. Gerhard Kittel, trans. Geoffrey W. Bromiley, vol. 5 (Grand Rapids: William B. Eerdmans, 1985), s.v. *parakupto* (Wilhelm Michaelis).

puzzling exchange of names, and a prohibition on touch. Immediately after the angels in the tomb address her, Jesus approaches her. In this recognition scene, her sight is not only dismantled, but other senses are altered in the process of searching for the body of Jesus.

The John text presents a series of turnings, raising the question of whether and when Mary is facing Jesus. Mary's witness is complicated by her positioning in relationship to Jesus. She is in search of his body. She first ran to the disciples, announcing that his body was stolen. Explaining her tears to the angels in the tomb, she makes a similar claim. I do not know where he is, she pleads to them. And then the text tells us that she turns around:

> She *turned* around and saw Jesus standing there, but she did not know that it was Jesus. Jesus said to her, "Woman, why are you weeping? Whom are you looking for?" Supposing him to be the gardener, she said to him, "Sir, if you have carried him away, tell me where you have laid him, and I will take him away." Jesus said to her, "Mary!" She *turned* and said to him in Hebrew, 'Rabbouni!' (which means Teacher). (John 20:14–16, emphasis added)

In her first turning, she is facing Jesus, but oddly she does not recognize him. He addresses her the same way that the angels did—by calling attention to her tears. He speaks to her through her tears, and she responds in misrecognition. Although she faces him, she does not recognize his face—or his voice. Again, she is caught up with the location of the body. Assuming that he works around the gardens, she thinks he might have some information about the body. They speak to each other face to face, but she cannot "see" him.

There is a slight confusion in the text about Mary's positioning. It says that Jesus speaks her name and that she turns around and responds to him. But isn't Mary already facing Jesus? At first she was looking into the tomb, speaking to the angels. Then she turns and speaks to him (without recognizing him). When he speaks her name, we assume that she is facing him. But the next verse calls this into question. It says that she turns and responds by speaking his name. Somewhere between speaking to him as the gardener and speaking his name, did she turn away? Commentators acknowledge the confusion in her turning.[8] Many explain it by saying that the second turning is not literal; it merely emphasizes Mary's comprehension of Jesus' identity. This turning highlights her moment of recognition. Although a textual difficulty is noted, it is not figured into the interpretation of the encounter between Mary and Jesus. As soon as they begin speaking to each other, it is assumed that they are face to face.

---

8. See Raymond E. Brown, *The Gospel According to John XIII–XXI*, Anchor Bible (Garden City, NY: Doubleday, 1970): "The use of Mary's name draws her attention because obviously the gardener knows her personally. Yet Mary had already turned towards this man (same verb) in vs. 14. Those who try to deal with the duplication without resorting to literary criticism (i.e., the joining of once independent accounts) usually suppose that Mary had turned away in the meantime" (991). See also Dorothy A. Lee, "Turning from Death to Life: A Biblical Reflection on Mary Magdalene," *Ecumenical Review* 50, no. 2 (1998): 112–20.

The textual confusion, I suggest, cannot simply be smoothed over. Instead, it raises the question of whether Mary recognizes Jesus through seeing and facing him or whether she recognizes him without seeing him. Could it be read this way? She has turned away (a turning that is not written in the text) and she is facing the tomb again, her back to him when he calls her name. She hears her name from behind her back, she turns around, and then she speaks his name. He calls, "Mary." And she recognizes his voice, a voice she couldn't identify when she was facing him. Her name spoken from behind sparks her recognition. If there is a turning between the two, it is not dependent on her seeing. The sound of her name breaks through the obstructions of sight.

The turning problem in the text introduces the idea that recognition is not dependent on sight.[9] If it comes, it must come a different way. The darkness, the tears, and the turning raise questions about the credibility of Mary's witness. What really is she able to see? The moment of recognition is, startlingly, not dependent on sight. The text indicates that her inability to see does not hinder her witness. Instead, I suggest, it redirects us to interpret her witness in a different way.

In this encounter, there is also an exchange of names that leads to Mary's recognition of Jesus. "Jesus said to her, 'Mary!' She turned and said to him in Hebrew, 'Rabbouni!' (which means Teacher)" (John 20:16). It is the dramatic moment of recognition. He calls to her, and she replies. But this moment is not without its difficulties. The text presents us with an address that requires a translation. The Aramaic term *Rabbouni*, spoken in Mary's native tongue, has always sparked curiosity.[10] Yet *Rabbouni* is neither straightforwardly *rabbi* (teacher in Greek), *rabbuni* (the vocalized form of the Aramaic), or *kurios* (lord, the name she reports to the disciples later). Instead, the written form of the Aramaic is inserted in the text; it is accompanied by a parenthetical explanation ("which means Teacher"), and a footnote in English translations (telling us that the term is Aramaic). It is important to note that what is often depicted as an intimate moment of recognition is forged through a series of translations.

Her recognition is different from what we might expect. Instead, there is a distance to this exchange of names. First, Mary's titular reference to Jesus marks a distance in the encounter between them. Although it is differentiated from "rabbi" and often interpreted as an address of endearment, it is, nonetheless, a title. As many scholars note, the caritative form points to Mary's familiarity with and affection for Jesus.[11] Yet this familiarity is nonetheless conveyed through the use of a title. The intimacy is qualified by his designation as her teacher. Intrinsic

9. One of the very problematic interpretations of this double turning of Mary is that, as Jane Schaberg notes, it "is sometimes read as a turning back towards Judaism, then turning in a spiritual conversion from it" (Schaberg, *Resurrection of Mary Magdalene*, 329).

10. Brown, *Gospel According to John*, 991–92.

11. See Robert Crotty, "The Two Magdalene Reports on the Risen Jesus in John 20," *Pacifica* 12 (June 1999): "*Rabbouni* is a caritative, a diminutive form of endearment. For John, *rabbouni* is a title used by disciples during Jesus' lifetime with overtones of familiarity and closeness" (165).

to the use of a title is a certain distance. Raymond Brown comments on the use of the title, contrasting it with the proclamation of Thomas. He writes, "Certainly, it falls short of Thomas' 'My Lord and my God' in 28. One is tempted to theorize that by using this 'old' title the Johannine Magdalene is showing her misunderstanding of the resurrection by thinking that she can now resume following Jesus in the same manner as she had followed him during the ministry."[12] Thomas's response is personal, confessional, and possessive; Mary's call names Jesus, but she names him through an external designation. Brown goes on to say that her later proclamation to the disciples, "I have seen the Lord," reveals her true recognition of Jesus. Brown emphasizes Mary's reliance on an "old" title to identify Jesus, distinguishing between two moments of her witness.[13] But perhaps the titular address preserves a distance that is constitutive of her witness rather than a sign of her failed witness.

In her moment of recognition, another distance is introduced as well. The sound of his name on her tongue is familiar. But her cry of recognition prompts a translation by the writer. An explanation of *Rabbouni* is inserted. This charged moment indicating Mary's familiarity with Jesus marks the reader's distance. In what is often interpreted as the climactic moment of the encounter, the strange disorientation expressed in the early scenes is not completely overturned. Now it is experienced by the reader. The readers of the text do not recognize this term *Rabbouni*, as suggested by the parenthetical insertion. Her moment of recognition is the reader's moment of misrecognition.

But Jesus' call to Mary is also unusual. Jesus speaks to Mary twice. He first addresses her as "woman": "Woman, why are you weeping?" he asks. Addressing her as a weeping woman, she does not recognize the address. Neither these words nor the sound of his voice prompts her recognition. But then he calls her name. "Mariam!" he says. Only at this second time when she hears the sound of her name does she know who he is. Although the English translation indicates that he calls out to her as Mary, the Greek text indicates a variance in his address. Up to this point, he has identified her as "Maria."[14] This, we assume, is what the disciples and those around her also call her. When Jesus speaks her name here, it is different. This distinction is lost in translation. He speaks her name distinctively. It is not simply the medium of sound taking over where sight has failed. Here, she recognizes him by the distinctive speaking of her name. It is neither sight nor sound directly, but somehow the unseeing and the alteration of sound—the particularity of her name spoken by Jesus—that gives rise to recognition. Much has been made of her call to him in Aramaic; less has been made of the variance

12. Brown, *Gospel According to John*, 1010.
13. Ibid.
14. Until this passage, Mary Magdalene had been addressed as "Maria" (19:25; 20:1, 11). In 20:16 this shifts to "Mariam" and is repeated again in 20:18. "Mariam" is used when attached to the adjective, to Mary the Magdalene. It stands alone in these two later verses in John, which is unusual. For the significance of this shift, see "The Woman Who Understood (Too) Completely," in Schaberg, *Resurrection of Mary Magdalene*, 126–27, and Brown, *Gospel According to John*, 990.

in his speaking her name. He speaks, but it is "Mariam" that prompts her cry, "Rabbouni!"

This moment of recognition is followed by a startling prohibition of touch.[15] Although her search for his body has come to an end, she encounters him still at a distance. She has frantically looked for him, reporting to the two disciples and the two angels the crisis of Jesus' missing body. Then he appears to her, and the question of placement persists. Although he stands in front of her, she still is unable to secure his location. With the exchange of names, it would seem that Mary's concern about the placement of Jesus' body is satisfied. His body is not missing or stolen. He is here, and they have recognized each other. But this recognition through sound does not address the problem of placement. The physical presence of Jesus before her is not reassuring. Instead, the placement of Jesus is denied to Mary once again. The text communicates this by the strong statements of Jesus to Mary about his location. The first is the imperative, "Do not touch me."[16] The second is his reference to his ascension. Even though he stands before her, his words direct her away from seeing him in that place. She cannot locate him, despite the fact that he is physically standing in front of her. How are we to read this denial of placement? The content of his message to Mary reinforces her failure to locate his body. She cannot secure his location. Jesus is here, but is he? The words he speaks to her, his command to her, all point to him not being here. "You cannot locate me here," he seems to be saying to her.[17]

The unseeing and the tangles of translation make it impossible to understand Mary's witness as straightforward and direct. We typically associate witness with seeing and, subsequently, with testifying to what one has seen. This is not the case here. Mary's witness is dominated by unseeing; it is not direct, clear, or easy.

15. Harold W. Attridge writes, "The encounter between Jesus and Mary Magdalene in John 20:11–18 is a dramatic episode with an enigmatic touch" ("'Don't Be Touching Me': Recent Feminist Scholarship on Mary Magdalene," in Levine and Blickenstaff, *Feminist Companion*, 2:140). Attridge provides an excellent overview of different feminist readings and finds those who work closely with 20:17b to be most provocative; the problem is not with Mary, but "with the situation of Jesus' transitional state. On his way back on high, he was simply not fit to be touched" (165–66). See also Jacques Derrida, *On Touching—Jean-Luc Nancy*, trans. Christine Irizarry (Stanford, CA: Stanford University Press, 2005). "Jesus the savior is 'touching,' he is the One who touches, and most often with his hand, and most often in order to purify, heal, or resuscitate—save, in a word. . . . It seems that these literal allusions to touching are rarer and even absent in the Gospel according to John. Why?" (100, 102–3). Schaberg notes, "The command of the risen Jesus in John 20:17, however, is most often taken to signal Mary Magdalen's spiritual and intellectual inadequacy, her earthiness" (*Resurrection of Mary Magdalene*, 329). Note that Ambrose interpreted the *noli me tangere* as the prohibition of women teaching in the church (Katherine Ludwig Jansen, "The Vita Apostolica," in *The Making of the Magdalene: Preaching and Popular Devotion in the Later Middle Ages* (Princeton, NJ: Princeton University Press, 2000), 54, citing *Expositio evangelii secundum Lucam*, ed. C. Schenki, Lib. X, *CSEL* 32 (1902): 519.

16. Gail O'Day in the *New Interpreter's Bible* reads this not as a prohibition against touching but as a prohibition against "holding on to" Jesus.

17. Referring to Brown and Schnackenburg's insights, O'Day says, "The awkwardness of Jesus' words, 'I have not yet ascended to the Father,' arises from the awkwardness of having to give linear, narrative shape to something that transcends and transforms temporal categories for the Evangelist" (ibid., 842–43).

The text dismantles sight, sound, and even touch as vehicles constituting Mary's witness. What we normally understand as witness would, applied here, be interpreted as a failure. If Mary witnesses to something taking place, she is doing so through darkness, through her tears, and through her inability to see, hear, and name Jesus face to face. Repeatedly, her witness challenges what we traditionally understand as witness.

But Mary's witness also signals the question of reception, in two ways. First, she runs to tell the male disciples what she has seen, and then she disappears from the account, only to reappear outside the tomb several verses later. There is no register in the text that her proclamations to the others— "They have taken the Lord out of the tomb, and we do not know where they have laid him" (20:2) and "I have seen the Lord" (20:18)—are received. Do others hear and believe her testimony? The text does not say. But this question of suspended reception is also constitutive of the interpretive history of Mary Magdalene which, Jane Schaberg claims, has been one of "silence, conflation, distortion, [and] legend."[18] Not only is Mary's message—her proclamation—questionably received; the figure of Mary, as witness, is questionably received. She becomes a figure subject to multiple elisions, using the terminology I invoke in chapter 1.

What does Mary Magdalene tell us about what it means to witness? In Mary's witness, there is an unusual orchestration of the senses or what we might call a sensorium surrounding her witness. One sense is stepping in for another in a curious way, and in her encounters with "questionable" corporeal beings (the angels and Jesus), she testifies between spirit/flesh, as understood in opposition, to an "unlocatable truth." It is frequently noted that Mary's testimony is suspended without response; the fact that Mary was a woman delivering this news would have been, of course, a cause for suspicion.[19] This questionable reception may tell a distinctive truth, though, about the events taking place; she provides a testimony to elisions surrounding the act of witnessing. Instead of interpreting her witness as an imperfect or flawed attempt to account for what is taking

18. This is the section heading that Schaberg uses to describe the interpretative history of Mary within the Christian tradition. The reception of the figure of Mary Magdalene has been extremely mixed in the tradition; the central image attributed to her is that of a prostitute or wanton woman: "But in fact no other biblical figure—including Judas, and perhaps even Jesus—has had such a vivid and bizarre post-biblical life in the human imagination, in legend and in art. . . . Fundamental questions concerning sexuality and the spirit, guilt and transcendence, authority and love, and unspoken questions too, have been addressed by her changing image" (*Resurrection of Mary Magdalene*, 68).

19. There is a difference here, as well, between the canonical Gospels and the gnostic gospels, in which Mary's witness is perceived as primary and presented as superior to that of the male disciples. See Karen King, *The Gospel of Mary of Magdala* (Santa Rosa, CA: Polebridge Press, 2003). About Mary Magdalene's witness to Jesus' teaching to her, King writes, "As she finishes her account, two of the disciples quite unexpectedly challenge her. Andrew objects that her teaching is strange and refuses to believe that it came from the Savior. Peter goes further, denying that Jesus would ever have given this kind of advanced teaching to a woman, or that Jesus could possibly have preferred her to them. Apparently, when he asked to her speak, Peter had not expected such elevated teaching" (5). King is clear in her view that the *Gospel of Mary* "exposes the erroneous view that Mary of Magdala was a prostitute for what it is—a piece of theological fiction; it presents the most straightforward and convincing argument in any early Christian writing for the legitimacy of women's leadership" (3).

place, we can read it as the shape of witness to an event such as this (see chap. 1). It is also important to note the ways in which her witness is elided, unreceived, and suspended. Mary's inability to directly access the events taking place does not reveal something about her credibility as a witness but instead the nature of what she is witnessing. She points to a different kind of presence, whose form cannot be readily identified or can only be received through multiple experiences of misrecognitions. She encounters not simply the absence of Jesus, but a mixed terrain of his absence and presence. He is there but not there; he is present in a way that she has not known before.

BELOVED DISCIPLE

He is the last witness mentioned standing at the foot of the cross and one of the first to peer into the empty tomb. He is the eyewitness who testifies to Jesus' pierced side and the disciple who follows behind Jesus and Peter at the end of the Gospel narrative. Referred to in some places in the text as the "other" disciple, and in others as the one whom Jesus loves, this unnamed disciple is a primary witness to the events of the cross and the resurrection.[20] He appears five times in the concluding three chapters of the Gospel. Although he holds primary status as a witness to the passion events, his anonymity is puzzling. He does not have a formal name throughout the narrative. He is often placed alongside Peter in the text, the disciple whose dramatic betrayal of Jesus before the crucifixion and dramatic profession of love in the postresurrection appearance only accentuates the anonymity of the unnamed disciple. He is both privileged and hidden, known for the love that Jesus has for him yet easily overlooked among the others. His significance is only evidenced when examined closely. At the foot of the cross, the tomb, and the postresurrection appearance, he remains as an eyewitness to the death and resurrection.

The beloved disciple's narrative begins in John 13, when he is introduced, reclining against Jesus at the Last Supper; he is introduced there as the disciple whom Jesus loves.[21] His narrative ends the Gospel. He is wandering behind Jesus and Peter, following them at a distance along the shores of the Sea of Tiberius. The beloved disciple's narrative begins and ends with pictures of

20. The term "beloved" is believed to be a later insertion. The Johannine community came to refer to this disciple as the beloved of Jesus. Raymond Brown notes, "The textual witnesses show variation in the clause 'the one whom Jesus loved'; it is almost certainly a parenthetical editorial insertion, for in vs. 4 and 8 this man is called only 'the other disciple,' the more original designation" (Brown, *Gospel According to John*, 983).

21. The text indicates that Jesus' spirit was troubled, and he declares to the disciples that someone will betray him. The disciples are confounded by Jesus' statement. But instead of asking Jesus directly, Peter points to the disciple sitting next to Jesus, directing him to ask the terrifying question: "Lord, who is it?" Leaning against Jesus' chest, he poses the question. The closest one to Jesus asks about the betrayer. The beloved disciple's entrance into the John text begins at the moment when one of Jesus' intimate followers betrays him.

intimacy and distance. Reclining on Jesus' chest, spotting him from a boat at a distance, and walking behind him on the shores of the Tiberian sea—these clips raise the question of the proximity of the beloved to Jesus. Is he close, or is he, somehow, always at a distance? As with Mary Magdalene's account, I couple an early and later scene of the disciple—the scene at the tomb and the scene at the shores of the Sea of Tiberius—in order to explore the nature of his witness.

> *Then Peter and the other disciple set out and went toward the tomb.* (John 20:3)

Two disciples run to the tomb after Mary has informed them that the body of Jesus is missing. The beloved disciple, here referred to as the "other disciple," outruns Peter, and he arrives first at the tomb. Immediately, the text tells us that he does not enter the tomb. Although he arrives first, he is not the first to enter. Instead, he peers into the tomb. This is the same word used to describe Mary's first glance (*parakupto*), and it carries the same uncertainties as it did in her account. We do not know why he does not enter the tomb, and we do not know the significance of his partial seeing. With limited vision, he sees the burial wraps, evidence of the missing body. He bends over to see inside; he peers in, looking but not quite seeing. What he deduces from the burial cloth is unclear. All we know is that he does not enter.

Instead, Peter bursts onto the scene, bypassing any brief glance as he enters the tomb. The beloved follows him inside. Looking this time from the inside of the tomb, the text says that the beloved not only sees but believes. Outside the tomb, he glimpses the linen wrappings. Inside the tomb, we do not know what he sees; the text does not say. We know that Peter sees two sets of linen wrappings inside the tomb, but there is no indication that the beloved disciple sees the same thing or anything at all. What is distinctive about his witness is that he experiences two moments of seeing at the tomb—inside and outside. The first, like Mary's, is limited and obstructed. The second, from inside, is absent of any identifiable content.

The Johannine text distinguishes the two witnesses at this point by indicating that even though both Peter and the unnamed disciple see inside the tomb, only the unnamed disciple sees *and* believes. Typically, when paired with Peter, the focus is not on the beloved. The experience of Peter is immediate, and the experience of the beloved always involves a certain degree of distance. Perpetually seconded in relationship to Peter, there is a tendency to interpret his witness as somehow secondhand or of secondary importance. Given this, attributing belief to Peter would make more sense, since Peter is the first one to enter the tomb and also the one who identifies the contents of the tomb. Instead, the one whose movements and sightings at the tomb are more unsteady is identified as the believer.

Through the witness of the beloved, the Gospel writers underscore a gap between seeing and believing. Belief does not appear to be dependent on content or evidence. This is not an unusual interpretation, given theological interpretations of the nature of belief as placing faith in what we cannot see. The Johannine text points frequently to the understanding of belief as adhering to what one cannot see.[22] But the testimony of the beloved suggests something else. Belief, in his case, involves not just the inability to see but an initial experience of unseeing. The delay in the beloved's entrance and the initial experience of seeing only partially provides a way of thinking about belief in a slightly different way. His witness suggests that belief entails an initial confrontation with what is unknown. The beloved disciple's witness points us to this double aspect of belief—the fact that a preliminary experience of "missed" understanding is constitutive of what it means to be a believer.

This initial unseeing suggests something else about witness: that witness is not directed at an identifiable object of witness. His witness is not focused on the evidence. Instead, his seeing and believing are tied to what has not yet been understood. When the text says that he "saw and believed," it is immediately followed by this statement: "for as yet they did not understand the scripture, that he must rise from the dead" (John 20:9). The unlocatable truth might, instead, suggest an encounter with the ways in which an event cannot be immediately comprehended. Is the truth of that event ungrasped in this moment (the disciple does not initially see, the Scripture has not yet been linked to what is taking place), yet received through witness? Could the displacement of an identifiable content of witness turn our attention away from the evidence to the witness itself? The truth may not be contained in some body that they seek, but instead somewhere else, even in their seeking bodies.

> Peter turned and saw the disciple whom Jesus loved following them; he was the one who had reclined next to Jesus at the supper and had said, "Lord, who is it that is going to betray you?" When Peter saw him, he said to Jesus, "Lord, what about him?" Jesus said to him, "If it is my will that he remain until I come, what is that to you? Follow me!" (John 21:20–22)

In this strange postdeath terrain, the crucified yet risen Jesus cooks fish for the disciples. In the farewell discourse preceding his death, Jesus tells them that he will be leaving them. He tells them that they will not comprehend the things that will take place, but that they will, in the aftermath, be accompanied by a paraclete who will guide them into the truth. Feet sinking in the Tiberian sands, they are now trying to make their way forward in the wake of events that, as forecast in the farewell discourse, they did not fully comprehend or grasp.

22. But Thomas (who is called the Twin), one of the twelve, was not with them when Jesus came. So the other disciples told him, "We have seen the Lord." But he said to them, "Unless I see the mark of the nails in his hands, and put my finger in the mark of the nails and my hand in his side, I will not believe."

   A week later his disciples were again in the house, and Thomas was with them. Although the doors were shut, Jesus came and stood among them and said, "Peace be with you." Then he said to Thomas, "Put your finger here and see my hands. Reach out your hand and put it in my side. Do not doubt but believe." Thomas answered him, "My Lord and my God!" Jesus said to him, "Have you believed because you have seen me? Blessed are those who have not seen and yet have come to believe" (John 20:24–29).

In this scene, the beloved disciple first glimpses Jesus from a fishing boat. The fishermen have not had a successful night of fishing, and Jesus calls to them from the beach: "Children, you have no fish, have you?" (John 21:5a) After a few words of exchange, the beloved recognizes Jesus, saying to Peter, "It is the Lord!" (John 21:7a). The moment of recognition is contrasted to Mary's; she is near Jesus when she recognizes him. Although I suggested an indirectness in her encounter, the beloved's encounter with Jesus is even more indirect. For the beloved, there is really no encounter at all. Once Peter hears the declaration of the beloved, he jumps in the water and begins to swim to shore. Two things are striking about this account. First, the beloved identifies Jesus from a distance. He never speaks to Jesus directly. The one who once reclined against Jesus now points to Jesus from afar. Second, recognition by the beloved does not result in his own encounter with Jesus. His recognition does not ensue or restore physical closeness with Jesus. Instead, Peter has the promise of proximity, out-swimming the beloved to meet Jesus on shore.

In the closing lines of the Gospel, Peter and the beloved are paired again. After breakfast, Peter and Jesus are walking along the beach, engaged in conversation. The beloved is walking behind them. Jesus asks Peter, "Simon son of John, do you love me more than these?" (John 21:15b). Peter answers affirmatively, "Yes, Lord; you know that I love you." Jesus replies, "Feed my lambs." Jesus repeats his question to Peter two more times and each time, after Peter's affirmative responses, Jesus gives him the instruction to feed his sheep. This threefold exchange about love is often read as a contrast to Peter's threefold betrayal of Jesus before the passion. Here, the love exchange ends in Jesus' prediction of Peter's death.[23]

The love questions are connected to death. Peter has followed Jesus throughout his life and ministry. Jesus' words indicate that he will follow Jesus to the death. Just as Jesus met his death, Peter, as a follower of Jesus, will meet the same fate. This is a very familiar model of discipleship and witness, but not the picture that closes the Gospel. The conversation does not end with Peter following Jesus in his death. Instead, the conversation is interrupted by Peter's awareness of the beloved disciple walking behind them. "Lord, what about him?" Peter asks. Jesus replies, "If it is my will that he remain until I come, what is that to you? Follow me!" Jesus again gives the imperative to Peter to follow, but it is contrasted now with the status of the beloved disciple. The repetition of this curious question shifts to the figure of the beloved, the one named throughout the Gospel for the love that Jesus has for him.

This interruption in the conversation is significant. In the midst of the conversation with Jesus, the presence of the beloved disciple who is following them

---

23. "Very truly, I tell you, when you were younger, you used to fasten your own belt and to go wherever you wished. But when you grow old, you will stretch out your hands, and someone else will fasten a belt around you and take you where you do not wish to go." (He said this to indicate the kind of death by which he would glorify God.) After this he said to him, "Follow me" (John 21:18–19).

distracts Peter. Suddenly the focus turns from a conversation about his death to the figure of the beloved and his fate. Love, in the scene between Peter and Jesus, ends with the imperative to follow, but the focus now is on the one following behind both of them. The focus is not on following but on remaining.

Jesus' statement to Peter could easily be read as a rebuke. Instead of Peter facing the weight of what Jesus has just said, Peter decides to change the subject. Jesus is sharply refusing this change. His concern for the status of the beloved is distracting Peter from the imperative that Jesus delivers to him. Instead of being concerned about the status of the beloved, Peter should focus on what Jesus would have him do, which in this case is to follow. But perhaps we could read this as something more than a rebuke of Peter. Perhaps we can read this as a continuation of the preceding conversation rather than as a change of subject. The interruption of the beloved turns the love question in a different direction. What if this question—what is it to you that he remains—is Jesus' fourth attempt to ask Peter the love question? Jesus directly asks Peter three times about his love for Jesus. Now attention is turned to the one who, throughout the Gospel, is known for Jesus' love for him. The love question is not going to be asked directly this time, but it takes shape through the figure of love.

Instead of reading the statement as a rebuke, the question can be reframed to capture another picture of what it means to remain in the wake of Jesus' death. The reference to remaining is not just about the particular fate of the beloved but part of a broader question of what it means to be one who is loved.[24] If read as the fourth love question posed to Peter, the question could also be posed in this way: "What is it to you that he remain? What does his remaining have to do with you?" Jesus infers that Peter will die a martyr's death, but the conversation does not end there. The series of love questions is not connected to death but to what remains beyond death. The figure of love is a figure of survival.

Reexamining the pairing of Peter and the beloved, the beloved is always a step off, either before or behind Peter. He does not receive a name throughout, and due to this anonymity he always seems to be a minor character in the major drama. On the beach at the end of the Gospel, the beloved again follows behind Peter. Peter, a second time, appears to be the one who sees first, engaging Jesus directly. The beloved becomes the third person in this discussion, but he does not speak. Instead, he is spoken *of*. Although he is present in the scene, the conversation proceeds as if he is not there.

Yet this positioning, as with the earlier scene, is curiously reversed at the end of the Gospel. The beloved upstages Peter. In the tomb scene, belief is attributed to him. In this final scene, the beloved is the one who will outlive Peter. This second scene could also reveal something significant about the texture of belief. The beloved is not the one who will imitate Jesus in his death, but perhaps more important, he is the one who remains, as the sign that love, even in

---

24. The earlier question is whether Peter loves Jesus. The question surrounding the beloved is, in fact, reversed: "What does it mean to be loved by Jesus?"

its anonymous designation, persists. Love, through the figure of the beloved, becomes bound up not in death but in survival. Believing is not focused here on sacrifice but on testimony. The text reads, "This is the disciple who is testifying to these things and has written them, and we know that his testimony is true" (John 21:24). His role as witness is highlighted at the end of the Gospel.[25]

The question that lingers at the end of the Gospel and remains unanswered is the fourth love question: what is it to you that he remain? This question is handed over in written form and becomes the question posed to the readers of the Gospel. This question, I argue, is inevitably tied to the figure of the Spirit. When Jesus speaks to them in the farewell discourse about remaining, he speaks about a way of being in the aftermath of death. Whatever remaining (*menein*) they will do, they will do it in connection with the usual partnership that the Gospel references—a partnership with the spirit-paraclete that will dwell in them.

What does the beloved disciple tell us about what it means to witness? In the first scene, I suggested that his secondary position, both temporally and physically, in relationship to the events at the tomb turn us away from an understanding of witness as exclusively tied to a clear and deliverable message. Given the fact that belief is attributed to him, it raises the question as to whether the process of initial unseeing is constitutive of what it means to witness in the aftermath of the passion. In the second scene, I suggest that his anonymity and positioning in relationship to Peter pave the way for a different interpretation of the Gospel's ending. Instead of privileging Peter as the one who follows Jesus to the death, the witness of the beloved disciple disrupts this familiar reading, pointing us instead to a different conception of love. Love is linked to remaining rather than to dying. Figured in the beloved disciple, the Gospel presents to us the new shape of love: witness.

It is important here to state the obvious. If Mary and the beloved are chief eyewitnesses to the events that are taking place, the reliability of their witness is in question. Yet, I suggest, they reveal the ways in which witness is distinctively configured at the intersection of death and life. They are not simply witnessing an event of death but, rather, the reconfiguration of life in relationship to death. They are witnessing something of death's remainder that will be carried forward into life. This sounds, at first, as if I am speaking about their witness to resurrection. Instead, I am marking out, in the pairing of scenes, a distinctive conceptual middle space that challenges our interpretations of death and life, passion and resurrection. This middle space calls attention to the complexities of witness, but it also raises significant questions about the object of witness.

The text tells us that Mary recognizes Jesus; the beloved is designated as the one who believes. But in both cases, distance and disruptions exist in their tes-

25. The Johannine Gospel is different from the other Gospels in that the figure of the beloved and references to the Johannine community close the Gospel. At the end of the other Gospels, Jesus is still present with them. Here, the focus is on those who remain to witness to Jesus in his absence.

timonies. They see, but never directly and with persistent obstructions. They locate Jesus, but even then they do so at a distance. Their witness tells us something important about the events being witnessed. The events themselves are ungraspable in any straightforward way. Their witness speaks to a truth about the passion: that it cannot be so neatly contained in the past but continues on, marking life in ways that cannot be cognitively grasped. The event of death is known precisely for the ways that it escapes cognition. The witnesses to the death point repeatedly to the ways in which Jesus is neither dead nor alive, neither absent nor present.

I draw attention to the complexities of their witness in order to raise a couple of questions. First, is Jesus the object of their witness? Second, are they witnessing someone or something at all? What looks like failed witness is a new territory of witness in which the experience of death makes impossible any simple access to Jesus. Instead, what is glimpsed, in both the witness narratives of Mary Magdalene and the beloved disciple, is the displacement of attention from the figure of Jesus. The content of their witness is continually elided. The obstructions through which they witness indicate that direct access to the person of Jesus is no longer possible in the wake of his passion.

They do not, however, witness directly to his resurrection—to his presence with them. This is not a witness *to*, but a witness without a clear referent. Balthasar's witness in *Heart of the World* depicts this through a series of questions. Is it this *or* that, the witness asks. The questions move from one opposition to another, revealing the insufficiency of our frameworks of understanding. Not life or death. Not a beginning or an ending. The witness searches for language to capture what is taking place. He ends up with a curious blend of descriptions—trickling weariness, wellspring in the chaos.[26] It is unmappable terrain in which something is emerging, but the question of content persists. Something survives a death; something remains. Even though the body of Jesus returns, it is a body that Mary Magdalene and the beloved recognize only through initial unseeing and at a distance.

What happens in these series of displacements is that the focus of witness turns from the figure of Jesus to the figures of witness and their movements. They are present, testifying to the movements of life in the aftermath of death. In the trajectory of reading from passion to resurrection, this tangled set of movements is rarely interpreted for what it tells us about the way in which death persists, refusing any promise of life ahead. These movements depict, for us, what it means to be one who remains in the aftermath of death.[27] Remaining cannot

26. Hans Urs von Balthasar, *Heart of the World*, trans. Erasmo Leiva (San Francisco: Ignatius Press, 1979), 152.

27. Esther de Boer distinguishes the Johannine Mary from the other Gospels by emphasizing her persistence, a term that is often understood as synonymous with remaining. See Esther de Boer, *Mary Magdalene: Beyond the Myth* (Harrisburg, PA: Trinity Press International, 1997). "What is most typical about John's description of Mary Magdalene is the emphasis placed by the Gospel on her persistence" (54).

be so easily integrated into a framework of resurrection life. As the Gospel closes with the surviving figure of the beloved, so Mary Magdalene's witness leaves her in a precarious position, her witness suspended: Was her testimony received? Who will remain to receive it?[28]

Mary Magdalene and the beloved disciple are presented, in the Johannine text, as primary witnesses to the passion and resurrection.[29] According to a familiar model of witness, they can be understood as recipients and conveyers of these events. Present at the foot of the cross, they report the events as they see them. They subsequently proclaim the truth of the events to others. My readings call into question the following: in what way and with what degree of clarity do they receive and convey the death event in the moments following death? Looking more closely at the particularities of their witness positions, I suggest that they cannot be understood as those who simply receive and pass on the news of Jesus' death and resurrection. Instead, their witness reveals an indirect encounter with what they do not fully comprehend of the event. This indirect encounter is not failed witness but, instead, witness to movements that I identify with the figure of the Spirit.

The witness of Mary and the beloved demonstrates an encounter with the three aspects of witness that I outlined in chapter 1. In both of their cases, the timing, the positioning of bodies, and the communication are off. They present a picture of the experience of witnessing in the aftermath of death. This picture of witness, however, is not isolated to their accounts. We have some clues about the shape and texture of their witness from preceding passages in the Gospel, in both the farewell discourse and the crucifixion account. These texts forecast the witness of Mary and the beloved by introducing us to two critical terms: *menein* and *paradidonai*. The farewell discourse employs the term *menein*—to remain or to abide—in order to mark out a distinctive kind of presence in the aftermath of Jesus' death. Remaining will be linked to witnessing through the figure of the paraclete-spirit. The arrest, trial, and death accounts also contribute to the concept of witness as I have developed it thus far. When Jesus speaks the word, "It is finished," he bows his head and hands over (*paradidonai*) the spirit. The term *paradidonai*, meaning to hand over, indicates an exchange taking place. It implies some form of transmission. This verb turns attention to those present at the moment of Jesus' death and to their attempts to discern a form of life arising out of death.

These two terms provide us a broader context in which to make sense of the witness of Mary Magdalene and the beloved disciple. This framing is connected

---

28. The text reads, "Mary Magdalene went and announced to the disciples, 'I have seen the Lord'; and she told them that he had said these things to her" (John 20:18). This ends the scene, and it immediately turns to an account of a meeting of the disciples in which Jesus appears to them.

29. Raymond Brown explains, "C. Masson, 'Le temoinage de Jean,' *Revue de Theologie et de Philosophie* 38 (1950), 120–27, reminds us that throughout the Gospel John prefers the language of witness or testimony (*martyrein*) to that of proclamation or of evangelizing in order to describe what Jesus was doing." See Brown, *Gospel According to John*, 1128.

to the figure of the Spirit, which means two things. First, if framed in this way, they are not exclusively witnessing to the events of Jesus but, instead, to another form of presence, the presence of the paraclete-spirit. Second, the Spirit's presence is enacted in their witness. They witness Jesus' absence, but they do more. They attest, in their movements, to what lives on.[30] When placed within this Johannine vocabulary, the witness of Mary and the beloved provides us with a glimpse into the texture of pneumatological witness between the passion and resurrection, death and life.

Through these two terms, we witness the disciples ushered into the precarious space of witness. They are handed over to the spirit—the *pneuma*—in the space of death, and they are situated differently in relationship to word and body as a result. They are present to witness the ways in which death makes impossible any simple access to either. The promised paraclete figure hovers in the aftermath, the interim figure whose arrival is indeterminate. This spirit, though, is not clearly figured as the Holy Spirit; this follows in chapter 20 when Jesus formally gives the Holy Spirit to the disciples. Here, between death and life, we encounter a different expression of spirit, both human and divine. *It is the persisting and remaining presence of divine love figured in and through their movements of witness.* It is not a viewable object but instead an enacted presence. The power evidenced in them is the power to persist, not triumph—to bear with and not to conquer. Between old and new, past and present, death and life, spirit persists. The pressing question is: will these movements be witnessed?

FAREWELL

> *"I will not leave you orphaned; I am coming to you. In a little while the world will no longer see me, but you will see me; because I live, you also will live."*
>
> John 14:18–19

Before the crucifixion and the witness accounts in the Gospel of John, Jesus speaks to his disciples about the lives that they will lead following his death. The Johannine farewell discourse is situated within the context of Jesus' final meal with the disciples. It begins just after the revelation of Judas's betrayal and ends before Jesus' prayer to the Father and his entrance into the garden where

---

30. Return, again, to Derrida's comments on *survivre* (see his chap. 1) in which life is conceived of in its excess, in the ways in which death exceeds its limits, constituting life in a different form. See Jacques Derrida, "Living On: Border Lines," in *Deconstruction and Criticism*, trans. James Hulbert (New York: Seabury, 1979), 75–176. He explores the boundaries of a text and the process of interpretation as an over-living, "as a sort of overrun [*débordement*] that spoils all boundaries and divisions and forces us to extend the accredited concept, the dominant notion of a text" (83–84). In the Gospel text, the event of Jesus' death overruns, placing them neither on the territory of his death (his absence) or his life (his presence), but instead in a curious relationship to what remains.

he is arrested by Roman officials. The farewell discourse contains a series of brief teachings that Jesus directs very specifically to his disciples. His words are similar to parting words that people speak to those they love as they anticipate their own death. They often speak their hopes and wishes for those who will survive them, envisioning, for those they love, a future. This is certainly true of the farewell discourse, and it is reflective of the genre of testament in which it is placed.

Yet distinctive aspects of this discourse contribute to the concept of witness as I have introduced it. First, Jesus delivers these words with full acknowledgment that the disciples will not comprehend what he is saying. They will only understand them at a later time. In John 14:25–26, he tells them that he is speaking these things now, but the disciples will be taught and reminded of them later by the paraclete. In John 16:12, he tells them that they will not be able to bear all the things he has to tell them now, but they will be guided into the truth of them sometime in the future.[31] Jesus suggests, in these words, that his upcoming death will be experienced by the disciples but will, in large part, escape their comprehension. They will go through it, but they will miss something of it.

Second, the timing is unsteady. The verb tenses change throughout, and what will take place and when is not clear. This recognized lack of comprehension is coupled with mixed references to time. The discourse interprets an event before it happens, Gail O'Day notes, thus breaking from its familiar Johannine narrative style. Past, present, and future mix throughout in unusual ways, presenting us with a different temporality.[32] The discourse is situated within a period of time referred to as the "hour": "Now before the festival of the Passover, Jesus knew that his hour had come to depart from this world and go to the Father" (John 13:1). It is not a literal hour but rather a period of time that uniquely marks the movements of Jesus to his death. The text indicates that Jesus knew that it was his designated time to leave. The "hour" marks both an ending and a beginning. Jesus lived among his disciples, taught those who gathered around, healed the sick, cast out demons, performed signs that distinguished him as a holy man, spoke words about a coming world, and instructed those who listened to see the world around them in a new way. But these activities come to an end. The ordinary marking of days ceases, and the hour begins. Yet the hour is, as Gail O'Day and Susan Hylen point out, frozen: "It is as if time stands still for a moment, so that Jesus can prepare those he loves for the life they will lead during and after the events of his hour."[33]

31. John 16:12–13a: "I still have many things to say to you, but you cannot bear them now. When the Spirit of truth comes, he will guide you into all the truth."

32. Gail O'Day, "I Have Overcome the World" (John 16:33): Narrative Time in John 13–17," *Semeia* 53 (1991): 153–66. "In a very real sense, the whole farewell discourse is out of place in the progression of narrative time in the Fourth Gospel. . . . It is not simply that certain parts of the farewell discourse disturb the temporal sequence of the narrative, but rather the discourse itself disturbs the sequence of the gospel narrative" (156).

33. Gail R. O'Day and Susan E. Hylen, *John* (Louisville, KY: Westminster John Knox Press, 2006), 143.

Other temporal references are used throughout, such as "in a little while" and "the time is coming." Yet despite references in the future tense, Jesus is speaking about what is already taking place. Jesus speaks to them about his departure, and we assume that this will take place in the future. Then he forecasts things and then tells the disciples that they are already happening. In the discourse, Jesus speaks to them as the risen Christ.[34] The question of his own status with them—whether he is present or absent, coming or going—is continually in play throughout the discourse, and it is reflected in the changing temporal references.

Third, Jesus speaks about his departure by appealing to a third figure, the paraclete, who will be present with the disciples in his absence.[35] The paraclete both is and is not familiar to the disciples. Jesus tells them that he will send them another paraclete, indicating that the disciples have known, in him, something of this paraclete before: "And I will ask the Father, and he will give you another paraclete, to be with you forever" (John 14:16). Yet this is the first time in the Johannine Gospel that the paraclete is mentioned. In the midst of the epistemological suspensions and the peculiar temporality, Jesus promises the disciples that they will not be alone. In his absence, he will send them an advocate, a witness, who will teach them and guide them in relationship to the events of the past. This figure of the paraclete is distinctively Johannine, and it appears in the farewell discourse to communicate something about God's presence beyond the physical presence of Jesus. This paraclete is both the promise of his continued presence and the memory of him in his absence.

In light of these three aspects, Jesus' parting words do not appear to provide closure for the disciples. Instead, they open up to a new framing of life in relationship to death. He confronts them with the inseparability of past and present, departing and arriving, endings and beginnings; he crafts their lives as witnesses to what remains.

34. "That is, the voice that we hear throughout the farewell discourse is the voice of the risen Jesus. . . . It is this post-resurrection perspective that makes the farewell discourse a narrative out of time" (O'Day, "I Have Overcome," 157).

35. Gail R. O'Day, "The Gospel of John: Reading the Incarnate Words," in *Jesus in the Johannine Tradition*, ed. Robert T. Fortna and Tom Thatcher (Louisville, KY: Westminster John Knox Press, 2001). "'Paraclete' is the transliteration of the Greek noun *paraklētos*, the noun FE [Fourth Evangelist] uses to speak of the Spirit. This noun can have many meanings—'the one who exhorts,' 'the one who comforts,' and 'the one who helps'—all of which FE seems to employ in his discussion of the identity and function of the Spirit in the life of the faith community. The Spirit/Paraclete will remain in the community after Jesus dies and returns to God. . . . The Spirit/Paraclete will continue the revelation of God begun in the incarnation. . . . The Spirit thus makes it possible for succeeding generations of believers to come to know the God revealed in Jesus" (30).

REMAINING

remain, v.: To be left after the removal or appropriation of some part, number or quantity; to continue in the same place; to abide, stay.[36]

In the midst of his departing words, Jesus speaks about remaining. *Menein*, meaning to dwell, abide, or remain, is employed throughout the Johannine writings and features most prominently in the farewell discourse and in the final chapters of the Gospel. It is a relational term, in that it is always directed toward an object. Jesus tells them to remain in or remain with. Although the term "abiding" is the most common English translation, most Greek lexicons translate *menein* as "to remain."[37] I employ "remaining" in order to connect it more explicitly to testimonial literature; there, the word "remain" is directly linked to the experience of survival. To translate *menein* in this way is to retain the link to death that can often be lost in translating it as "abiding." When Jesus speaks to the disciples about his leaving, he is addressing them as those who will not only remain after he has left them but will, in fact, survive his crucifixion. To remain—to *menein*—is to be one who survives Jesus and the horrifying events of the cross. The weight and the severity of the death are conveyed in the references to remaining. Jesus tells the disciples that they will be survivors of his death. But the term *menein* conveys more than this. It also links to witnessing life reshaped through death.

At the beginning of the discourse, Jesus tells the disciples that he is leaving but promises to provide a place for them to *menein*, to dwell or reside. He tells them that there are many dwelling places in his Father's house and that, in his absence, he will prepare a residence for them. Jesus is leaving, but they will not, in a sense, be homeless. But that place is not, as it turns out, some place far away. Instead, in the course of his talk, he tells them that they will *be* that residence; they become the site in which God will come to dwell. Later, he instructs them to remain. "Remain in my love," he tells them.[38] In both cases, the promise and the imperative, *menein* is coupled with the figure of the paraclete. Jesus indicates that remaining is only possible because of the presence of a third party. This verb is linked to the unique figure of the paraclete-spirit. The power to remain *is* made possible through the paraclete.

---

36. *Oxford English Dictionary Online* 2000, s.v. "remain," http://dictionary.oed.com/.

37. Joseph C. Dillow, "Abiding Is Remaining in Fellowship: Another Look at John 15:6," *Bibliotheca Sacra* 147 (2001). "The English word 'abide' means '(1) to wait for; (2) to endure without yielding, to bear patiently, to tolerate, to withstand; (3) to remain stable or in a fixed state, to continue in a place.' These are also the meanings of the Greek word *menein*. However, the slightly mystical connotation in English Bible translations has freighted it with overtones of faith or dependence. Most Greek lexicons suggest that *menein* simply means 'to remain'" (48).

38. John 15:9: "As the Father has loved me, so I have loved you; abide in my love."

The paraclete is mentioned at five points throughout the discourse and is introduced, first, as a gift to the disciples.[39] In John 14:16, Jesus says that he will ask the Father to give them another paraclete, who is the Spirit of truth, that will dwell in and with them. This gift is given in light of Jesus' imminent departure. The *paraclete*, then, is the promise of God's continued presence with the disciples in the physical absence of Jesus. The paraclete will comfort the disciples and is the one who is called alongside. Yet Jesus' words do not simply assure them of his continued presence. The paraclete is not merely a substitute for Jesus while he is absent. The role of the paraclete, as Jesus describes it, exceeds this. The paraclete will carry forward the disciples while maintaining their link to Jesus. "I have said these things to you while I am still with you," Jesus says. "But the *paraclete*, the Holy Spirit, whom the Father will send in my name, will teach you everything, and remind you of all that I have said to you" (John 14:25–26). The paraclete takes up residence in them and provides a critical link between past, present, and future.

The paraclete is a teacher and a guide, but is also referred to as a witness, without which the disciples could meet perilous ends. John 14 closes with the picture of the paraclete as the one who resides within the believers as a teacher and guide. John 15 closes with a different picture. Two things are significant here. Jesus employs *menein* in a different form—as an imperative and with a series of conditional statements. Using the metaphor of the vine and the branches, Jesus commands them to remain. He indicates that remaining is more than a statement about a new condition; he speaks about it as something that must be practiced or exercised: "Remain in me as I remain in you. . . . Those who remain in me and I in them bear much fruit, because apart from me you can do nothing" (John 15:4–5). The stakes here are high. If you *menein* in me, you will have life. If you do not *menein* in me, you will die, just like the branch that is cut off from the vine. Remaining is not optional; it is commanded. It is also tied to the commandment to love.

Second, up to this point, Jesus has been describing the relationship between the disciples and God; he introduces here a new relationship that the disciples will have with the world. When the paraclete comes, the paraclete will come as a witness. "When the *paraclete* comes, whom I will send to you from the Father, the Spirit of truth that comes from the Father, he will testify on my behalf" (John 15:26). Again, the paraclete is introduced as the Spirit of truth. This Spirit testifies on behalf of Jesus and does so in the face of the world and its opposition to him. The paraclete will transform them, as well, into witnesses (John 15:27). In this chapter, housing the paraclete is not static. Instead, the spirit's residence within them transforms them into witnesses. But their witness is tenuous; it is a witness that they will have to give in his absence and in the face of opposition. If the paraclete resides in them, this figure will place them at the cusp of death and life as witnesses.

39. Five passages in John speak about the paraclete (14:16–17, 26; 15:26–27; 16:7–11, 12–15).

Menein is inextricably tied to witnessing. Although this is most evident in the later references to the paraclete and the function of witness in relationship to the world (John 16), I suggest that the relationship that Jesus is describing to the disciples involves their continual witness to what cannot be fully known. It is clear, in the introduction of the paraclete, that this figure is promised because of this lack of knowledge and comprehension. In commentaries, a frequent interpretation of *menein* is that Jesus is instructing his disciples to walk in fellowship with him.[40] He is asking them to maintain that relationship in the midst of all the things that are going to take place. This is often interpreted in terms of belief. Jesus is asking the disciples to continue to believe in him, even when he has left them. This interpretation misses something critical about both the context and the urgency of Jesus' parting words. They are being asked to do more than maintain belief in him. They are, instead, placed on the other side of his death and asked to witness love there. Remain in me. Remain in my love. They are asked to see love from the position of one who remains. This is not captured in the interpretations of "maintaining belief in Jesus."

The paraclete bears witness to the things that Jesus did, and the paraclete will remain in and with them to remind them of these things. The disciples, in turn, are instructed to love and to witness. The presence of Jesus with them and the call to remain in him is delivered in a context of death. This death context not only indicates that they will be survivors—those who remain—but that they will operate in the world in a particular way—remaining—in the aftermath of death. In the *Oxford English Dictionary* definition presented earlier, "remain" refers to what endures, survives, or is left over after everything else falls away. It also refers to the practice of waiting or enduring.

I suggest that both waiting and enduring are vital to interpreting the kind of life that Jesus is forecasting for the disciples. Jesus is telling them that they will be those who remain, but they will do so in and with a spirit—a paraclete—who persists with them. But linked to the commandment, he instructs them to remain in the spirit. What does it mean, both to be one who remains and to remain? *Menein* is a way of communicating a different kind of presence that will be required in the wake of Jesus' death. It is a presence that takes the form of bearing with, of enduring, and of persisting. It is an accompanying and attending presence that always carries with it the marks of suffering and death. Jesus introduces them to a series of new relationships (often referred to as "mutual indwelling") in which divine presence is reconfigured. This presence is enacted in their witness. The presence that he speaks about in the figure of the paraclete is a witnessing presence. But, as we have seen through the witness of Mary Magdalene and the beloved, this presence is rife with elisions, missteps, and misrecognitions.

40. For example, see Jürgen Heise, *Bleiben. Menein in den Johanneischen Schriften*, Hermeneutische Untersuchungen zur Theologie 8 (Tübingen: Mohr-Siebeck, 1967). He defines the Johannine use of *meno* as the instruction to walk as Jesus walked.

In connecting them to the figure of the paraclete (as the one who remains in and with them), he is shaping their lives as those who will bear the events that are taking place. Yet they do not do this, as we see with Mary and the beloved, with full comprehension of what is taking place. The beloved disciple, in the final scene of the Gospel, becomes the figure of *menein*. By extending the relationship of mutual indwelling to the disciples, there is also a very embodied aspect to what is taking place. The spirit of Jesus does not expire but continues. It does so, however, through the bodies and movements of the disciples who are receiving something of Jesus' death. Yet, as I displayed through the witness of Mary Magdalene and the beloved disciple, their witness at the postdeath scene continually presses the question of content. What are they receiving?

HANDING OVER

When Jesus had received the wine, he said, "It is finished." Then
he bowed his head and [handed over] his spirit.

John 19:30

Paradidonai means "to hand over." In the Gospel, the term is most associated with Judas, the disciple known for betraying Jesus, for handing him over to the authorities.[41] *Paradidonai* points to a rejection of Jesus and his claims to revelation. Instead of being recognized as one who has authority, Jesus is handed over as a condemned man; his fate is in the hands of the authorities. In John 19, Pilate hands Jesus over for the final time; John 19:16 reads, "Then he handed him over to them to be crucified."

The word is employed again at the end of the chapter, but this time the agency shifts. Jesus is no longer handed over but is the one who hands over. The text places us at the moment of his death, and it tells us that he "hands over his spirit." All of the other Gospels refer to the moment of death by referring to the cessation of breath. In those accounts, he breathed his last breath (Luke 23:46; see also Mark 15:37; Matt. 27:50). But the Johannine Gospel narrates it differently, drawing on the earlier use of *paradidonai*. Some scholars suggest that the Johannine writers are pointing to Jesus' active and voluntary approach to death. He is not a passive victim but instead voluntarily hands himself over, as one obedient to the will of his Father.

There are two important things to note. First, the term *paradidonai* is paired with *pneuma*, meaning spirit. The text tells us that he hands over his spirit—*pneuma*—on the cross. There are differing opinions as to whether this is a specific reference to the Holy Spirit or whether *pneuma* refers to Jesus' life breath. The first, of course, would imply that something more symbolic is taking place here—namely, that Jesus is giving the gift of the Holy Spirit. But this gift of the

41. Mentioned eight times in reference to Judas and his betrayal—"handing over"—of Jesus.

Holy Spirit comes later in John 20:22. It does not make sense for Jesus to give the Holy Spirit twice. The other alternative is that the *pneuma* is simply a reference to Jesus' life spirit. The reference to *pneuma* is merely a synonym for breath. It is curious, however, that another term is not used. The reference to spirit bears, in either case, some weight; its significance has not been clearly determined.

More significant, however, is the suggestion of an exchange taking place. Jesus is handing something over. The Johannine use of *paradidonai* implies a recipient, but unlike the other Gospels, the recipient is not clearly identified.[42] Jesus does not just release or give up the spirit; he hands over the spirit.[43] With the use of *paradidonai*, the text suggests a transmission of something *to* someone. The term directs us to potential recipients. Who is receiving this *pneuma*? To whom is Jesus handing over his spirit? It begs the question of who or what will receive what is being handed over. Do those standing at the foot of the cross receive something here? If so, what do they receive? This is not a simple ending; it implies that something extends beyond the moment of his death.

This leads us back to the first point. If Jesus is handing over the spirit, what form does this spirit take? It is not the formal gift of a holy Spirit. That occurs at a later point in the Johannine Gospel. It is not the breath of new life, since it appears at the point of death. It is, paralleling the other Gospel accounts, the final breath, the death breath. In the Johannine text, it is referred to pneumatologically. Although it cannot be simply equated with the Pentecost Spirit, it may point us to another dimension of the divine Spirit operating at this point in the narrative. The spirit breath is released at the site of death. Spirit is released into the middle; the pneumatological focus turns to those who witness its release. As the biblical witnesses suggest, in the Gospel and in Balthasar's account, the release of the spirit prompts a unique testimony to what remains. *Paradidonai* implies a movement of spirit in the aftermath of death, but the implication of an exchange places the question of reception at the fore. We return to the image of the oozing wound at the opening of the chapter, in which the water—a symbol of life—mixes with the blood in the postdeath piercing. A witness is there to testify to this strange occurrence; does this witness receive what is being handed over?

Jesus' death breath is handed over. The significance of the death breath is not in what is being handed over—an object. Instead, I want to suggest that the significance of the death breath lies in the "truth that it tells," a truth about remaining.[44] This truth is that something of death remains. Death is somehow

42. Brown writes, "It will be noted that, unlike Luke who specifies that it was into his Father's hands that Jesus committed his spirit, John does not *identify* a recipient" (Brown, *Gospel According to John*, emphasis mine, 910), and "although Matthew and Luke also describe Jesus' death in terms of his yielding up his life spirit, John seems to play upon the idea that Jesus handed over the (Holy) Spirit to those at the foot of the cross, in particular, to his mother who symbolizes the Church or new people of God and to the beloved Disciple who symbolizes the Christian" (931).

43. The significance of the term *paradidonai* is lost in English translation, losing the very specific ways that it is employed throughout the Johannine Gospel.

44. A guiding question for Caruth is "how we can listen to trauma beyond its pathology for the truth that it tells us." *Trauma: Explorations in Memory*, vii–viii.

handed over, or, in Balthasar's words, oozing into life. "Is it life? Is it death? Is it a beginning? Is it an ending?" The key question facing the potential recipients is this: what does it mean to witness the ways in which death, handed over, persists in life? The significance is that there is no clear ending to death here. Instead, something of death persists. The focus, given the term *paradidonai*, is not on death but on its potential reception. In the context of the Johannine text, remaining is not optional. The crisis of truth is a crisis of reception, in that what is being received is not fully comprehended and not fully seen.

I suggest that there is something pneumatologically distinct and significant conveyed through the use of *paradidonai*. The handing over at the site of the cross implies two things. First, the Johannine passion account does not have a clear-cut ending. There is, instead, an unclear beginning. Death and life are, in this space, unmarked. The significance lies, however, in the fact that death is witnessed not as something conclusive but, instead, as something that continues. Second, nothing is formally given at this point, but something is present nonetheless. The key question is whether and how it will be recognized and received. The *pneuma* marks this space of witness to both death and life. What form this spirit takes is still unclear. It is not clearly identified with the Holy Spirit.[45] But the clue could be in the verb itself; the spirit is not clearly Jesus' spirit or the Holy Spirit but, instead, a middle spirit witnessed in the aftermath of death. The movements of Spirit are less definable and discernible.

The term *paradidonai*, by refusing us any conclusive ending, suspends us in this moment beyond death. Like *menein*, it turns our attention to those who remain in the aftermath of death. These terms, as I develop them here, become middle terms, marking out a distinctive territory of witness. They come to new meaning in the wake of Jesus' death and position the disciples in such a way as to draw them into a different understanding of death and life. The terms become critical in developing a pneumatological way of being in the world that takes seriously both the inextricability of death and life and the centrality of witness arising from this middle territory. These terms highlight the unusual events following the passion, and each frames the life that follows in a particular way. Jesus tells the disciples before he leaves them that their lives will take new shape in his absence. But his words fall on deaf ears. They are unable to comprehend them as they are being spoken. He hands over words to them before they are ready, and when he hands over his spirit on the cross, the question of their reception becomes a question marking their very breath. Will they be recipients of a message that they do not yet know? What does it mean to receive what is being handed over in death?

45. "And the satiation of Jesus' physical thirst, an event peculiarly linked to the fulfillment of Scripture (19:28), elicits the climactic announcement from Jesus himself that 'It is finished' (19:30)—at which point he yields up—what? His spirit? The Spirit? (Greek simply has *to pneuma*)" (Moore, *Literary Criticism and the Gospels*, 161). The point I am interested in here is that John differs from the other Gospels in the reference to Jesus' death breath. It is not a moment in which he gives the disciples the Holy Spirit, but it does seem here that he hands over something to them about his spirit that is distinctive.

TOWARD A MIDDLE SPIRIT

In the Johannine farewell discourse, Jesus hands over final words to the disciples in anticipation of his death, just as he will hand over his spirit on the cross. I want to stress here that this handing over (*paradidonai*) marks a middle space of witness in which the Spirit remains in and through the witness of the disciples.[46] While the broader Johannine Gospel is often known for its high Christology, and the farewell discourse is used to support this, the pneumatological strain in the Gospel comes to unique expression if read through the lens of trauma. It is often occluded in service of this high Christology. Although I acknowledge these dominant interpretations, I also suggest that the Gospel attests to a distinctive pneumatology of witness circling the cross. Developing this strain does not lead us to the cross but to the surrounding events and its peculiar temporality. The Johannine text points to something that exceeds death but that is not yet configured as life. The paraclete figure and the death breath provide a testimony to the ways in which death is carried forward and witnessed in the wake of the cross. This alternative and pneumatological reading provides critical scriptural testimony, I suggest, to the realities of death as it is experienced and witnessed in human life.

The departure discourse sets us up to read the landscape of the Johannine Gospel as a landscape of witness and survival in which is posed the central question: "What does it mean to be one who remains?" Remaining—a term unique to the departure discourse—is defined within the context of Jesus' death. But the Johannine text is distinctive in that remaining is coupled with the forecasting of the spirit-paraclete. Mary and the beloved disciple testify to the truth that death is *not* contained and *not* comprehended, but instead is handed over into the fragile territory of remaining. Yet the departing words of Jesus suggest that something—a spirit—will survive this death. The biblical text indicates that Mary and the beloved witness a death, but they also witness something else: a spirit that remains, that persists in the aftermath.

As I indicated in chapter 1, witness to trauma involves a transmission or handing over of what is not known about an event of violence. Remaining, in the Gospel texts, is invoked by the Johannine authors in the farewell discourse; it is defined, then, in respect to a departure and, in this case, to Jesus' death. But what we have is a unique kind of survival narrative: a biblical testimony to what it means to remain in the aftermath of death without the assurance of life ahead. We can see a unique testimony arising from the biblical and theological texts: Something survives a death. Something remains, even in the depths of hell.

---

46. If pneumatology is read from the middle, there are two figures of spirit here: the first is the paraclete who remains suspended over the middle territory; it is unclear when this spirit will come and what form the spirit will take. The second is the death *pneuma*, released on the cross. These figures or instances of Spirit are rarely noted. Instead, theologies of the Spirit that draw from these death-life accounts typically identify the Spirit with resurrection and Pentecost. What would it mean to interpret the handing over of breath before the formal gift of breath?

In this chapter, I examined through the lens of trauma the events in the Gospel of John between death and life, cross and resurrection. The crisis of trauma, as I noted in chapter 1, is a crisis of what does not go away. Trauma is the crisis of what remains after a radical ending. It is the crisis of what persists beyond its end. Turning to the language in the biblical text, I probed the context of death precisely for its testimony to this persistence, this remaining. But it is precisely in this remaining that life is redefined. The promise of the biblical language is that it provides a vocabulary of witness, including the peculiar figure of the paraclete-spirit and a commandment to remain. It is language that emerges when we resist reading the death and resurrection—death and life—in binary and oppositional ways.

I examined the Johannine figures—Mary Magdalene and the beloved disciple—in order to show that there is no straightforward conception of what it means to witness the passion event. Is the primary role of the witness to convey a message about the events observed? If so, Mary and the beloved seem, at many points, to not observe fully the events taking place; they seem to miss repeatedly a crucial element of what is taking place, either because they are positioned in a particular way, either to Jesus or to those around, or because they have impaired vision and cannot see clearly. Yet witnessing, given the context of death, is a layered process of encountering an event whose impact is not immediately known or recognizable. In these texts, this encounter takes embodied form, as Mary and the beloved try to discern what is taking place. As witnesses, Mary and the beloved disciple experience the dismantling of sight, sound, and touch in the wake of the passion; it is through, rather than despite, these obstructions that they witness to life where life is not recognizable as such.

Throughout the chapter, I have been highlighting the difficult aspects of the witness of Mary Magdalene and the beloved disciple, suggesting that the difficulties, if recognized, tell us something significant about the relationship between death and life as it is narrated in the Christian Scriptures. It points us to what persists in the places where death and life are indistinguishable. If we account for the difficulties in their witness, rather than smoothing them over, we see the unique meeting point not only of death and life but the witness arising between them. There, the Johannine text tells us, a testimony is birthed (John 19:35).

The difficult witness of the two disciples points to realities that are often elided in readings of the biblical narrative and its theological interpretations: Death persists. Life is not victorious. There is no life after the storm but only life reconceived through the storm. There is, I insist in my reading, a biblical testimony to this remaining. But this testimony always threatens to go underground; the forward pull of a certain reading of redemption, as we see in the following chapters, is strong. Read through the lens of trauma, the witness of Mary Magdalene and the beloved points to the impossibility of envisioning life ahead. They depict the messy and inconclusive experience of living beyond a death. But in the aftermath of Jesus' death, their survival is haunted by Jesus' words of farewell and his instructions about remaining. Survival is given shape through the curious imperative to remain and to love.

In the aftermath of overwhelming violence and suffering, accurate accounts of the events are not fully accessible or recoverable. The truth of the events cannot be communicated directly. A different form of communication takes place, as something of the past returns and seeks expression in the present. This communication is a vital testimony to the fracturing of body and word in the absence of other forms of communication. Mary and the beloved disciple witness the death of Jesus in this way. The struggle to locate and identify his body and the difficulties of translation and communication are enacted in their accounts; both, as well, experience delays in their witness. These disciples are depicted in relationship to a death event, and more than an account of that event, they provide a testimony to what remains. This testimony, if framed pneumatologically, is more than a landscape of despair. It is a testimony to the movements of love as it moves in and through the bodies and breath of the witnesses. This witness, this movement of love figured in the promise of the paraclete-spirit, cannot simply be translated into classic interpretations of resurrection life. Mary and the beloved disciple testify to a death event in and through which a different conception of life emerges—a picture not of victorious new life but of persistent witness to love's survival.

Chapter 4

Middle Spirit

No one saw the hour of your victory. No one is witness to the birth of a world. No one knows how the night of that Saturday's hell was transformed into the light of the Easter dawn. Asleep it was that we were all carried on wings over the abyss, and asleep did we receive the grace of Easter.[1]

In the pages following Hans Urs von Balthasar's description of Holy Saturday in *Heart of the World*, he presents the Spirit as a winged creature flying over the abyss of hell. This passage implies that knowledge of the middle events is somehow erased; travelers are said to know nothing of what has just occurred. A transformation has taken place, and the experience of Saturday was somehow missed—unseen, unwitnessed, and unknown. Just as the narrator repeats the haunting words, "No one," to open the chapter, he repeats declarations about the Spirit just pages later. He writes,

> Who can describe what it means to say: "The Lord is Spirit"? *Spirit is* the invisible reality that asserts itself more manifestly than all that is sensible. *Spirit is* the invisible fragrance of the Paradise that has arisen in our very midst. *Spirit is* the great invisible wing which we recognize by the blowing of the wind and by the keen desire that overflows us when we are but grazed by its down. *Spirit is* the Paraclete, the consoler, whose tenderness

1. Hans Urs von Balthasar, *Heart of the World*, trans. Erasmo Leiva (San Francisco: Ignatius Press, 1979), 157.

makes the word of remorse be muted unsaid, absorbed like the drop of dew in the sunlight. A great white mantle, light as silk, is laid about your body, and under it the clinging garments of despair fall to tatters of themselves.[2]

Spirit is the invisible means of transport blowing between Holy Saturday and Easter Sunday. This movement introduces a different kind of knowledge not dependent on vision but, instead, on an unusual play of senses. The movement is experienced but somehow not experienced.

A kind of pneumatological body is awakened in the passage from death to life. Contrasted with the emptiness of the previous picture, the picture of the Spirit is full, vivid, and even erotic. The imagery for Spirit is rich: fragrance, wings, clothing, and sorcerer. We smell the fragrance; we feel the down of the wings brushing up against us; we feel a touch as light and smooth as fine silk. Though invisible, the Spirit is connected to creation, bearing the powers of a master gardener able to make the most infertile soil productive. Overnight, we, as passengers, are transported into an almost fantasy-like world by this winged creature—the Spirit.[3]

Yet the scene changes in Balthasar's text. Suddenly, we are back in the space of death, staring into the empty tomb: "Only a while ago you still knelt at the empty grave, a sea of tears. And all you knew was that the Lord was dead, that the life of quiet joy you shared was dead. You only stare into the void of the cave."[4] The blowing wind of the wings is now the "cold and chilly wind exhaled from your soul."[5] There is no garment, no covering, for the despair in the wake of death. Suddenly, we, the readers, are Mary Magdalene outside the tomb, experiencing a parallel and paralyzing set of questions to that of the witness at the foot of the cross in the Holy Saturday scene. Mary asks, "What is now the meaning of faith? . . . What is now the meaning of hope? . . . And love?"[6] Her questions are about the nature of life and about what lies ahead. Transported to the space of the tomb, we stand in the precarious space of resurrection.

Balthasar juxtaposes these two scenes—the dreamlike transport and the tomb scene—and introduces the Spirit in both as a winged creature. In her dialogue with the resurrected Christ, named here as Love, Mary is given these instructions: "Proclaim," Love says. "Go and proclaim it to your brothers."[7] In this encounter, Love speaks to her, giving her a new name:

2. Ibid., 157–58. Italics added.
3. "You live in the realm of miracles, you go about as children do in a fairy-tale—in bliss and as a matter of course. All of your past is like a dream which one can no longer recall precisely, and the entire old world hangs within the new space like a picture in its frame" (ibid., 158).
4. Ibid.
5. Ibid.
6. Ibid., 158–59. Earlier, the witness asked, "Is that God? . . . Is that death? . . . Is it the end?" (ibid., 150–51).
7. Ibid., 160.

> Already I see your wings beating impatiently. Go, my dove, my Easter mes-
> senger, proclaim it to your brothers. For in this do resurrection and life
> consist: in further proclaiming the Good News, in carrying on the flame,
> in being a useful instrument in my hand that I may build up my Kingdom
> in men's hearts, in letting my Heart go on beating in yours.[8]

In Balthasar's presentation of Mary's encounter in the garden with the risen Lord and his Spirit, he transforms her into a winged creature—a dove. It is a Spirit of life and resurrection, an instantaneous and jolting transformation of the old to the new. Christ's breath re-creates her: "Spoken to me, breathed forth with a smile and a promise . . . In a thunderclap I am the new creature."[9]

Yet Mary's wings carry us back. In the flashback to the tomb, Balthasar links Mary to the winged Spirit of Saturday. Separating the two scenes, it appears that Mary is, as the winged messenger, called to proclaim new life and resurrection. Connecting the scenes, her witness is simultaneously pulled back to the winged voyage over the depths. Without a clear narrative break between the two scenes, Balthasar invites us to link these Spirit figures—the Spirit of the descent and the Spirit of resurrection. Read together, the voyage in the abyss is inscribed into the witness to resurrection. The wings of the middle day reshape the message of redemption into something other than what we might anticipate.

The passage from death to life, as it is narrated in the crucifixion and resurrection accounts in Christianity, is more complex if viewed through the lens of trauma. There is no smooth passage from death to life. The narrative of Holy Saturday and the descent into hell provide a picture of what persists between death and life. The rhetoric of the descent into hell, in Balthasar and Speyr's texts, is not unlike a trauma narrative; the language of death, forsakenness, abandonment, and hopelessness is present. The middle day provides a fitting landscape to speak about the razed terrain of trauma, providing us a theological view from Deacon Lee's backyard.

Yet there is movement there. When viewed through the lens of trauma, the movements of witnesses discerning what persists in this space are not immaterial. In the Johannine texts, the movements of the disciples and the figure of the paraclete speak to the more tenuous nature of life in the absence of Jesus; this tenuousness can often be glossed over by a victorious account of resurrection. In the previous chapters, the Spirit appears as a figure uniquely positioned between death and life. In both cases, this Spirit is easily elided. Who or what is this middle Spirit? If the middle describes the space in which persons find themselves in the aftermath of trauma, the middle Spirit provides a vision of God's presence in the abyss.

8. Ibid.
9. Ibid., 159.

SPIRIT OF LIFE

Jürgen Moltmann claims that there is one constant and uncontested sign of the Spirit's presence: where there is life, the Spirit of God is there.[10] Where there is death, God's Spirit is absent. For Moltmann, the Spirit is the force of life pulsing through all things. The Spirit creates. The Spirit renews. The Spirit also liberates, bringing life in the form of resistance to counter the forces of death. In Moltmann's dialectic of cross and resurrection, death and life stand in opposition. One stands over and against the other. The good news of Christianity is that life conquers death; it is victorious over it. This dialectic of death and life, and the overcoming of death by life, has pervaded much of Christian theology, particularly readings of redemption. It is difficult to contest this concept of Spirit; after all, it seems wrong to claim that God's Spirit is a Spirit of death. But the sole association of Spirit with life may prevent us from seeing the critical relationship of the Spirit to death.[11]

In the previous chapters, I gestured toward a theology of the Spirit that exceeds this death-life opposition. Experiences of trauma expose this oppositional understanding of death and life as insufficient to account for both the nature of death and life in the aftermath of trauma. Looking through the lens of trauma, the line between death and life is no longer, in Susan Brison's words, "clear and sustaining."[12] My claim is that if they are read in terms of remaining, a unique pneumatology arises. I call this the "middle Spirit." This understanding of Spirit is not so clearly aligned with life. Instead, this Spirit occupies a more tenuous position between death and life. The Spirit remains and persists where death and life defy ordinary expression; death is neither completed nor in the past, and life is neither new nor directed toward the future. This middle Spirit is often elided in the association of the Spirit with new life and resurrection. I aim to retrieve it, developing the contours of this Spirit by reviving biblical concepts that speak to pneumatology in this different key.

In this chapter, I develop a theology of the middle Spirit. I begin by engaging the work of theologian Catherine Keller, who probes the primal beginnings and constructs a theology of the Spirit, as the figure hovering in the depths before

10. Jürgen Moltmann, *The Source of Life: The Holy Spirit and the Theology of Life* (Minneapolis: Fortress Press, 1997), 19. See also his *The Spirit of Life: A Universal Affirmation* (Minneapolis: Fortress Press, 2001). It is beyond the scope of this project to fully engage Moltmann's pneumatology, but it is interesting to me that while Moltmann asserts the Spirit as the drive to life (especially in *The Crucified God*, trans. R. A. Wilson and John Bowden [New York: Harper & Row, 1973]), he always includes an autobiographical testimony to his encounters with death in his pneumatological works. There is an undertow to his pneumatology that speaks to middle Spirit as I develop it here.

11. Mark Wallace and Jane Linahan explore this in and through Moltmann's theology of the cross. See Wallace's *Finding God in the Singing River* (Minneapolis: Augsburg, 2005), and Jane Linahan, "The Grieving Spirit: The Holy Spirit as Bearer of the Suffering of the World in Moltmann's Pneumatology," in *The Spirit in the Church and the World*, ed. Bradford E. Hinze (Maryknoll, NY: Orbis Books, 2003), 49.

12. Susan J. Brison, *Aftermath: Violence and the Remaking of a Self* (Princeton, NJ: Princeton University Press, 2002), 8–9.

creation is spoken into being. I probe the territory of second beginnings—the territory of redemption. I transpose Spirit into re-creative territory and claim that this Spirit is best understood in its witness to the depths. I bring images of breath and paraclete together to form a pneumatology of the middle in which the Spirit is figured as the breath of witness between death and life. Although witness is typically framed in ethical terms, I make the case that witness is expressed aesthetically as the capacity to imagine beyond an ending. The Spirit searches for forms of life when life cannot be recognized as such. Through the witness of Spirit, redemption and healing are suspended and recast in different terms.

SPIRIT OF THE DEEP

From the revisioning of apocalyptic to her *tehomic* explorations, the Spirit has been central to Catherine Keller's theology. Developing a theology of the Spirit at the convergence of process theology and poststructuralism, she defines the movements of the Spirit as oscillations between the absolute and the dissolute. The Spirit is the figure that resists dualisms by keeping things in flow; the Spirit disrupts binaries by creating a third way, an alternative path between oppositions.[13] This is consistent with contemporary moves in pneumatology in which, as Mary Grey says, the Spirit is interpreted as a "way through false dichotomies."[14]

Keller develops a "pneumatic space" most fully in *Face of the Deep*, in which she probes the *ruach elohim* in the first chapter of Genesis.[15] Through multiple discourses, from French philosophy to kabbalah to American literature, she traces the figure of Spirit, vibrating in the *topos of the Deep* (*tehom*) before the words of creation are spoken.[16] According to Keller, the narrative of creation, as it has developed in the Western Christian tradition, has tamed the *tehomic* waters of the Hebrew Scriptures, securing a notion of God's relationship to the world that sustains and fosters earthly hierarchies and dominations. These claims have proliferated under the concept of creation *ex nihilo*. *Ex nihilo* asserts that nothing existed before God spoke creation into being. Keller attempts to reveal the costs of this theological development and the elisions—of gender, race, and religion—enacted under the framework of *ex nihilo*. The logic beneath this claim is as follows: if there is something in existence before creation, then God's power, conceived in a particular way (as omnipotence), is threatened.[17] *Ex nihilo* secures this creative territory, by drawing it under divine control; nothing can come before.

13. Catherine Keller, *Face of the Deep: A Theology of Becoming* (New York: Routledge, 2003), 167.

14. Mary C. Grey, *Sacred Longings: Ecofeminist Theology and Globalization* (London: SCM Press, 2003), 110.

15. See also Catherine Keller, "Be This Fish: Creation in Process," in *On the Mystery: Discerning Divinity in Process* (Minneapolis: Fortress Press, 2008), 45–67.

16. Keller, *Face of the Deep*, xvii.

17. The idea of creation from nothing, she claims, "settled the dogmas of omnipotence: not just of the biblical lord of great if somewhat unpredictable power, but an immutable, unilateral All-Power clothed in the attributes of a single male Person (or two; or . . .)" (ibid., 15–16).

For Keller, the *ruach elohim*, the Spirit of God, opens up the territory of the deep and disrupts the orthodoxies of pure beginnings. These orthodoxies have been colonizing, operating to secure power and to elide differences. The Spirit decolonizes the textual waters of Christian theology, opening up readers of the biblical texts to divine dis/closure, to the continual opening of God. Working with the ideas of Gilles Deleuze, she constructs the Spirit as the "difference in relation" that connects multiple voices and bodies without colonizing them.[18] Through a pneumatology, Keller exposes theology's entrenchment in certain patterns of thinking, revealing the ways in which theological commitments and orthodoxies silence, erase, and hold captive what is unfamiliar and different. This third space, an in-between space of the Spirit, keeps the divine open and in process: "The bottomless deep will not stop opening; the divine manyone will not stop unfolding."[19] The work of the Spirit makes possible this unfolding, always breaking open the logic that threatens to close down and seal off the multifold life of God.

Catherine Keller's pneumatology of the abyss informs my reading of the middle Spirit. She places the Spirit in a similar position—in the tenuous places that are easily elided and covered over in Christian theology. In her case, the Spirit oscillates in the abyss of creation; in my work here, the Spirit oscillates in the abyss of re-creation and redemption. Christian interpretations of redemption have also been governed by certain orthodoxies. And, as Keller points out in relationship to interpretations of creation, redemptive narratives can serve to elide differences, covering over the complex realities of human experiences.[20] The narratives of victorious new life following death have often served to silence stories that attest to the less victorious realities of ongoing violence and suffering. To disrupt these interpretations—these "orthodoxies"—is to witness what often falls between the cracks of these overarching narratives.[21]

At the heart of any articulation of the Spirit are the following questions: Who or what is the Spirit? What does the Spirit do? I explore the nature and activity of the Spirit between death and life. In the previous chapters, I pointed to the Spirit as a figure of witness. Through my readings of the disciples in the Johannine Gospel and Balthasar and Speyr, I have displayed a more complex understanding of what it means to remain in the aftermath of a death that was not fully grasped. Despite the christological renderings, I suggested that this witness, in its unique configuration, is better understood pneumatologically. What exactly

18. Ibid., 177.
19. Ibid., 231.
20. See ibid., xv. Keller writes, "Does this sheer exteriority, this bounding boundlessness, wash out every signifier of human difference?"
21. The terms "orthodoxy" and "orthodoxies" appear throughout Keller's work, and in most cases they are negatively cast, representing a particular closure of thought or a movement within the Christian tradition to seal truth. For example, Keller says, "Theologies of creation have followed the orders of various orthodoxies and run almost dry" (Keller, *Face of the Deep*, 40). "Yet among the deep folds of Christianity, even of a certain orthodoxy, a different interpretive tradition survives" (200).

does it mean to say that the Spirit witnesses the abyss? The timing, positioning, and movements of Keller's *tehomic* Spirit bear a great similarity to the middle Spirit hovering in the abyss of Saturday.

Three aspects of the middle Spirit serve as conceptual handholds for interpreting the movements of the Spirit between death and life: First, Spirit is breath. Second, Spirit moves differently in time. Third, Spirit is love. These affirmations of Spirit are not inconsistent with the classic affirmations of Christianity. Yet they come to mean something quite different when they are interpreted from the middle. When read through the lens of trauma, they alter prevailing conceptions of redemption.

Spirit Is Breath

The Spirit is God's breath. The Hebrew term, *ruach*, used throughout the Hebrew Scriptures means spirit, wind, and breath. Catholic theologian Yves Congar frames his three-volume study of the Holy Spirit with the image of breath. He writes, "In the Old Testament especially, but also quite often in the New, to translate it [*ruach*] as 'breath' gives a realism and an emphasis to the data reported, and to the biblical texts that our word 'spirit' does not suggest so well."[22] Congar traces this breath, from Genesis to the Johannine writings, from patristic and medieval writings to contemporary expressions. In the biblical accounts of the Spirit, breath moves in and through living creatures, taking different forms, depending on where the Spirit lands and with whom it interacts. In all cases, it signals God's presence in and with creation.[23] Whether in the mouths of prophets, blowing over the primal waters, or giving rise to a cacophony of languages, the breath is the sign of God's connection to the world. This relationship is living and dynamic. The breath is the power of life surging through all things, animating and sustaining them. God is depicted as a breath-giver. The *ruach* animates creatures, bringing life to the otherwise lifeless forms. The recovery of *ruach* as gendered in the feminine brings many things to the meaning of the term, one of which is to evoke the imagery of childbirth, of God's Spirit as not only the breath of life but as the laboring breaths that bring about life. *Ruach* attests to a God who labors, who pants with creation to bring about something new.

Pneuma is the term for spirit as it emerges in the Christian Scriptures, in the translation from Hebrew to Greek. The article shifts from the feminine to the masculine, and *ruach* is interpreted within a new context, in which the breath becomes tied to the person of Jesus. It also is gendered in the masculine. As the breath becomes tied to the breath of Christ, this aspect of the Spirit birthing creation can be lost. The *pneuma* hovers over Jesus at his baptism, descends

---

22. Yves Congar, *I Believe in the Holy Spirit* (New York: Seabury Press, 1983), 3.
23. For a compelling discussion of divine presence in the Jewish and Christian traditions, see Michael Lodahl, *Shekhinah/Spirit* (New York: Paulist Press, 1992), 44.

upon him, and accompanies him during his ministry. He is guided by this spirit, empowering him to teach, preach, and perform miracles. As the resurrected one, he gives this breath to the disciples, breath that powers them to do similar work.

Between passion and resurrection, we encounter this breath in the context of death. Jesus gives up his spirit, his breath, on the cross. This is not the life breath but, instead, the breath of death. If we interpret "Spirit" as breath at this point, we need to examine more closely the exchange of breath taking place here. The term *paradidonai*, to hand over, alters the significance of what is taking place. The handing over of breath conveys a sense that something of death itself is handed over. Jesus hands over this breath. But to whom? Where does this breath go? These questions are central to an articulation of a middle Spirit. The risen Jesus, we are told in the following passages, breathes the Holy Spirit in the Upper Room, saying, "Receive the Holy Spirit." But this prior exchange of breath reveals something quite different about the Spirit. We are witnessing a different moment, a different expression of the Spirit. It is not unlike when Keller places the *ruach elohim* back into a more chaotic territory. For Keller, the Spirit of God cannot be simply aligned with the declaration of creation. Neither can the Spirit of God be simply aligned with declarations of resurrection. We linger, then, in the space of the abyss, of death. The breath that we encounter there represents the cessation of life as the beginning of another form of life.

John 19:30 tells us that Jesus delivers his final words, bows his head, and hands over the spirit on the cross. In the other Gospel texts, this handing over is described as Jesus' exhalation, as his last breath before his death.[24] The Johannine language of "handing over" connects the breath to other significant exchanges in the surrounding passages. Jesus is handed over to the political officials to be put to death. He also hands over his mother to the beloved disciple in the moments preceding his death. If set within this broader context, the *paradidonai* of the breath raises a series of questions. What is being handed over? To whom? Biblical scholars disagree about what is being handed over. Gail O'Day says that this spirit refers to life: "As in Matt 27:50, 'spirit' ($\pi\nu\epsilon\tilde{\upsilon}\mu\alpha$, *pneuma*) is used here as a synonym for 'life.'"[25] Jesus, then, breathes out his life-spirit, indicating only that he is dead.

But others read this moment—this breath—as more significant. It is not simply a statement signaling that he is dead; it is a description of Jesus' gift to those standing by the cross.[26] Those at the foot of the cross, Raymond Brown notes,

24. "Then Jesus cried again with a loud voice and breathed his last" (Matt. 27:50); "Then Jesus gave a loud cry and breathed his last" (Mark 15:37); "Then Jesus, crying with a loud voice, said, 'Father, into your hands I commend my spirit.' Having said this, he breathed his last" (Luke 23:46).

25. R. Alan Culpepper and Gail R. O'Day, *Luke/John*, vol. 9 of *The New Interpreter's Bible* (Nashville: Abingdon, 1995), 833.

26. Raymond E. Brown describes this moment, this giving of Spirit, as symbolic. He writes, "Although Matthew and Luke also describe Jesus' death in terms of his yielding up his life spirit, John seems to play upon the idea that Jesus handed over the (Holy) Spirit to those at the foot of the cross, in particular, to his mother who symbolizes the Church or new people of God and to the

receive this spirit before it is "actually given" in chapter 20. In these interpretations, the last breath of the crucified is the first gift of the Spirit. The second breath is a more formal gift, breathed from the mouth of the resurrected Jesus into the disciples. This latter breath is accompanied by the words "Receive a holy Spirit." In John 20, the resurrected Jesus hands over the Holy Spirit to the disciples, and through this breath he instructs them to receive the spirit. It is the vivifying, life-giving power breathed into the disciples in order for them to continue the ministry that Jesus started among them. Gail O'Day writes, "For the Fourth Gospel, as John 20:19–23 makes clear, the gift of the Spirit and the articulation of the community's mission are intimately and inseparably tied to the resurrection and ascension of Jesus."[27] Brown notes, of John 19:30, that there are no words and there is no indication that the breath is received.[28] What, then, do we make of the release of the breath in John 19:30? It could be explained, as Brown does, by claiming this first breath as symbolic and the latter actual. But it could also mark a moment of *paradidonai* in which the divine breath (in this case, the death breath) is curiously intermingled with the breath of the witnesses. It is an exchange that cannot be simply comprehended.

In the middle territory, breath is impossible to delineate. Because of the nature of breath, it is difficult to calculate where one breath ends and another begins. The spirit-breath is exhaled on the cross, but this exhale—released in the territory before resurrection—marks a pneumatological beginning distinctive from that of resurrection. The exhale and inhale, if interpreted from the middle, suggest a movement that exceeds death and yet precedes the event of life that resurrection narrates. This unleashed breath—this exhale—is no longer contained within the body of Jesus; it is handed over at the moment of death. In Mary's and the beloved disciple's search for the body, they are confronted with the impossibility of locating the divine presence bodily. The presence is now continued through the breath. But what is interesting is that this does not render presence a purely ethereal thing. Instead, the focus of the text is on the witnesses' bodies, their turnings, and their movements. They physically testify to the absence that they are witnessing. Mary testifies through her tears, the beloved through his repeated trips to the tomb. The released breath enters them, but it is not the formal entrance that we witness in John 20:22. The breath of death blows in and

Beloved Disciple who symbolizes the Christian. In vii 39 John affirmed that those who believed in Jesus were to receive the Spirit once Jesus had been glorified, and so it would not be inappropriate that at this climactic moment in the hour of glorification there would be a symbolic reference to the giving of the Spirit. If such an interpretation of 'he handed over the spirit' has any plausibility, we would stress that this symbolic reference is evocative and *proleptic*, reminding the reader of the *ultimate* purpose for which Jesus has been lifted up on the cross. In Johannine thought the actual giving of the Spirit does not come now but in xx 22 after the resurrection." Raymond E. Brown, *The Gospel According to John (XIII–XXI)*, The Anchor Bible, ed. William Foxwell Albright and David Noel Freedman (Garden City, NY: Doubleday, 1970), 931.

27. O'Day, *Luke-John*, 847.

28. "It will be noted that, unlike Luke who specifies that it was into his Father's hands that Jesus committed his spirit, John does not identify a recipient" (Brown, *Gospel According to John*, 910).

within them. But the breath becomes in them more than the breath of death; it becomes a breath of witness to what remains. Within their bodies and their movements, the breath is transformed. They mark a critical moment in the narrative of redemption that is often overlooked. It is a moment in which breath testifies, not to life, but to something less discernible. It is the breath that moves between death and life, hovering over the deep not as a mastering or commanding presence but as a testimony to the inextinguishable remainder of divine love.

This breath powers a testimony to what is unknown, unaccounted for. This breath powers witness to what is unsaid, unspoken, and inaccessible through language. Witnessing in this space between death and life, those who stand there experience the inarticulable terrain of middleness. Witnessing what cannot be contained within speech, they demonstrate a unique relationship to language. If they are to witness to these depths of experience, they must confront the reality that these experiences are inexhaustible within language. These experiences exceed the limits of language. This is why the language of the Spirit, as the Pauline writings describe it, is too deep for words and is therefore expressed more fittingly through sighs and groans.[29] The language of the Spirit is the language of witness. The new language, the language that the Pauline text describes through the word "prayer," is language that can testify to that shattering. Breath is what blows between shattered words, perhaps as it does through the dry bones in the valley of death in Ezekiel. Breath disrupts words, thus testifying through their rupture to what remains beyond their shattering.

The primal breath of God persists. But between death and life, it is instanced in its fragile release, without the guarantee of life ahead. The affirmation of Holy Saturday is that God is dead. There is no apparent sign of breath or life. But in the middle, this release of breath is witnessed. It is carried on the breath and in the bodies of those who move in the aftermath of death. The farewell discourse has already connected this witness to the figure of the paraclete. The words of the farewell discourse hover in this middle territory. When will the promised paraclete-spirit arrive? Has this paraclete already come? With the release of breath, the disciples remain in the context of the forecast paraclete, whose arrival and movements indicate a series of new relationships linked both to the past and the future. The primal breath witnesses, in Keller's rewriting of the deep, to less tidy and chaotic beginnings. This is the same in middle territory, in which the assurance of resurrection and new life cannot be grasped. Yet the breath of God is handed over in the context of death, and its reception is linked to the figure of the paraclete and the witnesses. Those remaining in the aftermath of death witness the release of the divine breath. What does it mean to witness this ending?[30]

In chapter 3, I suggested that the Johannine reference to Jesus handing over his spirit (the *pneuma*-breath) turned attention to the movements of divine

29. Rom. 8:26.
30. Remember that it is precisely this tenuous exchange that concerned Balthasar, which is why it was important to him to secure the Spirit in the holding position, preserving the relationship between Father and Son.

Spirit following the cross. I queried the movement of Spirit, from this death-breath breathed out on the cross to the giving of the Spirit to the disciples. This language of handing over (*paradidonai*) resonated with the concept of transmission in trauma discourse. This transmission was not dependent on cognitive apprehension of what was taking place. The disciples are being handed over something that they do not comprehend. They, speaking concretely, inhale the death-breath. This breath becomes indistinguishable from their breath, and it positions them in relationship to an event whose effects will unfold within them, shaping them in relationship to both past and future. This transmission reveals a distinctive pneumatological moment—a middle moment in the narrative that often remains unnarrated.

In the farewell discourse in the Johannine text, the figure of the paraclete is forecast, but its arrival and form are indeterminate. The critical role of the paraclete lies in its witness in and to interim periods when Jesus, and evidence of his presence, are inaccessible. Jesus promises that the paraclete will come after he has left them, but the paraclete will also carry the memory of Jesus, connecting them to an earlier time when Jesus was present with them. Yet the paraclete also reminds them of the fact that Jesus was never fully known to them. A different kind of knowledge, we are told, will unfold in the paraclete. With Jesus' reappearance in the resurrection, another interim period is initiated, between his departure and his purported return. In these absences, the paraclete will remain in and with them. Speech about the paraclete arises in the tenuous spaces in which the disciples find themselves, but it also links the disciples to a new form of life arising in the aftermath of death. In a sense, the promise and indeterminate arrival of the paraclete hovers over the final chapters of the Gospel.

Bringing together the images of breath and paraclete, I envision the Spirit as the breath of witness oscillating in the territory of remaining. The Spirit, as in Keller, disrupts the tidy claims of re-creation as something radically new and separate from the abyss. The Spirit, as breath, witnesses in and to the abyss, the chaos between death and resurrection. Yet this breath is not isolated to the figure of Jesus. It is instanced in the curious and uncertain encounter of death handed over. The notion of weariness, evoked in the brief passage in Balthasar's *Heart of the World*, conveys the weight of the death-context, but weariness, as a movement, suggests something beyond an ending. He asks, "And is this wellspring in the chaos, this trickling weariness, not the beginning of a new creation?"[31] Yet the term "new life" does not properly identify it. It is life conceived outside of the binary framework of death and life, of endings and beginnings.

Keller rethinks the form of Spirit against familiar and what she understands to be problematic conceptions. First, the Spirit is not a fixed essence, or Being. The Spirit, in Keller, is defined by its movement and not by its essence. The Spirit is the vibration, the flow, the flight, and the unfolding of God that is

31. Balthasar, *Heart of the World*, 152.

unending and unconfining. Second, the Spirit is not immaterial. Traditional understandings of Spirit as a disembodied entity have been "asphyxiating," cutting off the primal breath of Spirit. Employing images of breath, sap, and bird, she ties Spirit to matter, contrary to the ethereal picture of Spirit in the tradition that divorced spirit from matter. She writes, "This pneumatological materiality, far from effecting a spiritual disembodiment, a flight from the earth, suggests in its very birdiness a dynamism of embodiment."[32] She insists that Spirit is connected to matter, not separate from it. Spirit moves in bodies, flesh, and breath.

What form does Spirit take between death and life? In this middle territory, the Spirit remains in those who witness to what remains. This remainder is neither death nor life in contrast to each other but, instead, the meeting of the two in the landscape of survival, of the middle. In the farewell discourse, Jesus tells them that the Spirit, as paraclete, will abide, remain, and persist in them. This occupation in and by the Spirit means that the Spirit, the divine breath, will find form in them and will continually take form in them as they move in the aftermath of death. With the release of Jesus' breath, the breath of those who remain is altered.

The breath powers them, directs them. It powers them to give form to the chaos, to transform it. Balthasar and Speyr continually speak to the formlessness of Holy Saturday. The challenge, then, is to find form. For them, the form is provided in the Christ-form. Speyr's body became important insofar as she imitated the Christ-form. But as we saw evidenced in their work, her bodily testimony merely served to point to and support a greater truth. Framed pneumatologically, she witnesses to what it means to *menein*, to remain. The palpability of her witness is the pneumatological power of the middle.

I am gesturing toward a pneumatological form or, more precisely, pneumatological movements that give rise to new forms of life. Spirit is the breath that gives rise to form. This cannot be exclusively tied to the figure of Christ but is tied to the breath of witnesses, to those who remain. The images of breath and paraclete do not have definite form. Breath infuses matter, yet it is formless. The paraclete is connected to Jesus, but is a dislocated presence, indeterminate and difficult to translate. Both of these figures—breath and paraclete—point to divine presence witnessed in its fragility. It is witnessed in its handing over, its transmission. When Jesus speaks about abiding and remaining, he identifies the disciples in such a way that links them to him but only indirectly. This tenuous link is what it means to abide. They will, in the abiding, become sites in and through which the breath of God moves.

This is purposeful breath in that it marks them as witnesses, connecting past and future. In them, the Spirit continually moves between formlessness and form, witnessing to the chaos (to shattered form) and giving rising to new and unimaginable forms. Mary Magdalene and the unnamed witness in Balthasar's *Heart of the World* stand in this unimaginable space and, through their move-

32. Keller, *Face of the Deep*, 232.

ments, powered by breath, they give rise to form. Their breath is not simply the indication of life but something much more dynamic; breath is the power in and through which life must be imagined.

It is significant, then, that bodies remain. We can interpret the figures of the middle day—Mary, the beloved disciple, and Adrienne von Speyr—as those who, with their breath, give rise to new expressions of life. Alongside the language of trauma, this testimony borne somatically makes sense. The Spirit is enfleshed as a knowledge borne within the body that has not been brought into speech, and the significance of Balthasar's activity of witnessing is that he insists on interpreting God's presence as it comes to expression in the body of Adrienne von Speyr; he insists that God's Spirit seeks new expression and takes new forms.[33]

The experience of traumatic suffering is intensified by the invisibility and unspeakable nature of violence.[34] A witnessing presence in trauma will make visible what is rendered invisible. In traditional therapies, the story is recovered. If a person who survives trauma can put words to that experience, the process of healing can take place. In more body-oriented therapies, the process of making visible is somatic. A person literally learns to move in the world again, rather than being paralyzed by it. Theologically, the image of breath speaks to a necessary stage in this process of making visible. Breath is necessary for life. But this witnessing breath is necessary for the reconstitution of life in the aftermath of trauma, a kind of rebirthing through suffering. As the breath of witness, the Spirit oscillates between formlessness and form, making visible what has been repressed, but never with a certainty that form will come. Keller distinguishes confidence from certainty, and this distinction is important in respect to trauma. The power, or confidence, of this Spirit lies in the capacity to imagine life where it cannot be envisioned as such.

The witness of the Spirit gives rise to forms of life. To pull the Spirit back to the territory between the death-breath and the Pentecost-breath is to acknowledge the necessity of this imaginative moment, and the importance of making visible and giving new form to what remains in the aftermath of death. In the work of trauma healing, the capacity of imagination is not a poetic luxury but, instead, a necessary component of survival and healing. Imagination is essential to revivification, drawing on a theological term. What can be elided in the linear redemptive narrative of death to life is the reality of lingering death. Also

33. The Spirit is the "ever-greater" mystery and love of God. See John Sachs, "Deus Semper Major—Ad Majorem Dei Gloriam: The Pneumatology and Spirituality of Hans Urs von Balthasar," *Gregorianum* 74, no. 4 (1993): 631–57. There Sachs writes of Balthasar, "The Spirit is the objective witness in person of the fact that the divine love as absolute is *in itself* absolutely inexhaustible, eternally new. . . . In the Holy Spirit, as the ever-greater 'excess' or 'fruit' of the love between Father and Son, there is something like a living 'history' and an open 'future' of the divine love, even in the immanent Trinity" (641, 644–45). Sachs notes that this pneumatological "ever-greater" in Balthasar is an innovation on the classical tradition, drawn from the work of Herbert Mühlen.

34. A nice display of this can be found in Elaine Scarry, *The Body in Pain: The Making and Unmaking of the World* (New York: Oxford University Press, 1985).

elided is the importance of imagining life amid lingering death. The imagining moment is, then, a necessary moment in the aftermath. The Spirit, as the breath of witness, testifies to the importance of giving rise to life, of imagining it rather than assuming its arrival. Because life cannot be envisioned and guaranteed, it must be imagined in new forms. This prior moment of imagination is the breath of witness before the breath of life.

Breath is both invisible and uncontainable. The breath oscillates in the space preceding the birth of conceptual categories, before the creation of divisions and orderings, which define the scriptural narratives to follow. The preresurrection territory is fraught with the interpretive tangles of identifying, naming, and speaking. How can witness, then, be understood apart from speech? If this figure and territory are outside the bounds of language and speech, then they appear inaccessible to us. But what the preceding chapters have demonstrated is a reworking of an understanding of witness that isn't primarily constituted by speech. Both Mary Magdalene and the beloved disciple depicted—through what we normally might understand as failed attempts at witnessing—a kind of witness to what cannot be defined and contained through speech. Instead, they witness to the unwitnessable territory, to the unboundaried temporal and spatial middle landscape, in which experiences can no longer be directly comprehended. They show us that these spaces are accessible to us indirectly. This is not simply to say that they are mysterious and cannot be accessed at all; it is to say that access to them requires reworking our familiar conceptions about divine presence and redemption. If witness looks like the witness of Mary, if presence is now to be understood in terms of breath, and if sight is redefined through a veil of tears, then the middle territory does not simply shatter these concepts; it re-offers them to us through their very shattering.

In the middle territory of the Johannine text, it is difficult to see, touch, and feel what is taking place. Divine presence is difficult, if not impossible, to discern but is witnessed through disciples like Mary Magdalene and the beloved disciple. They enact movements out of death. The difficulty of their witness is not attributed to a failure but, instead, is attributed to the nature/phenomenon of what they are witnessing. Through their tangled testimonies, focus is shifted from the content of their witness to the activity of witnessing itself. The territory that they inhabit in the wake of the cross makes it impossible to simply locate or name what is taking place.

The movements of the divine can be traced in this breath. In the Johannine account, the divine figure is the paraclete, who remains as a witness in the aftermath of death. In Keller's *tehomic* territory, the *ruach elohim* oscillates before beginnings. This oscillation does not cast a shadow over the light, but rather testifies to the depths and, in Keller's words, to the undertow. The breath of witness is not an active and creative presence of life but a movement in the deep and inarticulable middle. This figure is translated as a breath-spirit, whose essence is not defined except through its movement. A passing between, a giving, a transmission, and a handing over—each of these marks the movement of breath. What is significant is that these figures mark a movement that precedes beginnings, opening up a territory in which the uncontainable depths of human experience can be witnessed. Marking the inarticulable space not with a controlling presence but with a breath, these texts witness an aspect of the divine that is easily smoothed over or neglected. It is not the Spirit of life, creatively and actively moving in the world; it is the breath of love witnessing through its passing to what remains. This oscillation between death and life is the movement of love.

Keller claims that Spirit seeks new forms of speaking and writing to reflect the uncertainties of our contemporary world. She writes, "Theological discourse, if it will live, will speak in the interstices between its historical densities of text and its creative creaturely hopes."[35] Pneumatology is tied to finding new forms of theological writing, to the practice of finding new ways of speaking beyond platitudes and dogmas. But the oscillation serves an important function in that it marks the irreducibility of God to certain frameworks of thought. "At its shore, the very edge of the *tehom*, the ancient oscillation of religious language between assertion and negation, utterance and silence, takes on a tidal rhythm."[36] The Spirit, instead of securing, navigates a third way in more tenuous terrain; in this way-making, Spirit initiates a new language, a poetics. The image of breath is also helpful here. Without breath, speech cannot arise. Breath wraps around words (rhythm), disrupts them (stutters and gasps), and contains the weight of words (silences). Breath cannot be reduced to words, but it can reconnect body and word.

Between formlessness and form, the language of the Spirit is distinctive. It is connected to words but has a different relationship to them. The oscillation, as Keller describes it, disrupts the static Word. The creation narrative, Keller reveals, is highly scripted according to theologies of presence, which are often logocentric, tied to the Word. As I have already shown, the redemptive narrative is also closely aligned with the Word, the Christ-form. The Spirit of the deep continually opens up this form. The Spirit, she claims, is the possibility of a discourse of theology after the death of God. She writes, "For beyond the nostalgia for a premodern grandeur of the doomed utopias of modern reason, what is the actual work of theology—but an incantation at the edge of uncertainty?"[37] Her pneumatology opens to a different way of reading and writing theology, one more likened to poetics than logic. The Spirit continually seeks form rather than securing it. In this, Keller points us back to the early witness of Speyr and Balthasar that was elided. The struggle to find form, as evidenced in Balthasar's early writings about Holy Saturday, is an imaginative activity. To imagine life beyond an ending, as I present it here, it is a necessary pneumatological activity.

35. Keller, *Face of the Deep*, xviii.
36. Ibid.
37. Ibid.

Spirit Moves Differently in Time

Between death and life, the movements of Spirit cannot be read forward. Instead, the middle disrupts a progressive narrative; the movements of Spirit are non-linear. Keller locates Spirit in the chaotic territory of creation. The Spirit hovers in the deep. Her reading of the *ruach elohim* directly challenges traditional Christian understandings of time. The event of creation, conceived in terms of pure origins, initiates the beginning of salvation history. Counter to this, Keller asserts that Spirit-time is the time of continual becoming. The straight line from origin to end depicts God's action in history as linear and progressive. She writes, "The figure of the recapitulatory spiral of this chapter suggests a model for time itself: each moment in process recapitulates its history and yet adds its own fresh becoming, its flow neither linear nor circular but helical. Spirit-time is the time of our shared becoming, unfurling beyond our knowledge."[38] The significance of helical time for Keller is that there is not just one creation, one single beginning. Instead, the movements of the Spirit attest to multiple beginnings and continual moments of beginnings and endings. The Spirit disrupts the temporality that secures one origin and one way of reading the Christian story. Becoming, then, is the term that counters the beginnings and endings, revealing the unfolding of God that cannot be confined to human conceptions of time and history. She writes, "So this becoming theology continues a deconstruction of the paradigm and presumption of linear time: the bottom line of origin, the straight line of salvation history, the violent end of the line of time itself."[39]

My readings of the Johannine Gospel in chapter 3 point to the unusual temporality surrounding the passion. The farewell discourse precedes the event of death and forecasts life on the other side of it. The event becomes the center of a new form of self-understanding. But that event is said to be unknowable; it will unfold in the disciples with the accompaniment of the paraclete. The timing of the Spirit in the Johannine text does not align with linear accounts of salvation history. Instead, the timing there is complex, and this complexity surrounds the figure of the Spirit. I showed, in chapter 3, that the mis-timings and dislocations experienced by Mary and the beloved constituted a new conception of witness. In their oscillatory witness, they do not point in a single direction—to life. Instead, their oscillations testify to death-in-life and life reconceived as *remaining*. If we release the straight line of salvation history, we can see their movements as enacting multiple and ongoing moments of witness. If death is conceived as an event continually unfolding within the disciples rather than an event of the past, then they will make sense of their lives in relation to, rather than apart from, death. The paraclete, accompanying them in Jesus' absence, is the figure of this unfolding.

In the "second chaos," the re-creation, the Spirit oscillates, turning not simply

38. Keller, *On the Mystery*, 174.
39. Keller, *Face of the Deep*, xvii.

forward but back and forth.[40] The abyss of Saturday, Balthasar claims, is time-less. In this suspension of time, the Spirit disrupts the forward movement from death to resurrection. Resurrection can no longer be expressed in terms of a clean break from death. The narrative of redemption often reads in a linear way, as a temporal progression from death to life. The placement of the Spirit before beginnings calls this timing into question. For Keller, the time of the Spirit is not linear. This is signaled in the first lines of *Face of the Deep*: "Beginning is going on. Everywhere. Amidst all the endings, so rarely ripe or ready."[41] She reclaims the concept of infinity, or infinities, to unmask a temporal template placed on biblical texts.[42] The creation and redemptive narratives have been indebted to a certain reading of history, of progress. With the rise of the new sciences and with a strong critique of modernist optimism about things getting better and better, the Christian conception of time has been called into question. Keller is among those theologians who see this telling of time as limited and problematic.

The notion of oscillatory witness is extremely helpful when looking through the lens of trauma. The central problem of trauma is that an experience repeats. The past intrudes into the present in such a way that belies clear delineations of time. This is the site of suffering for those who survive trauma. Their ability to be in the present is severely hampered. The linear narrative of the movement from death to life does not sufficiently address this repetition of time. Instead, it has the tendency to elide it. Could this helical conception of time provide a way of addressing the repetitions of trauma? Keller's critique of linear time is shared and enhanced by Flora Keshgegian, who connects the problem of linear time directly to trauma. The nature of trauma, Keshgegian writes, is "being outside of linear time."[43] As long as Christian theologians are wedded to a linear reading of salvation history, they will be unable to address the disruptive temporality in trauma. Keshgegian explores the recent theological engagements with tragic time and apocalyptic time in order to find a better way of engaging the particularities of traumatic experience. She writes, "Tragedy points toward a different quality of time that interrogates the ubiquity and adequacy of linear and teleological notions."[44] Tragedies have no clear beginnings or endings; instead, they narrate events as if they are part of an endless cycle of existence.[45] The category

40. Balthasar, *Mysterium Paschale: The Mystery of Easter*, trans. Aidan Nichols (Grand Rapids: William B. Eerdmans Publishing Co.), 173.

41. Keller, *Face of the Deep*, 3.

42. "Perhaps for a beginningless and endless cosmos, where every novum takes place *in medias res*, creation is indeed best noted in passing-in process. Discourse of 'the creation' does invariably reinscribe 'talk of the beginning and the end'" (ibid., 4).

43. Flora Keshgegian, *Time for Hope: Practices for Living in Today's World* (New York: Continuum, 2006), 102.

44. Ibid., 112.

45. Keshgegian quotes Kathleen Sands, another theologian who proposes tragedy as a genre for rethinking the Christian narrative: "Tragedy, as an aesthetic form, consigns trauma to a ritual space where, rather than being silently reenacted, it is solemnly voiced and lamented" (Keshgegian, *Time for Hope*, 113), originally in Kathleen Sands, *Escape from Paradise: Evil and Tragedy in Feminist Theology* (Minneapolis: Augsburg Fortress Press, 1994).

of apocalyptic has also been another site for countering linear conceptions of time. Here, Keshegian uses Keller's earlier work, *Apocalypse Now and Then*, as an example. By developing a counterapocalyptic theology, Keller seeks, in Keshgegian's words, "to move away from 'endism' to a more spirit-centered spirituality that values the present as both time and place, and that privileges life itself."[46]

Keshgegian suggests that the challenge of persons who experience trauma to be in the present may be hindered by a spirituality rooted in certain conceptions of the future—an endism. For Keshgegian, the linear narrative of salvation history dismisses the dislocations and displacements of trauma. It offers, as well, a problematic location to address suffering: the cross. A certain concept of time, a *telos*, even pulses beneath redemptive interpretations of the cross, the belief that God, in and through the death event, will bring all things to a close, to ultimate fulfillment. The problem of time in trauma, according to Keshgegian, cannot be approached in terms of problem and solution. She writes, "If we can try not to solve or 'heal' time and its wounds and if we do not cover them over with worn narratives as bandages, then the fractured time sense of the traumatized may serve to correct traditional, linear views."[47] She seeks different ways of witnessing to the "black holes" of trauma. The tragic and the apocalyptic speak to the temporal ambiguities of remaining. The linear form is worn.

The linear narration of redemption is also seductive. Keller implies that the pull of new beginnings and the desire to leave behind difficult experiences of the past is a very human desire. We want to get over and move past the negative experiences of our lives. Theological orthodoxies insofar as they provide the promise of new beginnings and clean breaks can facilitate this movement forward. But traumatic experiences refuse this clean break from the past. Keller's picture of the deep speaks to these losses. By lingering in this chaotic territory, she refuses to fold them into a narrative of pure beginnings. Theological narratives of creation, insofar as they present creation as a clean break from the *tehomic* depths, fail to testify to these losses. Keller believes that theology often reinforces the pull forward that operates within many of us. She writes,

> Much has been lost, inconceivably and irreversibly lost. We grieve our losses so that we ourselves will not get lost. Already in the grieving the generativity of genesis, the flow of beginning, begins. The undertow of *tehom* can be painful. The pull of new beginning may seem to add insult to injury: to rub in our faces not just in dead actualities but the lost possibilities, all that might have been but cannot be. The water wears a dark face: we are mirrored mysteriously back to ourselves, deformed and aswirl. We are out of our depths.[48]

The image of the undertow is a helpful one for thinking about the repetitions and returns in trauma. The force of the undertow is strong but it is not visible

46. Keshgegian, *Time for Hope*, 119.
47. Ibid., 121.
48. Keller, *On the Mystery*, 66.

on the surface. And, like trauma, the undertow represents powerful realities of traumatic experiences that are not visible on the surface of things.

I assert that insofar as redemptive narratives present resurrection as a clean break from the abyss of the middle, they participate in the forgetting that lies at the heart of trauma. One of the things I have been countering, in looking through the lens of trauma, is the tendency to rush to the proclamations of Easter and to its claims of new life and resurrection. In many Christian traditions, the movement from passion to resurrection, enacted liturgically, is seamless. Death is behind, and new life comes. Cornel West reveals the problematic dimensions of this approach. Speaking within the tradition of prophetic Christianity, he points to Holy Saturday as the day that most American Christian churches want to ignore.[49] They want victory and good news, he says. The proclamation of Saturday, "God is dead," stops us in our tracks by reminding us that victory does not come quickly, if it comes at all.[50] Smoothing over this day is tied to a larger smoothing over of oppression, violence, and the injustices of history. For West, the forgetting of Holy Saturday symbolizes the elisions of history, of the truths that are, so to speak, swept under the rug. Implicit in his reference to Saturday is the refusal to forget, the intentional remembering of the past. Holy Saturday thus brings the past to light, but it does so in a way that is not debilitating. It provides a way of being oriented to the past, holding it in such a way that it is recognized and yet, in that holding, transformed.

As part of the profession of Christian faith, Holy Saturday speaks to the persistence, the "keep on keeping on," that constitutes, in West's understanding, a way of being of a "blues people." West's image of African American history and spirituality is one of a journey without any assurance of a destination. This keeping on is infused with memories of past suffering and oppression. The movements and not the destination constitute a Holy Saturday people. Historical memory is very important here, and West understands that Holy Saturday is a theological site in which these dangerous memories are named and exposed. The language of resurrection is, in many senses, the language of the oppressor.

49. Cornel West, Lannan Foundation, lecture delivered in Santa Fe, NM, June 25, 2003. West said, "Deep disillusionment, deep disappointment, deep disenchantment, and yet what? Endurance through suffering. Struggle through darkness. Why? Because it's not about just winning. It's about testifying and bearing witness. You get this even in our dominant forms of religiosity in the United States, especially Christianity. American Christianity's a *market* form of Christianity, for the most part. It's all about identifying with a winner. That's why Easter Sunday the churches are full, but Good Friday they're empty. I'll show up when the winner pops up. But don't tell me about the main protagonist being treated like a political prisoner by the Roman Empire. Don't tell me about a senseless death based on injustice. And certainly don't tell me about the Saturday in which, echoing Nietzsche, God is dead, even for Christians. You don't get too much theo-thanatology in Christian thought these days. But God is dead that Saturday, and there was no thought of a bounce back."

50. In his opening note to the essay "Philosophical View of Easter," in *The Cornel West Reader* (New York: Civitas Books, 1999), West writes, "This piece is a favorite of mine, even though I now reject wholeheartedly its salvation-history perspective. The centrality of Good Friday—and especially Holy Saturday, when God is as dead for Christians as God was for Nietzsche—for me now prevents me from embracing Easter too quickly" (415).

He pulls back life onto this more fragile territory. And in this, West points to a different relationship with time. It is time of survivors, of those for whom the movements from death to life are uncertain and precarious.

How, then, do we understand our movements in this uncertain relationship to time? Past, present, and future converge in the middle. Jesus describes the figure of the paraclete at this point of convergence. The paraclete is the figure of memory. But abiding in and with the disciples, the memory of Jesus will take shape in them. This memory is haunted by all that was not known about Jesus, the memory of a death that they failed to comprehend in its happening. By attending to the middle Spirit, there is a way of resisting a linear time line of healing.

Spirit Is Love

What does it mean to say that middle Spirit is love?[51] What do these movements of Spirit between death and life tell us about the nature of love? In the middle, Spirit is imaged as breath, fragile breath in that it is depicted in process—between release and reception. Instead of interpreting this fragile breath as a diminishment of—or threat to—divine power, Keller points us to interpreting this fragility in relational terms. Love is not expressed through securing divine presence or controlling the chaos (as evidenced in the interpretations of *ex nihilo*). Instead, the fragility is evidence of God's fundamental connectedness to creation. In her development of the Spirit, Keller counters traditional conceptions of divine power that depict God as ruling the world while remaining detached from it. Divine love, when attached to this conception of power, is presented in hierarchical and charitable terms.

According to Keller, the *ruach elohim* attests to a different understanding of love. Keller identifies the oscillation of the Spirit as love, a "strange eros."[52] She draws on the language and images of *eros* (desire) to speak about the *tehomic* territory of the Spirit. She reconnects with Augustine's Trinitarian definition of Spirit as the bond of love between Father and Son. Keller affirms yet redefines this bond in respect to *eros*. Divine love, expressed through the *eros* of the Spirit, continually flows; Spirit is the movement of God toward creation. The movements of Spirit are erotic and rhythmic. Spirit pushes against ossifying and binary logic. This push and the space it creates constitute love. The oscillations of the Spirit in the deep reveal that God is entangled, related, and implicated in the becoming of the world.[53] The Spirit's oscillations are purposeful and dynamic, and they always involve risk. God is powerful, not in God's distance but in God's intimate connectedness to all things. In this, Keller aligns with one of the most

51. The connection of the Spirit to love is consistent with the classical Trinitarian formulations of the Holy Spirit as the bond of love, or mutual love, between Father and Son. See Augustine, *De Trinitate*; Thomas Aquinas, *Summa theologiae* Ia, q. 36, 37; Hans Urs von Balthasar, "The Holy Spirit as Love," in *Explorations in Theology*, vol. 3, trans. Brian McNeil (San Francisco: Ignatius Press, 1993), 117–34.

52. Keller, *Face of the Deep*, 230.

53. Ibid., 233.

distinctive claims of process theology: God is vulnerable to the world, affected by it. The Spirit, as the figure of divine desire, expresses power in openness and vulnerability.

The recovery of *eros* by Keller and other contemporary theologians is instigated by the dominance of conceptions of love that fail to speak to human loves and to the materiality of fleshly existence. These theologians claim that the casting of divine love in terms of *agape* has elided desire in pursuit of a love that is not subject to material existence. To reclaim *eros* and its middle position harks back to Plato's *Symposium*, where love is birthed from the parents, Plenty and Lack. It is the tale of love that has more tenous beginnings, and it is elided in Christian engagements with Platonism.[54] Reclaiming the precarious positioning of *eros*, these theologians assert that the claims of Christianity are not weakened by this retrieval; instead, Christian discourse is released to speak something true from the middle.

In the middle, the question is suspended over the abyss: can love—the breath—be extinguished? Balthasar and Speyr answered this question by interpreting the extinguished breath in terms of kenotic love. They provide us with a picture of love emptied out in the abyss of hell. Balthasar and Speyr espouse kenotic love as redemptive, a love that reveals itself in self-emptying. Their concept of love is attributed to a reading of the Johannine Gospel and the notions of sacrifice that permeate this Gospel. While the Gospel can support this reading, it can also be interpreted in a different direction. Love is not so clearly sacrificial. Instead, love, read through the middle, can be instanced as a movement of witness to what exceeds, what survives, death. If we preserve the link to death, reading the narrative backward instead of just forward, then love is not love sacrificed, fulfilled, or completed. Love is handed over (*paradidonai*); it remains. Love, when it becomes linked exclusively to the event of the cross, can easily reinforce notions of sacrifice. But the shift from cross to middle reshapes love in a different direction, in terms of witnessing and remaining.

As I mentioned in chapter 3, the verb *menein* has particular significance if read in connection to the language of trauma. Instead of interpreting *menein* as the promise of continued presence, I translated the term as the power of persisting in light of the event of death and its uncertain future. Exchanging the term "abiding" for its synonym "remaining," I turned us to think about Jesus' instructions to the disciples in terms of bearing witness. This process of bearing witness involved a continual encounter with what they could not readily see, touch, or identify. To remain in Jesus meant that they are connected to him but in a different way—through the figure of the paraclete. Interpreting this role through a traumatic lens, the disciples are placed at the precarious intersection of death and life, and they witness to what remains. "Remain in my love," Jesus instructs

---

54. Plato, *The Symposium* (Cambridge, UK: Cambridge University Press, 2008). See Pseudo-Dionysius, *Divine Names*, ed. John Farina and trans. Colm Luibheid (New York: Paulist Press, 1987). Pseudo-Dionysius is an exception. In sections 11ff. of chap. 4 he insists on referring to God's love as *eros*, believing that it expresses the nature of divine love in a way that *agape* cannot.

them. Their power to remain is made possible by the Spirit. In turn, the power of remaining is also connected to love.

Love, paraclete, and breath are tied together in the farewell discourse. Jesus delivers these words before his death, but they speak about life on the other side of death. The odd timing of the discourse begs the question of the reception of these words by Jesus. I suggested, in an earlier chapter, that Jesus indicates that they will not be able to receive his words as he is speaking them. The reception, framed in terms of cognitive knowledge of what is taking place, is deferred: they will not be able to bear his words now (John 16:12). They will come to know only later, and this knowledge will come about with the aid of the paraclete. This one will guide them into all truth.

The promise of the middle is that love remains. Breath is and is not extinguished. In its handing over, it persists. Witness unearths—makes visible—this love. Witness reveals a different configuration of love in the context of the aftermath. The witness, in this sense, revives the breath, but it does so in a way distinct from the breath of life. The breath of witness marks a necessary moment in which death and life are held together. The dynamics of traumatic survival reveal this moment as significant and necessary. This encounter of breath—the fragile breath of survival and the breath that witnesses to that survival—is equally an encounter with death and with the crisis of life, of living beyond death.[55] This encounter is narrated in the Gospel by Mary Magdalene and the beloved, who encounter the chaos of death's aftermath, and in their witness to it, reconfigure life differently as a result.

This witness is identified as love in the farewell discourse, and it is connected to the figure of the paraclete. Jesus frames love in relationship to the paraclete. This Spirit-figure will link his departure and return; his love for the disciples will persist, but it will persist in and through the paraclete. What we see is that the territory that the disciples are entering is not the triumphant terrain of resurrection life but the complex territory following a death. And instead of declaring that this is a difficult space that they have to endure in order to reach the triumphant life enacted by the resurrection, Jesus initiates a whole new vocabulary: new commandments to love and to remain, and a description of their lives in terms of vines being pruned and mothers suffering the pains of childbirth. It is not a temporary language given for them to endure the passage from death to resurrection. The word "commandment" conveys a more radical restructuring. Just as the lives of the Israelite people were structured around the double command of loving God and loving neighbor, the lives of the disciples now have a different definition through the middle territory between death and life. The commandment to love is tied to the imperative to remain: Remain in me. Remain in my love.

55. Cathy Caruth, *Unclaimed Experience: Trauma, Narrative and History* (Baltimore: Johns Hopkins University Press, 1996), 7.

The discourse is fraught with temporal and spatial difficulties, thus preparing the disciples for the territory in which they are to enter. Jesus is not simply foretelling the death here, as he has done before. Instead, he is foretelling a transformation in the way of understanding and relating in the world. This transformation involves the shifting temporal markers of "the hour," "on that day," and "until now." When is Jesus leaving? When is the paraclete arriving? The problem of locating and identifying what is taking place also arises throughout the discourse.[56] The disciples are repeatedly confused about Jesus' statements about coming and going. He announces the beginning of a life grounded in an event that they will not fully comprehend. Unable to make sense of the event of death, this beginning narrates a series of relationships constituted around what is not fully known.

Love finds new definition at the interstices of death and life. Love is reenvisioned through the discourse of death and becomes, in the process, a middle term between death and life. Love finds its definition in the middle, as the breath blowing between the two. The farewell discourse departs from a certain conception of love purely in sacrificial or kenotic terms and, instead, rewrites the disciples' lives (through the love command) in relationship to the movement of love making a way out of death. They will be empowered not exclusively by the Spirit of life, but by the breath of the middle Spirit oscillating in the territory of the aftermath. Rather than proclaiming life in the midst of death, they will be empowered to witness the deep abyss of human experiences, to bear something of that death within. Now they are to understand love not through the visible presence of Jesus, but through the breath, moving in and through them.

The new rhetoric of love is a language that acknowledges the complex dynamics of the death-event: the absence of knowledge, the failure of sight, and the impossibility of directly accessing the event as it occurs. The farewell discourse offers a way of framing their lives in the absence of their knowledge of the event of death. Death is the beginning from which their lives are now constituted; yet there is acknowledgment in the discourse that the disciples will always fail to understand the events that are to take place. The divine figure promised to them is a figure defined by the activity of witnessing; the paraclete-breath witnesses in the absence of full comprehension. The definition of love, then, is not only tied to death; it is marked by an unknowing. The dynamics of witness are set in motion through the discourse; the spatial and temporal parameters are broken down, the figure introduced is described in terms of witnessing (and the complexities of witnessing to both absence and presence), and love is birthed through a failure of comprehension. Think back to Cathy Caruth's discussion of the lovers in *Hiroshima mon amour* that I referenced in chapter 1. With bodies and words entangled, fragmented, and haunted by pasts not fully known,

56. A good example of this is in John 13:36. "Simon Peter said to him, 'Lord, where are you going?' Jesus answered, 'Where I am going, you cannot follow me now; but you will follow afterward.'"

something emerges from this encounter. For Caruth, it is the "new language" that Freud witnesses in his rereading of the death drive.[57] The Johannine text identifies this as love.

LOVE REMAINS/REMAINING LOVE

In *Heart of the World*, love remains as a residue. Balthasar and Speyr name this residue as cruciform love, a love that takes particular form in the crucifixion. Yet read from the middle, love becomes the name for a series of relationships rebirthed in the aftermath of death. A different conception of love emerges in the fragile intersection of death and life. It is introduced to the disciples as a new commandment, repeated twice (in 13:34–35 and 15:12–13) in the discourse. Between these two commandments, there is a statement revealing the new configuration of relations: "As the Father has loved me, so I have loved you; abide in my love" (John 15:9). Patterning love after the Father-Son relationship can be strongly supported by reading the farewell discourse. The writers claim that the disciples will know a love similar to the Father's love for the Son. It is at this point that verse 13 is often highlighted to describe the paradigmatic form of love: "No one has greater love than this, to lay down one's life for one's friends." (John 15:13). Love is displayed in the laying down of one's life for loved ones. The model of self-sacrifice, then, becomes a dominant model of love. Just as the Son sacrifices his life, the believers, too, should follow the model of self-sacrifice, displaying a willingness to lay down their lives for their friends. Sacrificial love is often presented as the highest form of Christian love. Raymond Brown explains, "Christian love does not simply *consist* in laying down one's life; but because it stems from Jesus, there is a tendency in Christian love that produces such self-sacrifice."[58] The weight of interpretations on the self-sacrificial model as the model espoused by Jesus in the farewell discourse is extensive. It is, after all, the closest Jesus comes to making a definitive statement about love—of providing some content to the term "love."

But this pattern of love is not exhaustive. The phrase "to lay down one's life" is reminiscent of the parable of the Good Shepherd in John 10, where it is used repeatedly. Jesus says, "I am the good shepherd. The good shepherd lays down his life for the sheep" (John 10:11). The verb τίθημι, meaning to set, place, or lay down, is used three times here to describe the relationship between sheep and shepherd. Jesus' reference to laying down his life and taking it up again in verse 17 is often read forward, as a prediction of his death and resurrection. But the extended parable of the Good Shepherd is not solely focused on this prediction. Instead, descriptions of the intimacy and protection between sheep and shep-

57. Cathy Caruth, "Parting Words: Trauma, Silence, and Survival," in *Acts of Narrative*, ed. Carol Jacobs and Henry Sussman (Stanford, CA: Stanford University Press, 2003), 47–61.
58. Brown, *Gospel According to John*, 664.

herd lead up to the statement about the shepherd laying down his life. There are an equal number of references (five) to the voice of the shepherd calling out to the sheep. Verse 3 says that the sheep hear the voice of the shepherd when he calls them out of the sheepfold by name: "The gatekeeper opens the gate for him, and the sheep hear his voice. He calls his own sheep by name and leads them out" (John 10:3). They know his voice, verse 4 says: "When he has brought out all his own, he goes ahead of them, and the sheep follow him because they know his voice" (John 10:4). This is contrasted with the lack of response to the strangers and thieves (John 10:8). The sheep know the voice of the shepherd, because he calls each out by name. It is not simply the voice that prompts their response, but the particularity of their name spoken by the shepherd.[59]

As if to summarize the relationship between sheep and shepherd, the parable reads in verse 14: "I am the good shepherd. I know my own and my own know me" (John 10:14). It is on the basis of this reciprocal knowledge—an intimate knowing through naming—that Jesus delivers the statement about laying down one's life. The shepherd's relationship with the sheep is defined by the activities of calling and listening. That relationship opens up into a more explicit discussion of Jesus' relationship to the Father, using the rhetoric of the parable. The parable moves into a description of how Jesus sees his life in relationship to the sheep and to his Father. The "laying down" references reflect the later shift to a specific understanding of Jesus interpreting his mission on earth; they quickly become linked to death. Yet the dynamics between sheep and shepherd are constituted by the activities of calling, hearing, and naming. Although this passage is interpreted in terms of Jesus' willful sacrifice of his life at the bidding of his Father, the reduction of the parable to this model would miss the power of the call and response of the sheep and shepherd. The sheep know and are known by the shepherd. The picture of love demonstrated in this passage cannot be explained solely in the sacrifice of the shepherd on behalf of the sheep. Instead, love is grounded in the process of speaking and listening.

This verse is frequently connected to the witness of Mary Magdalene; she, the sheep, hears the voice of the resurrected Jesus, the shepherd. Given the analysis of Mary's witness in the previous chapter, we can see how her witness cannot simply be folded into a sacrificial interpretation. Her process of recognition, as I have shown, involves the entanglement of senses. It is the process of attempting to receive what cannot be straightforwardly communicated, a truth handed over in death. As I describe in chapter 1, Dori Laub mapped the contours of this witness in a similar way, as he spoke about the transmission of an experience that has yet to be given expression, not just to the one who listens but to the one who speaks it. What does Mary's witness tell us about love?

---

59. This is reminiscent of my analysis of the encounter between Mary Magdalene and Jesus in chap. 2. The knowledge is not just prompted by the sound of Jesus' voice, but by the particularity of her name spoken by him.

Reading the commandment to love as the command to sacrifice one's life (patterned after the sacrifice of the Son at the will of the Father) would be to read love exclusively in the relationship between Father and Son and to read the cross as the culmination (*telos*) of that love. But love is presented in the farewell discourse through the promise of another paraclete, a witness. The relationship between Father and Son gives way to a series of relationships. John 15:9 features the word "remaining." This verb, as we have seen in chapter 3, is strongly tied to the promise of the paraclete. The patterning of the Father-Son relationship is accompanied by the figure of the spirit-paraclete. This verb *menein* disrupts a straightforward exchange between Father and Son. The laying down of one's life must be interpreted in light of the third figure, the Spirit. Raymond Brown notes that John's use of the phrase "to lay down life" may reflect the rabbinic Hebrew *ideio masar mafso*, "to hand over one's life."[60] Jesus is handing over his life to them through the promise of the paraclete-spirit. If love is demonstrated through the handing over of one's life not *in* death but in some way *through* death, love is intricately bound up in the spirit-figure. As I have shown, this handing over, if understood pneumatologically, can yield a figure of witness to what remains. The expression of the greatest love will not be understood exclusively through interpreting the sacrifice of love poured out in death or victorious love triumphing over death but through interpreting the love remaining in the abyss between them.

What model of love is generated from this Spirit? Balthasar writes, "The Christian love of one's neighbor is rather the result or outcome of self-sacrifice, just as God the Father made the redemption of mankind the outcome of his forsaken Son's self-sacrifice."[61] Balthasar heralds this love. Redemption occurs through seeing and knowing this love, a love displayed most visibly through the death of the Son. Love is displayed through sacrifice, through the complete emptying out of self as a demonstration of the depth and fullness of love. And it is one that Balthasar affirms, even as he shifts the dramatic kenotic territory from the cross to the abyss of hell.

The Johannine passion, of all the Gospel accounts, presents the events of the passion in terms of the Son's willed sacrifice of his life for the sake of love, for the completion of the Father's mission on earth. But the rhetoric of love in the farewell discourse exposes an equally powerful description of love as persisting witness beyond death. The focus is not on the demonstration of love at the point of death but instead the impossibility of love's survival. The rhetoric of love is projected into a future as a rhetoric commencing from the point of death, not finding its significance and culmination at that point but rather its starting point. We could read the rhetoric of remaining love as a displacement of kenotic readings of the passion. The central figure is not, then, the sacrificed Son or even the resurrected Son, but the remaining Spirit.

60. Brown, *Gospel According to John*, 386.
61. Balthasar, *Moment of Christian Witness*, 34.

Reading from the middle, the connection of love to death is preserved, but it is not rendered sacrificially. Instead, an orientation to death entails witness, not sacrifice. In the middle, love is reworked as a particular relationship to death. In the middle, we directly confront the reality that the divine breath can be extinguished. Countering the images of God's nature in Martin Luther's classic hymn, "A Mighty Fortress Is Our God," love is not a bulwark that cannot be penetrated. Instead, it is a fragile breath that can be—and is—extinguished. Its "never failing" aspect is bound up in its transmission—its handing over. The love that remains, that persists, that survives is neither triumphant nor sacrificial, neither conquering nor emptying. It is love that survives a death.

If breath released on the cross is handed over into the middle space, then love is the witness to this breath—the witness of breath. This encounter of divine and human at the site of death is, as we see with the beloved disciple, a disorienting experience. It involves the struggle to identify what is taking place. The ooze moving out of the space of death, in Balthasar's text, is the ooze of love. But this ooze, likening it to the sap of Keller's *tehomic* Spirit, is not simply the residue of the Son's love, but remaining love that witnesses the deep. The significance of the Johannine *paradidonai*—handing over—comes into play here. In its handing over, its curious release and reception, the Spirit is transformed into the power of remaining, a spirit of persisting.

The Spirit remains. The cross is an ending but, if read through the middle, finds a beginning in the territory between death and life. It is not simply an ending in which love is emptied out; it is a much more tenuous beginning in which the divine breath is handed over into the space where life is not evidenced as such. Through the farewell discourse, Jesus hands the disciples over into the territory in which their lives will be defined through this unique configuration of love. The divine Spirit is not extinguished but, rather, remains. And if we begin to think about the claim that the Spirit resides in us—that we, in some way, house this Spirit—we can think about what it means to carry this remainder within.

CONCLUSION

Redemptive love expressed in terms of sacrifice or victory—of love emptied out or love conquering—elides the truth handed over in the Johannine text: love remains. But this truth is not some content but rather a process of testifying to the precarious movements between death and life. In the middle, there is breath. Breath is not silence; neither is it speech. It is the movement between the two, the possibility of both, and the witness to the impossibility and the necessity of each. Love is a new commandment, and it calls witnesses into the abyss. This love is not demonstrated in the power to pronounce life but in the capacity to bear witness in and through death to the breath of divine love. In the middle, life cannot be seen; because of this, life must be witnessed. Neither love sacrificed nor love victorious expresses this dimension of witness.

In the previous chapters, I called into question the finality of the event of death, both in the biblical and theological accounts. I revealed the difficulty of witnessing to the inconclusiveness of the event of death. Balthasar's question— "What *is* it that persists between death and Resurrection?"—draws our attention both to this difficult witness and to the possibility of something emerging from death's excess.[62] Yet this question of what persists was wrought with its own elisions, as we saw in Balthasar's work on Holy Saturday. Nonetheless, he and Speyr opened up a theological territory and vocabulary that parallels the experience of traumatic survival.[63] The survivor occupies a space like Holy Saturday, between death and life, between an ending and a beginning. The stark opposition between events can no longer be maintained. This dissolution calls for a unique theological testimony to what survives.

A theology of the Spirit takes into account experiences that fall outside of speech, experiences whose "ongoingness" is dismissed and unrecognized. What remains there? What persists? As evidenced in chapter 2, Holy Saturday provides a vocabulary consonant with the experience of a survivor. It is a place of alienation, confusion, and godforsakenness. But it is also a place that is continually covered over, dismissed, rendered unintelligible, and therefore subsumed under operative narratives of the progression of death to life. It is important to mark out this space pneumatologically for precisely these reasons. Attributing theological significance to the middle involves resisting the forward pull of the Christian narrative, from death to life. The middle suspends this forward movement and, in so doing, provides a necessary witness to the struggles of living in the persisting storm of the aftermath.

Attending to the between, as Balthasar noted, threatened to untidy the theological landscape. Holy Saturday challenges the logic of redemption. But in what way is the logic challenged? For Balthasar, the logic still maintained its christological form. According to him, Jesus is the link between death and resurrection. The uniqueness of redemption on Holy Saturday is that Jesus' journey through hell is not his active victory over the abyss, but his entrance into it.[64] Redemption is revealed in the paradox enacted between the Father and Son—in emptiness, there is fullness; in darkness, there is illumination; in abandonment, there is consummation. The problem, according to Balthasar, was that theologians did not know how to express this paradox. But the challenge to logic lies elsewhere, not in a christologically rendered paradox but in its pneumatological excess. For Balthasar and Speyr, the Spirit maintains the love of Father and Son in the abyss

---

62. Hans Urs von Balthasar, "We Walked Where There Was No Path," in *You Crowned the Year with Your Goodness* (San Francisco: Ignatius Press, 1989), 90.

63. In fact, Speyr claimed that in these journeys to hell, she was transported to different places of suffering. The early years of her visions correspond to World War II, and several of her visions took her to concentration camps and other sites of genocide. Hans Urs von Balthasar, *Kreuz und Hölle* I, vol. 3, *Die Nachlasswerke* (Einsiedeln, Switzerland: Johannes Verlag, 1966).

64. "He it is who walks along paths that are no paths, leaving no trace behind, through hell, hell which has no exit, no time, no being; and by the miracle from above he is rescued from the abyss, the profound depths, to save his brothers in Adam along with him" (Balthasar, "We Walked," 91).

of hell; the Spirit makes possible the paradox without allowing it to collapse into a tragic drama. His reading of the Spirit is consistent with his Trinitarianism orthodoxy. But it should not foreclose other interpretations of the Spirit.

My claim here is that Spirit remains. The movement of the Spirit can be understood in terms of witness and love.[65] This witness does not adhere to a linear trajectory from death to life. The Spirit does not secure the Godhead in the way that Balthasar claims but instead remains as witness to both death and life; Spirit is the breath that gives rise to new forms of life forged through death. A theology of the Spirit, if developed in this way, will attest to the haunting losses and elisions that constitute traumatic experience. It will also attest to the power and necessity of imagining life in different ways given the persistence of death. I am not disputing the association of the Spirit with life, but I am disputing the opposition of death and life in which conceptions of the Spirit are often grounded. This middle Spirit provides a way of speaking about the persistence of death-in-life; in this way, it testifies to the realities of traumatic suffering and survival.

A theology of the Spirit equates this persistent witness with the concept of love. In the preresurrection depths, there is no assurance that life will arise. Instead of aligning the figure of the Spirit with life, I suggest that the figure of the Spirit witnesses to what cannot yet be envisioned as life. When the Spirit is so straightforwardly aligned with life, then the middle aspect of Spirit is lost. If the power of Spirit is only expressed in terms of the forces of life, or even the forces of life countering death, then the power of the middle Spirit testifying to what emerges between them is unexplored. In Genesis, the *tehomic* breath witnesses the eclipsed depths of divine mystery; in John, the Spirit-breath witnesses to the eclipsed depths of the enigma of suffering, both divine and human. Life becomes newly configured through a series of witnessing relationships, narrated in the farewell discourse between Father, Son, paraclete, and believers. Life becomes defined in light of death, and love is birthed at this interstice.

The Spirit is often referenced in terms of her indeterminate blowing and formlessness. This stems from the Johannine expression—the wind (*pneuma*) blows where it chooses.[66] This often gives the impression that Spirit is independent,

---

65. Hans Urs von Balthasar, "The Holy Spirit as Love," in *Creator Spirit*, vol. 3 of *Explorations in Theology*, trans. Brian McNeil (San Francisco: Ignatius Press, 1993). "Here Acts of the Apostles comes closest to the mystery of the Spirit who is breathed out from the Cross, proceeding from *the* testimony of blood and, as it were, filled and drenched in this testimony; while he bears witness to the dying love of the Son of God, he also allows the disciples to bear witness to this when they are in mortal danger; Stephen, who bears witness 'full of the Holy Spirit' (7:55) to his vision of the exalted Son, thereby draws his death by stoning down upon himself" (130). Note, as well, that his understanding of witness is aligned with death.

66. See John 3:8. See also Wendy Farley, *The Wounding and Healing of Desire: Weaving Heaven and Earth* (Louisville, KY: Westminster John Knox Press, 2005). "There is the third member of the Holy Trinity: Spirit. She is outrageous because of the kind of power that seems to spin off of Her. She is trouble-making, always stirring things up in crazy directions, and blowing wherever the hell She wants to: 'The wind blows where it chooses, and you hear the sound of it, but you do not know where it comes from or where it goes' (John 3:8). Most denominations try to keep quiet about Her,

chaotic, and even capricious. Yet Spirit's blowing is more purposeful and directed if interpreted from the middle. Spirit is not aimless but instead is continually searching out new forms of life amid the realities of death. At Caruth's insistence, there is ethical weight to this middle.[67] The middle Spirit refuses prescriptions of life or even the certainty of life. Instead, Spirit moves amid the uncertainties. Keller differentiates certainty and confidence, identifying Spirit with the latter. According to her, pneumatological confidence comes from an orientation between the absolute and the dissolute; it is resolute. This resolution describes the orientation of those who remain and their determination to imagine forms of life that are not clearly evidenced. This Spirit requires different capacities than the ones that Balthasar and Speyr map out. This Spirit does not require imitation but imagination.

I opened the chapter with the Spirit's winged transport over the abyss of hell. The Saturday voyage was juxtaposed with the testimony of Mary to the risen Christ. In the course of the chapter, I probed the significance of this juxtaposition. By turning attention back to the Saturday voyage, I have identified a territory of witness that precedes resurrection and the claims to life and newness associated with the resurrection event. I not only described this as pneumatological territory, I suggested that Mary's witness does not just extend forward but extends back onto this tenuous terrain. She moves in the abyss, carrying others, oscillating in the middle space. Her work is not solely the proclamation of what is new but the work of witness to what remains. Her testimony is, after all, elided; in the Gospel, her proclamation is suspended and it is unclear if her witness is received. Her breath and movements unveil a pneumatological sensorium at the interstice of death and life. This sensorium is shaped by an unseeing that shifts to seeing but only through hearing, and a hearing that requires altered naming; touch is suspended as well.[68]

Looking through the lens of trauma, the middle Spirit cannot be fully explained as an animating life force; neither can Spirit be clearly identified as the Spirit of resurrection or Pentecost. In the aftermath of death, the Spirit is expressed in terms like "remaining" and "persisting," conveying a more mixed

---

remembering Her flame only on the Sunday of Pentecost" (97). I make note of Farley's discussion of Spirit because she refers to the Spirit using the female pronoun, but she translates the *pneuma* in John 3 in impersonal terms, as wind. The power of Farley's claim of the Spirit as feminine is one that I share, but not in terms of Spirit as the feminine aspect of God or God as manifest in female attributes. See Elizabeth Johnson, chap. 3, in *She Who Is: The Mystery of God in Feminist Theological Discourse*, 2nd ed. (New York: Crossroad, 1992, 2002), 42–60. Instead, I take seriously the degree to which the Christian tradition has elided the female witness to the Spirit and I want to account for the ways in which female bodies incarnate and give shape to the divine breath. To use the female pronoun "She" for Spirit is a witness to the elisions of Christian history but should not essentialize the divine nature in terms of gender.

67. See Cathy Caruth, "Traumatic Awakenings: Freud, Lacan, and the Ethics of Memory," in *Unclaimed Experience*, 91–112.

68. Thanks to Catherine Keller, who pointed out this sensorium, a pneumatological body, in response to an earlier version of this chapter.

picture of death and life and, in turn, a different narrative of redemption. Between a radical ending and an impossible ending, the Spirit is witnessed in its remaining. Forms of life arising from this Spirit have yet to be imagined. These imaginative practices—of giving form to what remains—can provide new definition to the biblical concept of *menein*. A theology of middle Spirit recasts redemption. What would it look like to perform this theology of Spirit? What does it require?

Chapter 5

Remaining, in Love

The storm is gone, but the "after the storm" is always here.
Deacon Julius Lee

Remain in my love.
John 15:9b

The story of trauma is a story about the storm that does not go away. It is a story of remaining. Deacon Julius Lee says that people do not want to hear this story. Instead there is a lot of pressure to claim that New Orleans has recovered from Katrina. There is pressure to get on with it, to move to a happy ending. He tells us about the local government's frenzy to tear down buildings. There is a hunger to remove not only traces of the storm but the pre-storm realities. In the post-storm push for fresh starts, previous forms of life are threatened. The pressure to get over, to forget, to wipe away the past, is often reinforced by one particular way of reading Christian redemption. The narrative of triumphant resurrection can often operate in such a way as to promise a radically new beginning to those who have experienced a devastating event. A linear reading of cross and resurrection places death and life in a continuum; death is behind and life is ahead; life emerges victoriously from death. This way of reading can, at its best, provide a sense of hope and promise for the future. But it can also gloss over the realities of pain and loss, glorify suffering, and justify violence.

The rhetoric of "re"—rebuilding, restoring, recovering—comes at a cost. The promise of starting with a clean slate is, in Deacon Lee's understanding, a violation of the rich history of life in the Ninth Ward. The past cannot simply be

143

wiped away. Deacon Lee is not ungrateful for the support that outsiders are showing for the city, but he is suspicious of how far it can go and suspicious, as well, of promises made too quickly. There is no triumph for New Orleans, and no savior for the city either. But there is a way of remaining, of attending to the always here. In resisting a redemptive narrative of New Orleans, Deacon Lee is also resisting this common reading of his faith narrative and forging another.[1] I have been pointing throughout to what remains—to the movements between death and life that bring to light a dimension of existence that does not often breach the surface. I have attempted to give theological significance to what remains, to name the complex space of trauma and to speak about a middle Spirit. If we look between cross and resurrection, we are directed to a new way of being, to a form of life that is not triumphant. Instead, it is life configured *as remaining*. Deacon Lee's "always here" infuses the Johannine *menein* with new meaning and weight. Lee calls for a Spirit to testify to love making its way through death.

In this chapter, I attempt to listen for signs of the movements of the Spirit from within the stories of persons and communities remaining in the aftermath of trauma. What do they reveal about redemption from the middle? I trace the movements of Spirit in these stories in a similar way that I traced the witness of Mary, the beloved, Balthasar, and Speyr. There is a witness arising from the middle that cannot simply be translated into the logic of death or life, cross or resurrection. Instead, these stories reveal the unique language and movements of the middle, displaying the distinctive shape of remaining, in love.

Here I situate a theology of the middle Spirit within the context of contemporary discussions about suffering, the cross, and redemption. Recent theological critiques of atonement theology turn us to the narrative of death and life in order to reexamine a dominant way of framing the Christian redemptive narrative. They reflect deep concerns about redemption claims rooted in an event of suffering—the cross. I enter this conversation from the site of the middle, in the territory of remaining. What does redemption look like when viewed from the middle, from, in very literal terms, Deacon Lee's backyard? Interpreting from the middle, I claim that we are oriented differently in relationship to suffering. The middle does not yield a narrative that calls us to suffer but instead calls us to witness suffering in its persistence, its ongoingness. If viewed from the middle, redemption is about the capacity to witness to what exceeds death but cannot be clearly identified as life. Redemption finds new expression in the always here, in the persistent witness to what remains.

Yet as I employ the language of redemption, I recognize that the middle

---

1. Throughout this chapter, I use the word "redemptive" in some cases and "redemption" in others. When using the term redemptive, I am referring to a particular version of redemption, such as the one to which McAdams is pointing, i.e., the redemptive self. Redemption is a much more encompassing term under which the range of images and language for speaking about God's relationship to the world are contained.

does not simply deliver a reinterpretation of redemption. In the process of offering a critique of a dominant redemptive model, I am aware of the assumptions undergirding much Christian discourse about redemption.[2] Redemption is such a foundational metaphor for Christianity that it often remains unquestioned and untouched. Is a reworking of one model sufficient, or does trauma shatter the metaphor, confronting us with the shards of redemption? The vision from the middle is one of perpetual witness. Can it be contained within a redemptive framework? I believe this shattering moves us away from the language of redemptive suffering narrated from the site of the cross to the language of remaining narrated from the middle. On the razed terrain between death and life, the language of Christian theology confronts its own shattering, the shattering of the categories that we employ to frame the world. Hans Urs von Balthasar claimed that pursuing the question of what persists between death and resurrection, the question of the middle day, would threaten the tidy practices of theology. He warned that if we took seriously the middle, it would threaten to dismantle all our Archimedean drawings.[3] The question then is: what remains after this shattering, after this dismantling?

THE REDEMPTIVE SELF

When asked to tell the story of their lives, Americans tend to tell a similar story—a redemptive one. This is the central insight of Dan McAdams's book *The Redemptive Self*.[4] Interviewing hundreds of American adults, McAdams, a narrative psychologist, began to detect a pattern in the way that generative Americans tell their life stories.[5] McAdams draws on the work of Erik Erikson to identify adults who are committed to "promoting the welfare and development of future generations."[6] McAdams says that these American adults overwhelmingly "make

2. Implicit in a dominant model are certain assumptions about both the human condition and the nature of God that are challenged in light of trauma. One example of this is the idea that the human condition is best cast solely in terms of sin and guilt, while there is a growing literature in trauma studies that point to shame as a more fundamental aspect of human nature. What is striking in studying trauma is the degree to which we are confronted with the fragility and vulnerability of human persons and the degree to which we can wound and be wounded by others. Therapist Laura S. Brown writes, "But when we admit the immanence of trauma in our lives, when we see it as something more likely than not, we lose our cloak of invulnerability." Laura S. Brown, "Not Outside the Range," in Cathy Caruth, ed., *Trauma: Explorations in Memory* (Baltimore: Johns Hopkins University Press, 1995), 108.
   3. See the Holy Saturday sermon by Hans Urs von Balthasar, "We Walked Where There Was No Path," in *You Crown the Year with Your Glory: Sermons throughout the Liturgical Year*, trans. Graham Harrison (San Francisco: Ignatius Press, 1989), 87–92.
   4. Daniel P. McAdams, *The Redemptive Self: Stories Americans Live By* (New York: Oxford University Press, 2006).
   5. McAdams writes: "Almost everybody can find some kind of redemption in his or her life story. But highly generative American adults tend to see more of it and to attribute more significance or meaning to the redemptive scenes and situations they do recall" (ibid., 7–8).
   6. Ibid., 4.

sense of their own lives through an idealized story script that emphasizes, among other themes, the power of human redemption."[7] This idealized story is progressive and linear, and it has three distinctive movements: (1) a state of original innocence or goodness; (2) a subsequent fall, struggle, or separation; and (3) a rescue, recovery, or transformation. According to McAdams, these adults identify a pivotal turning point in their lives in which they encountered suffering and hardship, after which suffering is surpassed, yielding something greater. McAdams notes that there are secular versions of this notably religious concept (reflected in cultural idioms such as, "Every cloud has its silver lining" and "no pain, no gain"), but the prevalence of redemption images and language suggests that redemption is in the bloodstream of American self-identity, both individually and collectively.[8] McAdams writes, "Redemptive stories affirm hope for the future and a belief in human progress. No matter how bad the life situation may seem, these stories suggest, there is always hope that things will get better."[9] Eventually, something better—something new—comes about. Good eventually triumphs over evil; life triumphs over death.[10]

In many respects, this redemptive narrative fosters growth and success. Yet it can also elide suffering, covering over painful realities. In a chapter titled "When Redemption Fails," McAdams identifies certain dangers inherent to the redemptive self.[11] He witnessed a subtle negation of difficult, complex, and ambiguous experiences in the quest for redemption. Things that cannot, and should not,

7. Ibid., 7.

8. In "I Dream of Denver," an op-ed piece discussing the economic downturn of 2008–9, David Brooks comments on the results of a recent Pew study: "The first thing they found is that even in dark times, Americans are still looking over the next horizon. . . . In short, Americans may indeed be gloomy and hunkered down. But they're still Americans. They are still drawn to virgin ground, still restless against limits." David Brooks, "I Dream of Denver," NYTimes.com, February 17, 2009, http://www.nytimes.com/2009/02/17/opinion/17brooks.html?_r=1&emc=etal.

9. McAdams, *Redemptive Self*, 17.

10. These individual life stories mirror the collective American story, of westward expansion and Manifest Destiny, of the concept of America as a chosen nation. This belief in a happy ending achieved through struggle is a national story. The concepts of Manifest Destiny, freedom, and chosenness are central to the development of this nation's story; these concepts fueled westward expansion, providing a nation with a distinctive sense of identity and mission. Theological concepts of divine sovereignty and providence often undergird this; God oversees, cares for, and blesses God's chosen (Ibid., 7, 18).

11. "So . . . what could ever be *wrong* with a story this good?" McAdams asks (McAdams, 242). This redemption narrative reveals the best and worst of American identity. The redemptive narrative may, at its best, give us meaning and urge us to contribute meaningfully to the lives of those around us; at its worst, it can justify violence and mask self-interest. He found that the generative Americans, although they were committed to social groups and institutions and contributed extensively to these organizations, tended to be strong individualists. The need for distinctiveness and the belief in chosenness also fuel American exceptionalism, a belief that is increasingly problematic in developing partnerships and working collaboratively. Redemptive narratives can also "condone aggression in the name of redemption" (ibid., 256). He calls attention, for example, to political responses to the September 11, 2001, attacks. The conviction of innocence and goodness, interpreted on a national scale, can drive and justify violence internationally. The belief in an identity of being chosen can translate into American exceptionalism and the belief that we are good and that others are bad. Coupled with exceptionalism, this view of American identity, both individual and collective, can be extremely harmful.

be redeemed are nonetheless made to conform to a redemptive framework. He writes, "We live in a society that expects, even demands, happy endings to tough stories. I believe there is a kind of tyranny in the never-ending expectation in American life that bad things will and should be redeemed. . . . Suffering is to be endured, but not necessarily redeemed."[12] McAdams's warning about the underside of American redemption highlights the ways in which redemption can become a gloss or a kind of fantasy, turning us away from, rather than toward, the complex realities of human existence. When we think about this in terms of trauma, it is easy to see that traumatic suffering—the suffering that remains— can be elided in the quest for a redemptive ending.

Note that McAdams suggests that redemption is a narrative of the *generative*—those who can and have, at some level, recovered or experienced transformation. Theologian Sharon Betcher critiques a Christian redemptive framework indebted to an "ontotheological history of creation-fall-redemption,"[13] stating that a particular version of redemption glorifies perfection and wholeness as end points. Betcher reminds us that this redemption story may come with some built-in assumptions and interests. The drive to perfection, wholeness, and—I would add—newness as goals for human life may come at a high cost, serving the interests of those who are, for Betcher, able-bodied. She argues that a theology of the Spirit, insofar as it attaches concepts of healing with ultimate ends of wholeness and perfection, is not good news for those who are disabled. We need instead a "theology on the slant"—one that looks through the lens of disability studies in order to take into account what redemption might look like for those who are differently abled.[14]

In McAdams and Betcher, the push to assert redemption at all costs enacts a certain violence by grafting an ideal story onto human lives. If we live by and into these religious stories, we must know the contours and limitations of our narrative interpretations. This is nothing more than an insistence on doing theology in context. For persons and communities who live informed by sacred stories, it is important to track the ways in which those stories are told. What is emphasized? What remains untold? The trajectory of the dominant redemptive narrative that McAdams describes interprets death and life in opposition—the triumph of life over death, the victory of overcoming. In so doing, that narrative can push for a redemptive ending at great expense. This push underlies the messages that Deacon Lee receives as well: get over it, start over, start fresh, the old is gone, and the new has come.

A pneumatology of remaining implicitly critiques a redemptive glossing over of traumatic suffering. It offers an alternative to redemptive suffering rooted in

---

12. Ibid., 264.

13. Sharon Betcher, *Spirit and the Politics of Disablement* (Minneapolis: Augsburg Fortress Press, 2007), 43.

14. Ibid., 4. The power of Betcher's book is that it does not offer a theology just for disabled persons but rethinks Christian theology for all persons, using the lens of disability studies.

the cross, but it does this not by claiming a redemptive locus in resurrection. Instead, redemption is enacted from that middle. What, then, does redemption look like from here? Just as I examined the unusual movements between death and life in chapters 2 and 3, I want to return to the context of Deacon Lee's "always here" and the movements of Spirit in communities remaining in the wake of Hurricane Katrina. In the context of New Orleans, redemptive narratives are visible and operative, attributing meaning to human suffering. The vocabulary of redemption is heavily employed to make sense of the hurricane's destruction and the lives of survivors in its aftermath. But there is also a testimony to what cannot be so neatly contained within dominant accounts of death and resurrection. There are critical points that disrupt the logic and give way to a testimonial dimension of redemption. They are, in David Goatley's terms, improvisations of the Spirit.[15]

NEW ORLEANS—JANUARY 2008

It is a new year at Christian Unity Baptist Church in New Orleans. Before the storm, the church was filled each week; now, only one-quarter of the congregation is here. It reflects the neighborhood. Low-income housing has been torn down, displacing thousands of downtown residents. Several blocks from the church, Tent City has emerged, a gathering of homeless persons living under the Claiborne Avenue overpass near Canal Street. The church has had a difficult time tracking its congregants. Right after the storm, many individuals and families were bussed out of the city, transporting them to Atlanta, Houston, and other locales, where they were promised temporary housing until the situation in New Orleans stabilized. Many had no contacts back home and had no way of knowing whether they had homes to return to. With one-way tickets out of the city, they did not have return tickets home. The congregation was scattered. The Rev. Dwight Webster and his wife have been traveling between California and New Orleans since Hurricane Katrina. Over the past two years, they have been working with insurance companies, with little success, to get enough money to purchase another home. In the midst of their back-and-forth, it is clear that the congregation is thankful to have them both here.

The time for welcoming visitors at Christian Unity has been transformed into a kind of homecoming for those who have returned to New Orleans post-Katrina. A woman sitting behind me whispers, "Oh, there she is. I wondered what happened to her." Several people stand up and announce, "I am back." These testimonies follow a familiar exilic narrative: the waters of Katrina forced them from their homes, and now they have made their way back. Katrina clearly

---

15. See David Emmanuel Goatley, "The Improvisation of God: Toward an African-American Pneumatology," *Memphis Theological Seminary Journal* 33, no. 1 (Spring 1995).

has marked their lives. One of the pastors told us, "Life for people in New Orleans follows a new timeline: pre-Katrina and post-Katrina." Pastor Webster folds each of these stories back into his congregational welcome. The testimonies of homecoming are part of a long testimonial tradition in the black church. When words of truth are spoken, they are often sealed with this question: "Can I get a witness?" This Sunday in New Orleans, the practice is both old and new, a kind of improvisation from the middle. The witness of the congregation encompasses the realities of the always here.

Beginning with a soft hum of the organ, the choir sings a response to Pastor Webster's morning message. The music builds as voices break in: "The Storm Is Over Now." The familiar song stretches back to a time before Hurricane Katrina, but this song is now marked in post-Katrina time. The irony is difficult to ignore. In this context, they are singing about a God who shelters. As Pastor Webster writes his nth letter to FEMA to ask them to supplement the funds that he will never see from his insurance company, he hears the words of the choir. At present, he has no home; the effects of the storm persist. But the affirmation, carried in rhythm and song, becomes something different in the aftermath of Katrina. The proclamation is not grounded in the reality of the present but instead in a persistent testimony that links believers to another time.

Following the service, members of the congregation take our group to lunch. Vera is sitting next to several of us at one end of a long table. She, like many people we encountered in New Orleans, is ready to answer the "Where were you when Katrina struck?" question almost as instinctually as if she were asked to recite basic facts, like her birthday or Social Security number. She is just passing through, visiting from her temporary home in Baton Rouge. Her picture, unlike most others, made it onto the cover of *Time* magazine; it was one of the many heroic portraits that the media highlighted.[16] Vera steered her wheelchair-bound mother through the toxic floodwaters of Katrina. The water, she said, was up to her mother's chest. We couldn't imagine all the water, she told us; it came in so quick, so fast. She managed to get her mother to the overpass of I-10. Hundreds of New Orleans residents were gathered there, waiting for buses to take them out of the city. When the people arrived, though, the buses were not there.

Forced to spend the night on the overpass, Vera described the scene. The sky was blacker than you can imagine, she said. With the electricity wiped out in the city, the darkness was thick, except for the stars. She had never seen a sky like that. It was as if God spoke through those stars saying, "I am the light." Vera shared with us this vision she received on the overpass of I-10. Under that sky, people converged from all parts of the city and began to communicate with each other. Kelly, one of the members of our group, wrote an account of Vera's story: "Vera had filled a pillowcase with food, water, clothes and some other supplies so

16. *Time*, September 12, 2005, cover photo.

she had a little more to share. She said if someone said they had a cracker another person would shout out they had peanut butter."[17]

Like many of the featured stories, Vera's story follows the trajectory of the redemptive narrative, as presented by McAdams. Hers is a story of great courage and strength. But it is not redemptive in the sense of triumph, of happy endings. It is, instead, a story of survival that exceeds the parameters of that version of the redemptive narrative. Vera speaks about a God who has an overall plan, who saves, who works out all things for good, even the most horrible and devastating of events. But her story reveals something else as well. On the overpass of I-10, Vera discerned life on the canvas of a New Orleans sky. She sensed life in the absence of signs of life. "Was it lightning? Was it?" Her descriptions of that night resonate with the Holy Saturday witness in Balthasar's *Heart of the World*.[18] What is emerging out of death? Vera testifies to a wearier and less victorious story about death-in-life and life-in-death. The testimony of the Spirit remains, carried on the breath and in the movements of the middle witnesses.

If we interpret from the middle, we can begin to see things that we would not have seen before, parts of stories that suddenly take on new meaning. The next evening, our group gathers to talk about what we have experienced. In the two days that we had been in New Orleans, we heard a rash of conflicting stories about what had happened in the floods and predictions about the future of the city. From the complex combinations of political, racial, socioeconomic, and religious perspectives, we heard stories of the before and after. But what was clear in many of these is that the depths of these stories rarely break the surface. They are difficult and, in many cases, impossible to tell. They bear truths that few want to hear. Simone Weil provides an image of the experience of affliction as a mute cry.[19] The cry is so deep and so repulsive that it is locked within the one who experiences it.[20] The challenge of attending to affliction—what Weil likens to the love of God—is to hear this cry, to hear what is, in all respects, unspeakable. She says that it is, in fact, a cry that sounds at the heart of every human person; it is a cry that we all share but that we are not attuned to hear in another. In "Reflections on the Right Use of School Studies," Weil describes a "practice of attention" in which a person works with a problem, not to master it, but instead to learn how to encounter it without imposing his own narrative on it.[21] This practice of attention allows a person to speak her truth. To the person

17. In "One Woman's Story of Survival," from a blog titled Wading in the Water http://wadinginthewater.blogspot.com, Kelly Drescher wrote on January 7, 2008, "That was life on I-10 in the aftermath of Katrina. . . . Everyone, person and animal, was a part of this community on the overpass of I-10."
18. See chap. 2.
19. Simone Weil, "Human Personality," in *The Simone Weil Reader*, ed. George A. Panichas (New York: Moyer Bell, 1977), 313–39.
20. Weil notes that what distinguishes suffering from affliction is its social dimension—the absolute deprivation of connection with others. See "The Love of God and Affliction," ibid., 461.
21. Simone Weil, "Reflections on the Right Use of School Studies towards the Love of God," ibid., 44–52.

in affliction, the truth is about suffering that cannot be superficially accessed. In this practice of attending—what I call a witness to the undertow—different pathways of knowing the world can be forged.

The fragments of the stories that we heard in New Orleans left us with this question: how do we hold all of the competing stories together? Cat, one member of the group, says, "Perhaps the one thing we know about trauma is that there is no *one* story." Witnessing is not about attaining a correct and true story but, in fact, about a capacity to meet these stories, to hear them for all the ways in which they do not cohere. We heard a variety of competing theologies operating in New Orleans.[22] Like Vera's story of a God whose skies reveal God's providential care, there were many iterations of redemption. Like the communion service at Christian Unity Baptist Church, there were many iterations of atonement theology, of salvation achieved through the blood of Jesus on the cross. Yet looking from the middle turns us to see the movements of Spirit that exceed the triumphant logic of cross and resurrection.

There is an undercurrent running through these congregations, a deep rhythm that pulses alongside the redemptive narrative of life triumphing over death. When this undercurrent is witnessed, a more layered story of redemption is enacted. These are not redemptive stories per se. They are fragments, or what David James Duncan calls "river teeth," parts of stories that do not go away but cannot be expressed in full.[23] They carry a truth that is easily covered over but nonetheless remains. If we look through the shattered lens of the middle, we see things differently. The possibility of giving Deacon Lee's statement a theological home lies in this difference. He is pointing to, and enacting, a unique pneumatology, a pneumatological witness to what remains of death and a sense of life that is taking shape.

The work of the Spirit is bound up in attending to what remains. A distinctive pneumatology of the middle is already operating in contexts of trauma. The work of theology is to name and give theological significance to these movements. These fragments begin to reveal what it would look like to discern Spirit in concrete situations of survival. This testimony emerges between the cracks of familiar redemptive narratives. As I have suggested here, the middle testimony operates in such a way as to unearth what does not often rise to the surface. In this sense, a testimony to the middle runs alongside narratives of redemption, revealing new theological responses to traumatic suffering and pressing the edges of redemption in search of new vocabulary and images for framing our lives. To highlight these movements is to speak to the curious truth at the end of the

22. For theological responses to Hurricane Katrina, see Cheryl A. Kirk-Duggan, ed., *The Sky Is Crying: Race, Class, and Natural Disaster* (Nashville: Abingdon Press, 2006). Kirk-Duggan writes, "The theological danger of simple answers is that we may scapegoat and make someone or something other without fully grasping the entire situation. . . . For some situations and challenges in life, there are no satisfactory answers, though this does not mean we do not continue to ponder the parameters of the inevitable" (xvii).

23. David James Duncan, *River Teeth: Stories and Writings* (New York: Doubleday, 1995).

Johannine Gospel: "But there are also many other things that Jesus did; if every one of them were written down, I suppose that the world itself could not contain the books that would be written" (John 21:25). The truth of the events cannot be exhausted in a single account or in a single interpretation. The story is not exhausted in this account but, instead, is continually handed over to those who remain.

In a small jazz club on Frenchmen Street, the band plays Miles Davis's "So What." The trumpet player breaks in. It is the same eerie sound one hears when driving through the Lower Ninth Ward of New Orleans with the windows rolled down. Death hovers here; much has been lost. But the lone trumpet also sounds a note of something finding its way to life. Sharon Welch suggests that jazz provides an analogy for ethics from the middle.[24] In jazz, there is a rhythm of remaining. You find the rhythm of keeping on when you do not see any relief ahead. Just as the image of the undertow is fitting to speak about the effects of New Orleans's floodwaters, so, too, the imagery of jazz conveys the sense of the city, a sense both old and new, but neither in the ways that we have known before. Vera paints the canvas in the night sky, and the trumpet player riffs Miles Davis in a late-night venue. They are the sights and sounds that accompany Balthasar's weary trickle of love making its way toward life.

A LOVE STORY

Redemption is God's work of love to restore and renew all things.[25]

The term "redemption" is rooted in the concept of repairing or restoring what is damaged. Something or someone is freed from a situation of harm and changed for the better. Although redemption is described differently across religious traditions, in the Christian tradition it revolves around a series of images that speak of the process by which humanity and the natural world are taken from a situation of disrepair and restored to their original, if not perfected, state.[26] In the beginning, things were good, perfect, and innocent. In the middle, this goodness is compromised. Things go awry in that the primal condition of humanity is compromised by sin and disobedience. The harmony of creation is compromised, and the situation calls for repair. Redemption typically refers to God's

---

24. Sharon D. Welch, *Sweet Dreams in America: Making Ethics and Spirituality Work* (New York: Routledge, 1999). Although Welch does not use the vocabulary of the middle, the ethical landscape that she describes is very similar. She aims to find a way of describing what it means to stay in difficulty without a clear ending or way forward.

25. Esther D. Reed, "Redemption," in *The Blackwell Companion to Modern Theology*, ed. Gareth Jones (Oxford: Blackwell Press, 2004), 227.

26. The discussion of redemption has been highly anthropocentric. This charge runs through the work of Sallie McFague. See in particular *Metaphorical Theology: Models of God in Religious Language* (Minneapolis: Fortress Press, 1982), and *The Body of God: An Ecological Theology* (Minneapolis: Augsburg Press, 1993).

work of restoring a broken creation. God works on behalf of creation, and this work is expressed in a variety of ways, from God's covenantal relationship with the Israelite people to the incarnation of Jesus, his ministry, and his death and resurrection. Interpreted within a Christian framework, God takes on flesh and dwells among creation in order to bring about this restoration. In the end, all things will be restored to an original, if not perfected, state. Redemption is, in essence, a divine love story.[27]

While this love story may be told in a variety of ways, a dominant narrative of redemption has interpreted Jesus' death on the cross as the central locus of redemption. The story of Christianity was cast largely in terms of the problem of the fall and its antidote—the work of Jesus on the cross. Grace Jantzen writes, "If we think in terms of salvation, then the human condition must be conceptualized as a problematic state, a state in which human beings need urgent rescue, or calamity will befall."[28] This love story took a turn toward death. Jantzen claims that a logic of death pervades Western philosophy and theology: "I suggest that much of traditional philosophy of religion (and western culture generally) is preoccupied with violence, sacrifice, and death, and built upon mortality not only as a human fact but as a fundamental philosophical category." This thanocentrism, she claims, has overwhelmed a vision of flourishing that was equally present in the Christian tradition; a vision of flourishing was continually elided in respect to the dominant logic.

Historian of early Christianity Karen King echoes this as well in her work with gnostic texts. She writes,

> Despite the enormous variety of the early Christian literature that eventually came to reside in the New Testament collection, all the New Testament texts conform to one perspective: that the death and resurrection of Jesus and his coming at the end of time are central to salvation. The Nicene Creed emphasizes this point by making the death, resurrection, and second coming, along with the virgin birth, the central points that a Christian must affirm about Jesus.[29]

Other texts circulating at the time placed salvific emphasis elsewhere. However, in the end, the story of redemptive suffering "won the day."[30] Fourth-century creedal Christianity sealed this interpretation. King writes, "In view of the

27. David Kelsey's *Imagining Redemption* provides a helpful discussion of redemption as understood both within Christianity and in relationship to contexts of suffering. David H. Kelsey, *Imagining Redemption* (Louisville, KY: Westminster John Knox Press, 2005).

28. Grace Jantzen, *Violence to Eternity*, ed. Jeremy Carrette and Morny Joy (New York: Routledge, 2008), 209.

29. Karen King, *The Gospel of Mary of Magdala: Jesus and the First Woman Apostle* (Santa Rosa, CA: Polebridge Press, 2003), 163.

30. Citing Walther Bauer, King says that he "proposed that despite the seeming variety of historical narratives," they all presuppose certain things in common. These common features constitute what she refers to as the "master story" of Christianity. Creedal Christianity and "orthodoxy" are synonyms (ibid., 159).

centrality of this position, it is astonishing to learn that some early Christian communities didn't think Jesus' death had any saving value at all, and who were not looking for his return."[31] With growing attention to these gnostic texts, the master story is called into question, giving way to multiple ways of reading the religious landscape of early Christianity and to alternative notions of redemption.

The concern about redemption's death-focus also rose to the forefront of discussions in contemporary theology surrounding the cross. In the mid-1990s, classical doctrines of atonement were called into question by theologians across a range of traditions.[32] Many of these concerns focused on the impact of redemptive suffering on the lives of suffering persons and communities, what S. Mark Heim identifies as the "toxic psychological and social effects" of atonement theologies.[33] Feminist and womanist theologians, especially, were attentive to ways in which the violence of the cross maps onto human experience, especially experiences of oppression and trauma.[34] Womanist theologian Delores Williams, in her classic work *Sisters in the Wilderness*, argues that the Christian tradition has supported an understanding of redemption based upon Jesus as the ultimate surrogate figure who stands in the place of sinful humankind.[35] Williams rejects this surrogacy picture and insists that humanity is not redeemed through the death of Jesus but rather through his "ministerial vision of life."[36]

In *Proverbs of Ashes*, theologians Rebecca Ann Parker and Rita Nakashima Brock reject the suffering of Jesus on the cross as redemptive. They reveal the ways in which Jesus' death, read as the redemptive climax of Christianity, sacral-

31. Ibid., 164. Elsewhere, she comments on recent discoveries of early Christian writings. "They demonstrate that reading the story of Christian origins backwards through the lens of canon and creed have given an account of the formation of only one kind of Christianity, and even that only partially. The fuller picture lets us see more clearly how the later Christianity of the New Testament and the Nicene Creed arose out of many different possibilities through experimentation, compromise, and very often conflict. The Nicene Creed emphasized that salvation came through the virgin birth, death, resurrection, and exaltation of Jesus, but some forms of Christianity focused almost solely on Jesus' teaching and did not even mention these doctrines. Some of them rejected the idea of a benevolent God requiring blood atonement for sin, seeing Jesus instead as the living messenger of reconciliation and spiritual truth" (157).

32. See Heim's helpful series in *The Christian Century*. S. Mark Heim, "Why Does Jesus' Death Matter?" *The Christian Century*, March 7, 2001, and "Visible Victim," *The Christian Century*, March 14, 2001.

33. See S. Mark Heim, "Saved by What Shouldn't Happen," in *Cross Examinations: Readings in the Meaning of the Cross Today*, ed. Marit Trelstad (Minneapolis: Augsburg Fortress Press, 2006), 212.

34. Referring back to the cartographical imagery here and the ways in which teachings serve to orient persons in the life of faith. The concern here is that a certain rendering of the divine story of suffering will keep persons in situations of suffering. See Introduction in this volume.

35. Black women throughout history have been related to surrogacy roles. This explanation of redemption perpetuates these roles. Williams writes, "It is therefore fitting and proper for black women to ask whether the image of a surrogate-God has salvific power for black women or whether this image supports and reinforces the exploitation that has accompanied their experience with surrogacy. If black women accept this idea of redemption, can they not also passively accept the exploitation that surrogacy brings?" Delores Williams, *Sisters in the Wilderness* (Maryknoll, NY: Orbis Books, 1993), 162.

36. Ibid., 167.

izes abuse.[37] If there is redemption in the Christian Scriptures, it lies in the story of resurrection and other postresurrection encounters. The redemptive power is not in Jesus' death but in communities of resurrection. Brock writes, "Salvation comes from communal practices that affirm incarnation, the Spirit in life, and its ongoing promise of resurrection and paradise."[38] The master story of redemption interprets resurrection only in light of the "work" accomplished on the cross. The resurrection is a triumphant beginning, but its triumph is deeply rooted in death. According to Brock and Parker, Christianity with death at its center is not good news but, in fact, the wielder of bad news for those who suffer.

These critiques have powerfully and effectively called attention to the problematic readings of suffering and the construction of a redemptive gloss that can often elide the realities of suffering. By employing images of flourishing and paradise, these authors reject this death focus and attempt to reground theology in a logic that is more life giving. These earlier images, they claim, were elided in service of a largely Western logic of death. Death dominates the narrative. The power of these critiques is that they expose the history of Christianity and interpretive commitments driving the tradition. These theologians are well attuned to the elisions enacted by a dominant reading of redemption. Rejecting the cross as a redemptive symbol, they point to Jesus' life, his ministry, and his vision of community as sources of redemption. They assert life over death.

But this move to life may unwittingly enact its own elisions. By preserving a certain way of casting the relationship between death and life (namely in opposition), they exchange one set of images for another, albeit more nourishing and sustaining ones. In the search for pristine beginnings and the recovery of images that counter death, might these critiques fail to speak to the experiences in which death and life are peculiarly entangled? I have resisted casting death and life in opposition, in search of a testimony to what remains, to the ways in which death haunts life and life bears death within it. While these critiques are poignant and necessary, they can also perpetuate a reading of death and life that elides the territory of the middle. Even these critiques can participate in covering over the realities of remaining.

37. McAdams quotes Brock and Parker in a section on redemptive violence (McAdams, *Redemptive Self*, 259). Their most recent book, *Saving Paradise*, carries forward these insights and scours the history of Christianity in order to show that the death of Jesus as salvific was a later development in the tradition and not a pervasive or early claim. The vision of paradise was, in fact, an earlier and more pervasive vision of salvation in Christianity. This work is an attempt to show the erasure of paradise in the history of Christianity. See Rita N. Brock and Rebecca Ann Parker, *Saving Paradise: How Christianity Traded Love of This World for Crucifixion and Empire* (Boston: Beacon Press, 2008), and their *Proverbs of Ashes: Violence, Redemptive Suffering, and the Search for What Saves Us* (Boston: Beacon, 2001).

38. Rita N. Brock, "The Cross of Resurrection and Communal Redemption" in Trelstad, *Cross Examinations*, 250. It reiterates, in briefer form, their reinterpretation of redemption. Brock and Parker's recent book, *Saving Paradise*, is a comprehensive search for the narrative they claim is extinguished by the Western Christian obsession with death.

REDEMPTION FROM THE MIDDLE

I want to reapproach the question of redemption from the middle. It is true; death has pervaded the tradition, and suffering has often been problematically interpreted as a necessary component to redemption. In turn, life has been narrated as triumphing over death, as if death were merely a hurdle to life victorious. What if redemption is interpreted from the middle rather than from either the death or the life events? These critiques identify, but do not fully account for, what remains. Knowledge of trauma and traumatic suffering add something distinctive to this conversation. Exposing unique dimensions of suffering, it moves us to a different theological site to take up anew the question of redemption.

Studies in trauma contribute two key insights to these discussions. First, traumatic suffering is not contained in a single event. The double structure of trauma suggests that we must interpret the suffering beyond one event and address, instead, the persistence of that event and the enigma of its remaining. If we interpret the suffering of the cross traumatically, the trauma cannot be isolated to the cross. Instead, the site of suffering extends to the middle space, which means that theological discourse about trauma must press beyond interpretations of the cross—the death event. Instead, the death and resurrection events must be brought together around a new question, "What persists between them?"

Second, redemption has often been employed as a theological synonym for therapeutic terms like healing and recovery. Trauma studies challenge us to think about recovery differently and, in so doing, return us to its theological correlate—redemption. The temporality of trauma and the reality of its return make it difficult to conceive of recovery in linear terms, as something to get over or get beyond. Trauma teaches us that there is no clean break from the past, of death behind and life ahead. Trauma tells us that death returns, haunting the life that follows.[39] In trauma, "death" persists in life. The question is whether a framework of redemption can resist a forward pull, using Keller's language, in order to speak to the realities of this persistence. The term "redemption" has always expressed the ways in which God relates to the world. Dominant interpretations of salvation and redemption, filled with images of God's rescue and restoration, can easily join the chorus of voices that tell Deacon Lee and others to get over it. "All things work together for good." "This is part of God's will." These familiar assertions emerge from dominant redemptive narratives and may be complicit in covering over and eliding the suffering that remains.

Reading from the middle, any interpretation of redemption must acknowledge that death and life are inextricably bound, in such a way that theologians must account for death's remainder, death's haunting, so to speak. In his response

---

39. In early trauma studies, flashbacks represented the primary traumatic symptom. Visual images of the past, usually fragments and not full narrative sequences, intrude into the present. First witnessed in WWI combat veterans who appeared to be haunted by ghosts of the past, these images would take them back to the traumatic event, and they would manifest bodily responses in the present, suggesting that they were somatically reliving the past experience in the present.

to womanist critiques of the cross, James Cone acknowledges the importance of cross critiques but is cautious about negating the cross as a site of redemption. There is still something redemptive there for Cone. The cross, he acknowledges, haunts the Christian tradition; it is the symbol of the tragic memory of suffering. In identifying the cross with the lynching tree, Cone is inarguably speaking about the trauma of the black experience in America. Yet while Cone insists that we must gaze at the cross to confront the terrible memory of suffering, I insist that this gaze is not a straightforward one. The terrible memory of suffering cannot be addressed by gazing at the cross; instead, the gaze is from the middle. This gaze is a gaze of the cross as it is handed over to those who remain. Cone's vocabulary is a vocabulary of trauma—the terror of lynching, the haunting memory of brutal suffering. The questions that Cone poses to theologians are questions about what it means to be one who remains as witness to the terror of the cross. How do we receive this memory? How do we make sense of this event in its persistence? He asks these questions, but locates the transformation, the redemption, solely in the death event. He also locates it solely in the figure of Jesus, the terror and beauty of the lynched Christ.

Likewise, in the postlude to *Proverbs of Ashes*, Rita Nakashima Brock and Rebecca Parker write, "Christianity bears the marks of unresolved trauma. Jesus' resurrection and the continuation of his movement are not triumphs, but a glimpse of the power of survival, of the embers that survive the deluge."[40] In this statement, they pull the resurrection into the space of survival, thus resisting a triumphant narrative of redemption. They insist that healing cannot come from a narrative of death and violence. The promise of healing lay for the authors in the brief and fleeting glimpses of divine presence in the aftermath of trauma. Their epilogue is a testimony to the power of survival. Thus, it testifies to the strength of those who survive abuse. Yet the theological uniqueness of survival remains unexplored. The statement, however, is startling in the truth that it tells: Christianity bears the marks of unresolved trauma. Reading this through the lens of trauma as I have presented it here, it is interesting to think with Brock and Parker about a haunting and haunted narrative of redemption that persists in the Christian tradition.

While these theologians reshape traditional interpretations of the cross, they do so without accounting for the ways in which traumatic suffering shifts the locus of theological discussions about suffering and redemption. The discourse about traumatic suffering must extend beyond the cross to the middle territory of survival. The distinctive structure of trauma suggests that death and life cannot be held apart; instead, death exceeds the event of death. But this excess, this unintegratable aspect of the death event, cannot be folded into life. Instead,

---

40. Brock and Parker, *Proverbs*, 250. Instead, they depict a violent nonsalvific death followed by a resurrection that does not bring triumph, but rather instances the possibility of survival. They do not attribute any unique power to Jesus—to his death or to his resurrection. They identify redemption with life, but they displace redemption from sole identification with the figure of Jesus. It is redemptive insofar as it points to abundant life that is expressed within relationships of mutuality.

there is something distinctive about the experience of survival that calls for a different theological locus. By locating redemption either in the death or in resurrection, these theologians miss a critical site for theological reflection.

They agree that the cross haunts the Christian tradition, and that its ghosts must be exorcised in order for Christianity to be life giving.[41] However, the lens of trauma, in turning us to the aftermath of the cross, turns us to, rather than away from, this haunting. By this, I mean that the shadow cast by the cross and its haunting return is not simply the problematic consequence of the tradition—its pathology, using trauma terminology.[42] I claim that the haunting of the cross yields a truth about God and human suffering that cannot be contained within a redemptive reading of either Jesus' passion or resurrection. It is a truth that emerges from within the accounts of the passion and resurrection and challenges traditional redemptive readings of them. It is a truth about remaining. This truth is named, yet to some degree is elided by Brock, Parker, and Cone. Cone urges us to give meaning to the cross, to not turn away from it; I urge us to give meaning to what remains in its wake. Just as Cone finds promise in the paradox of the cross, I locate promise in its excess, in its transmission and witness. The theological meaning cannot be found in turning away or turning to the cross, but, instead, in the turning itself, the movements between that acknowledge a more tenuous relationship between death and life.

This haunting unearths a different orientation to suffering, one rooted in witness to the unspeakable realities that persist beyond death. To give this haunting theological significance is not to glorify it or to redeem it, but instead to receive it for the "truth that it speaks."[43] In *Ghostly Matters*, sociologist Avery S. Gordon explores histories of violence and claims that these histories live on inside persons and communities, constituting a "complex personhood" that is often unaccounted for in sociological research.[44] The ghosts of the past constitute present realities. If we attend to these ghosts, Gordon says, they communicate the unspeakable truths of the past. But they do more. For her, haunting is not solely negative because it has the potential to reveal a "something to be done" in

41. For Cone, the cross can be redeemed and, thus, still be redemptive. See James H. Cone, "Strange Fruit: The Cross and the Lynching Tree," *Harvard Divinity Bulletin* 35, no. 1 (Winter 2007). Reading the cross and the lynching tree together, they can be mutually liberative. "The cross and the lynching tree need each other: the lynching tree can liberate the cross from the false pieties of well-meaning Christians. The crucifixion was a first-century lynching. The cross can redeem the lynching tree, and therefore bestow upon lynched black bodies an eschatological meaning for their ultimate significance" (53). He speaks about the haunting of the cross as the tragic memory still waiting for theological meaning. For Williams, Brock, and Parker, the cross cannot and should not be redeemed. In his 2006 Ingersoll lecture at Harvard Divinity School, Cone emphasized the need for theologians to continue to seek the meaning of the cross. These urgings do not appear as prominently in the written form "Strange Fruit." He implored the students in theology who were present at the lecture to take on this task; it is a wonderful example of the handing over of the work of theology.
42. See Cathy Caruth, *Unclaimed Experience*, 4; *Trauma: Explorations in Memory*, 156.
43. I draw here on Caruth's language in *Trauma: Explorations in Memory*, vii–viii.
44. Avery F. Gordon, *Ghostly Matters: Haunting and the Sociological Imagination* (Minneapolis: University of Minnesota Press, 2008). See her notion of "complex personhood," 4–5.

the present.[45] Although Gordon distinguishes haunting from trauma precisely because of this something, I interpret the handing over in the biblical texts in a similar way: reading through the Johannine text, an imperative is transmitted, a something to be done. The dynamics of trauma and its transmission provide a way of recasting an interpretation of tradition, as a handing over of both what is known and unknown about the sacred stories that we live into and interpret. I want to press us to think about the cross as something that the Christian tradition continually receives, not as a symbol that traumatizes and retraumatizes but, instead, as a symbol that haunts, giving rise to an imperative to witness to the truth of death's remainder. Interpreting from this middle disrupts interpretations of redemptive suffering, moving us onto different theological ground and toward interpretations connected to witness and testifying. Theologizing from the middle also provides a way of comprehending the ways in which interpretations of redemptive suffering persist in the tradition, haunting us even while calling us to rework redemptive narratives, to press in and beyond them to speak to the undertow of human experiences.

In the aftermath of the cross, we are oriented to suffering in a particular way. We are oriented in the Spirit, in the haunted territory. In her reworking of the Trinitarian event of the cross in relation to women's experiences of reproductive loss, Serene Jones notes that the suffering itself is not the source of redemption.[46] Instead, she writes, it is "the persistence of love in the midst of suffering."[47] Reading in relation to trauma, this persistence moves us from a theology of the cross to a theology of the middle. Just as the suffering cannot be isolated to a death event, neither can love be solely located there. Locating this love in the middle and linking it with the figure of Spirit can disrupt problematic understandings of redemption and suffering that pattern themselves off the cross.

The undertow of a triumphant redemptive narrative is this: despite claims to victory and to overcoming, there are fragments—unintegratable aspects of suffering—that remain.[48] I have attempted to give texture and theological significance to this remaining by aligning it with the concept of *menein* and the figure of the paraclete. The suffering is accompanied; it is witnessed. Spirit maintains a connection to the events of cross and resurrection but dismantles a certain way of reading the relationship between the two. In the vocabulary that I have developed here, the transmission (the handing over of the death-breath) marks a more chaotic beginning than that of a miraculous resurrection. This beginning features the breath of witness to what remains. I have insisted that these fragments must be taken into account; they must be witnessed. The theological affirmation forged in the face of this reality is as follows: love remains. The middle Spirit that I have been developing testifies to death's persistence and also points

45. Ibid., 139.
46. Serene Jones, "Hope Deferred: Trinitarian Reflections on Infertility, Stillbirth and Miscarriage," *Modern Theology* 17, no. 2 (April 2001).
47. Ibid., 242.
48. See the remarks on "undertow" in chap. 4.

to distinctive movements of life in the aftermath. Fragments of death remain, yet the breath of witness remains there as well. The cross haunts the territory of remaining, yet this haunting is met with pneumatological possibility.[49]

Between death and life, the Spirit's witness can be described in two movements: tracking the undertow and sensing life. These movements of Spirit attend to suffering that remains long after an event is over. They also witness to forms of life that appear tenuous and fragile. As I described in chapter 2, Balthasar and Speyr patterned Christian life in terms of Christ's death; to witness meant to imitate Christ in his sufferings. But they also told another story, one that did not, in the end, register in the formal theology. They narrated a witness to the between—to the disorientation of discerning divine presence in hell and to the weary trickle of love trying to make its way toward life. The shape of life, in the Spirit, is precisely this work—the work of testifying to the oozing of love into the space of life and of discerning life where it is not.[50] The Spirit persists there. This persistence is an oscillation between death and life, tracking what remains and sensing a way ahead. This persistence, this abiding, is the witness not just to death's remaining but to love's survival.

TRACKING THE UNDERTOW

The first movement of Spirit is the witness to what remains of death. The image of the undertow is a helpful one for thinking about the ways in which death persists. An undertow refers to an underlying current that lies beneath the surface of the water. Though waves move toward the shore, the undercurrent pulls in the opposite direction. This pull is not visible, but its force can be great. Judith Herman, in her introduction to *Trauma and Recovery*, points to a pattern of recovering and forgetting that is constitutive of the experience of trauma. It is also true of the study of trauma. There will be periods of time when trauma will come to public consciousness, and there will be times when it recedes, when it is forgotten. Scholars of trauma, Herman says, must be attentive to these cycles. This pattern of recovering and forgetting translates well to the image of ocean tides. Part of the task of trauma work is to account for the force of the undertow. The task of theology is similar: to track the movements of the Spirit's witness to the undertow, to death's pull in life. Keller recognizes the force of the undertow in the *tehomic* waters: "The undertow of *tehom* can be painful." A theology of *tehom* attends to the losses, grief, and the chaos of life.[51] These realities remain but, in and through the Spirit, they are witnessed.

49. Speaking to Brock and Parker, this pneumatology—the Spirit of resurrection—must reckon with this haunting; it cannot be read apart from it.

50. Hans Urs von Balthasar, *Heart of the World*, trans. Erasmo S. Leiva (San Francisco: Ignatius Press, 1979), 152.

51. Catherine Keller, *On the Mystery: Discerning God in Process* (Minneapolis: Fortress Press, 2008). There, Keller writes, "Recovering the luminous possibilities of seascape, dwelling at the edge

Mark Lewis Taylor coins the concept of "tracking Spirit."[52] He explores the presence of the sacred in contemporary expressions of popular culture. In the rhythms and lyrics of artists like Bruce Springsteen and Arrested Development, Taylor seeks a way of linking theological discourse about the Spirit to the pulsing spirit of America's artists and musicians. He rewrites the theological task as one of tracking divine presence in these cultural expressions. As a theologian, Taylor connects the discourse of theology to cultural grassroots movements of artists and musicians that resist the death-dealing forces of American imperialism and capitalism. Taylor wants to situate theology in the space of cultural critique; he does this pneumatologically. "Spirit" is a shared term, rich in theological meaning and in cultural expression. He writes, "Theology is a searching and investigating reflection, attempting to discern the tracks of spirit. It searches for tracks left, for example, by liminal dwellers and spinners . . . , by integrative visionaries, and by those fighting and hoping for liberation."[53] Taylor urges theologians to tune into these rhythms of spirit for the truths that they speak.

By selecting the word "tracking," Taylor preserves the negative connotations of this term, noting the surveillance and stereotyping practices employed by the United States to stifle, stigmatize, and silence human spirits. A tracker knows that what she is looking for is not readily apparent. In this sense, tracking requires more than just taking a look. Tracking involves discerning what does not rise to the surface. It accounts for the force of institutions and persons that do not want certain truths to be told. In chapter 1, I noted that traumatic suffering is exacerbated by not having visible and concrete signs and evidence of violation. In the absence of evidence, the task of witnessing is equally challenging. Taylor's notion of tracking aligns with these dynamics in trauma and speaks to the kind of underground work of the Spirit. The witness of Mary Magdalene and the beloved disciple depicts this tracking work. With blurred vision and movements that appear to be missteps, they witness to the undertow in the territory of remaining.

SENSING LIFE

If death remains, then life cannot be conceived apart from it. Life is not miraculously new but instead is a mixed and tenuous process of remaining. I have distinguished between living and remaining to convey the sense of the nature of life as survival. I have also suggested that survival has a biblical correlate in the concept of remaining and abiding. "What is it to you that he remain?" This final

of the sea's mysteries—not forgetting its tragic aspects—is one way of experiencing the graced possibilities of sacramental poetics" (66–67).

52. See chap. 6, "Tracking Spirit: Theology as Cultural Critique in America," in Dwight N. Hopkins and Sheila Greeve Davaney, eds., *Changing Conversations: Religious Reflection and Cultural Analysis* (New York: Routledge, 1996).

53. Ibid., 137.

question of the Johannine Gospel reframes life in relation to remaining. Surviving Peter, the beloved disciple remains at the end of this Gospel and points to a different conception of life, not as shaped in terms of imitation and sacrifice but instead by the practices of testifying and witnessing. Life, as remaining, is handed over in a question. And this handing over is a transmission of what is both known and unknown about the event of death. Again, Jesus tells the disciples that they will not understand the events that will take place; but they will, in the Spirit, be guided in relationship to them. The movements of life are less certain, less prescribed, if we interpret life through this lens. In the aftermath of a traumatic event, practices and ways of life that people knew before trauma can never be fully recovered and restored as they once were. Instead, forms of life must now emerge with death as a shaping force.

The practices of sensing life are embodied practices of imagination. When Bessel van der Kolk speaks about the path of trauma healing, he says a primary bodily connection to the world needs to be restored. In the course of his research he has discovered that, of all the capacities lost in the experience of trauma, the loss of imagination is perhaps the most devastating. For trauma healing to happen, the capacity to imagine one's life beyond a radical ending, to imagine life anew, must be restored. "The degree to which we are successful, as clinicians, is the degree to which we can restore these capacities of delight, hope, and imagination," he says.[54] Restoring the sense of trust and meaning is not purely cognitive; it involves instead a different sense of the world. Sensing life is this kind of reconnecting process; it is an exercise of imagination in the face of what is unimaginable.[55]

This second movement of Spirit witnesses a process of coming into life, of sensing it again. The Spirit's witness, here, is to forms of life that are less discernible, more inchoate and tenuous, than visible and secure. In and through the witness to the undertow, a new sense of life emerges that is more sustaining and truthful than theological interpretations of resurrection life. There is no redemptive gloss, no prescribed ideal of life to which persons can cling. I describe this witness as a sense or sensorium emerging in the middle. When people refer to having a "sense of things," they are describing an orientation to their surroundings that is not altogether confirmed by what they cognitively know about their surroundings. Instead, this sense is a preliminary survey of the landscape. This sense reveals a curious interaction between what is there and something deep within—an inner sense, a spirit. The experience of witnessing to what remains of life is similar. It involves an encounter with what is not recognizable. In this encounter, there is a movement to reorient oneself in relationship to what is not immediately familiar. This movement involves interplay of the senses in an attempt to find one's way.

54. Bessel A. van der Kolk, "The Body Keeps the Score: Integration of Body and Mind in the Treatment of Traumatized People" (Lecture, The Trauma Center, Brookline, MA, January 24, 2007).
55. A good discussion of imagination can be found in Kelsey, *Imagining Redemption*, 97–106.

Sensing is a way of aligning oneself in the face of what is unknown. Balthasar's Holy Saturday disciple in *Heart of the World* depicts this movement of orienting oneself in the midst of chaos and darkness. Balthasar's rhetoric conveys this disorientation. In the absence of clarity and confirmation of what is taking place, a sensorium arises. The movements of Mary and the beloved—often seen as incidental to their resurrection witness—are signs of this unique pneumatological sense. The Johannine promise that the Spirit will guide the disciples into truth may be the biblical expression of this sense. What is unknown about the event of death moves into life. This movement, this sense, gives rise to different expressions and practices of life.

I refer to this sense in another way as well. Considering what we know about the ways in which traumatic experiences bypass the cognitive and conceptual pathways in the brain and are registered somatically, we can think about the movements of middle Spirit as sensual rather than exclusively conceptual. Trauma research also suggests that reconnecting people who have experienced trauma to the world around them cannot be achieved by assuring them that the world is a safe place. Cognitive assurance may be helpful, but it is secondary. Instead, safety has to be restored on a more basic level, a level of the senses. For those who experience trauma, the world is filled with sensory triggers. Reenactments of trauma can be triggered by thoughts, but they are more likely to be triggered by an experience of the senses—the sounds and smells of an earlier traumatic experience. To reconnect a person to the world in the aftermath of a traumatic event, it is essential to first reconnect a person to the movements of her body, enabling her to reestablish and navigate her physical connection to the world. Reconnecting people to their own breath is an essential first step in trauma healing. The pneumatological possibilities are rich here, given that I have imaged the Spirit as divine breath. For those who experience trauma, regaining access to one's own breath is a gateway to reconnection.

In the witness of Mary Magdalene, she does not recognize Jesus by direct access to any of the senses. Instead, there is a sensorium, a chorus of interaction between the senses taking place. The Spirit witnesses, enacting the senses—sight, sound, touch, and smell—attempting to align and orient her to a different way of being in the world. She is receiving the words of the farewell discourse as they are handed over in the context of death; she begins to sense life in the aftermath. To witness, as I displayed in chapters 2 and 3, involves trying to grasp a sense of things in the darkness, attempting to move toward life without knowing its shape. The spark, the faint glimmer that remains, is the movement of Spirit, witnessing to the depths. A faint breath, a weary love, persists. If we conceive of Spirit as breath, we can think about each of these senses as powered by breath. The Spirit's witness, then, is always a double movement of tracking and sensing, attending to what lingers of death and sensing life. Rethinking redemption from the middle calls for practices of tracking and sensing Spirit, pneumatological work.

THE TESTIMONY OF THEOLOGY

Language falters in the abyss; it fractures at the site of trauma. We need to find a different way of speaking from the depths, reclaiming the notion that language about God is always fractured language, always broken, and never complete. It is a truth handed over from Pseudo-Dionysius and Thomas Aquinas.[56] Mark D. Jordan suggests that negation, understood as a soul-forming practice, opens up new ways of speaking, new forms: "It broke language open in anticipation of God."[57] This way of speaking with wounded words is theological speech; in its movements of unsaying and saying, apophasis and cataphasis, it has the potential to witness to what remains—to the always here.

Thus, giving pneumatological significance to the middle presses questions about the language we use to interpret redemption. If read pneumatologically, redemption can no longer be contained within the bounds of a master story. Instead, the story itself must take different shape. It is more akin to testimony, a genre that, according to Elie Wiesel, emerges in response to the silencing force of violence. It is a genre that assumes that the whole story cannot be brought into speech.[58] Spirit, as witness between death and life, provides a necessary testimony to what remains. What is the form of this witness? If this is a space of witness, then the genre of witness and testimony is its fitting correlate. The Spirit breathes in and through our theological lexicons, reminding theology of the testimonial dimension of its discourse. A pneumatological reading does not necessarily replace the redemption narrative, but it operates alongside, disrupting the language of redemption, yielding a different vocabulary of truth telling, testimony and witness. The language of the middle, as we saw in Balthasar and Speyr's descriptions of the descent into hell, will always resemble a tracking process.

Taylor is skeptical, however, about the theological capacity for tracking. He likens this tracking to interpretive art, and theologians, bound to certain genres and styles of discourse, are unable to engage in the experimentation necessary to do this kind of cultural tracking. He writes, "The verdict is still out on whether or not the system-building integrative reach in systematic theology can work with, and not squelch, liminal intensity of spirit or the urgencies of liberating practice."[59] Rebecca Chopp shares this skepticism as well. If theology aims to respond to the realities of human trauma, it must reexamine its form of theological discourse. For Chopp, the work of testimony and truth telling must be met with a refashioning of theology as poetics:

56. See Mark D. Jordan's discussion of Thomas's rhetorical strategies in *Rewritten Theology: Aquinas after His Readers* (Oxford: Blackwell Publishing, 2006), 29–32.

57. Mark D. Jordan, *Telling Truths in Church* (Boston: Beacon Press, 2003), 62.

58. See John Beverly. *Testimonio: On the Politics of Truth-Telling* (Minneapolis: University of Minnesota Press, 2004), and the Latina Feminist Group, *Telling to Live: Latina Feminist Testimonios* (Durham, NC: Duke University Press, 2001).

59. Taylor, "Tracking Spirit," 142.

In response to the moral summons of testimony, theology gets fashioned through what I call "poetics." . . . Theology now explores domains of imaginative discourse, understanding its ordering discourse as reworking language, symbols, codes, images. In this work, theology is not simply adding or subtracting metaphors but reshaping the moral imaginary.[60]

In its modern forms, Chopp claims that theology screens out these truths. In this sense, it fails to witness. She envisions theology as responsive to these life stories; these stories *inform* theological discourse and shape it rather than *conform* to a master story. For both Chopp and Taylor, the possibility of theological witness lies in the degree to which theologians are willing to reexamine the form of theology.

Trauma theory presses questions about the practices of writing, reading, and interpreting texts. The nature and function of theological language, when viewed through this lens, becomes something new. But this "newness" is forged through death; it is a language that survives, a language that is haunted. Overarching frameworks of meaning are scattered on the razed terrain of the middle. Interpreters of these texts witness the shards of these frameworks and rediscover theological language as a language that calls from the abyss, as a language that survives. It is compelling language not insofar as it contains truths but insofar as it testifies to truths that cannot be contained. The promise of theology lies in its testimonial positioning instead of in its confident proclamations. Cornel West's words return here. "It's about a way of being, a way of witnessing."[61] Many familiar versions of the redemptive narrative skim the surface of the abyss. The gloss of redemption is, perhaps, the greatest enemy to those who survive trauma; it provides a promise often unaccompanied by forms of life that can deliver on that promise. Life, for many, does not triumph over death. Instead, life persists in the midst of death and death in the midst of life.

Traumatic survival is an experience at this interstice—between a radical ending and an impossible beginning. The middle is the world that remains after the collapse of the known world; it is the world of survival. In his book *Radical Hope: Ethics in the Face of Cultural Devastation*, Jonathan Lear frames his exploration of ethics around the testimony of Plenty Coups, the last chief of the Crow Nation; it is a testimony to survival. Plenty Coups's words, "After this, nothing happened," become the premise for Lear's ethical exploration. With these words, Plenty Coups narrates the end of life for the Crow Nation. These words spur Lear to conceptualize a different and radical form of ethics at the end of civilization, where the boundaries of familiar frameworks of morality dissolve.[62] The

---

60. Rebecca Chopp, "Poetics of Testimony," in *Converging on Culture: Theologians in Dialogue with Cultural Analysis and Criticism*, ed. Delwin Brown, Sheila Greeve Davaney, and Kathryn Tanner (New York: Oxford University Press, 2001), 66.

61. Cornel West, Lannan Foundation lecture delivered in Santa Fe, NM, June 25, 2003.

62. Jonathan Lear, *Radical Hope: Ethics in the Face of Cultural Devastation* (Cambridge, MA: Harvard University Press, 2006). Lear writes, "After this nothing happened: what could Plenty Coups's utterance mean? If we take him at his word, he seems to be saying that there was an event or a

experience of the Crow that Plenty Coups narrates is the gradual depletion of
resources of the Crow Nation and their movement to the reservation; he identifies this as the demise of identity and a way of life.[63]

> Insofar as I am a Crow subject there is nothing left for me to do; and there
> is nothing left for me to deliberate about, intend, or plan for. Insofar as I
> am a Crow subject, *I* have ceased to be. All that's left is a ghostlike existence
> that stands witness to the death of the subject. Such a witness might well
> say something enigmatic like "After this, nothing happened.[64]

For Lear, these words attest to a vulnerability of humanity, to the breakdown of
ways of life that are understood to be fundamental—guaranteed. "What would
it be to be a witness to this breakdown?" Lear invites us, through his analysis
of Plenty Coups's testimony, to think about ethics after the collapse of a world.
Attending to the middle entails confronting the loss of these familiar frameworks. Lear suggests that something emerges in this confrontation.

I invoke Lear's work because he moves us to think about the collapse of fundamental frameworks we have for understanding and framing our worlds. Lear
stands on the razed terrain of Deacon Lee's backyard. What remains, Lear suggests, is life structured traumatically. The Crow Nation ended. Yet the witness
of Plenty Coups points to what remains. The testimony of Plenty Coups haunts
Lear. Facing this ending, what is the possibility of life ahead? He writes,

> [Plenty Coups] is witnessing the death of the Crow subject, to be sure—but
> he does so in order to clear the ground for a rebirth. For if the death is not
> acknowledged there will most likely be all sorts of empty ways of going on
> "as a Crow." Only if one acknowledges that there is no longer a genuine
> way of going on *like that* might there arise new genuine ways of going on
> *like that*.[65]

Witness involves this encounter with a radical ending and the impossibility of
a new beginning. Lear's point is that "rebirth" is only possible with this witness.

The positioning of Plenty Coups, as witness, resonates with my depiction of

---

happening—the buffalo's going away—something Plenty Coups can refer to as a 'this,' such that
after this, there are no more happenings. Or, to get the temporality correct, Plenty Coups came to
see, as he looked back, that there was a moment such that after this, nothing happened. It would
seem to be the retrospective declaration of a moment when history came to an end. But what could
it mean for history to exhaust itself?" (3).

63. The experience of the Crow Nation and the ending of life as they knew it becomes a beginning for Lear's reflections on human existence more generally. Lear admits that receiving the full
impact of these words, "After this, nothing happened," is bleak. He admits, "What I am concerned
with is an ontological vulnerability that affects us insofar as we are human" (ibid., 50).

64. Ibid., 50. The ghostlike existence is similar to what Susan Brison speaks of as a "spectral existence." Susan Brison, *Aftermath: Violence and the Remaking of a Self* (Princeton: Princeton University
Press, 2002), 9. Both are speaking about a way of living beyond the dissolution of the boundaries
between death and life.

65. Lear, *Radical Hope*, 51.

the Johannine witnesses. What does it mean for Plenty Coups to witness beyond an ending? And what, as well, does it mean for Lear to witness Plenty Coups's words? Reading the Johannine text, the first question is an internal one, directed toward the disciples; the second is directed outward, to those who read and interpret the biblical text. "After this, nothing happened." The declaration from the cross—"it is finished"—can be read in a similar way. These final words haunt those who receive them. This radical ending cannot simply be followed by the proclamation of new life. Instead, the narration of redemption must be forged through the witness to this radical ending. Insofar as it elides this witness, it provides an "empty" form of life, using Lear's words.[66] Instead, to receive the breath released on the cross is to be oriented differently in the world. The radical ending of this claim and the reception of it recasts life in the shape of witness. By using the biblical language, I have attempted to unearth the vocabulary of remaining (*menein*) in order to find a way of theologically narrating the experience of life in the aftermath of trauma.

Both the narrative of Plenty Coups and the Johannine text speak about the loss of an intelligible world, of a recognizable form of life. Lear says that the loss of the intelligibility of a Crow world calls forth a new Crow poet. He asserts,

> What would be required, though, would be a new Crow poet: one who could take up the Crow past and—rather than use it for nostalgia or ersatz mimesis—project it into vibrant new ways for the Crow to live and to be. Here by "poet" I mean the broadest sense of a creative maker of meaningful space. The possibility for such a poet is precisely the possibility for the creation of a new field of possibilities.[67]

Plenty Coups creates a new field of possibilities. He does this, not because there are grounds for hope, but because there are not. Imagination is essential in Lear's vision of radical hope.

But what does this witness look like? In the previous chapters, I pressed us to think of witness in more complex ways. Reframing it through the dynamics of trauma, I have cast theological witness in relationship to traumatic survival. In post-Holocaust testimonial literatures, survival, as a form of life, is examined in great depth. What form of life can arise in the wake of a radical ending? The form of life is intricately linked to witness. There is a weight to life, an urgent and precarious dimension to it, as it is reconceived through the radical event of death. Yet many of these writers, from Elie Wiesel to Primo Levi to Lawrence Langer, insist that the ethical urgency of witness is not divorced from aesthetics. They are suspicious of logic.[68] Witnessing demands a relationship to life that

66. Ibid., 51.
67. Ibid.
68. See Cornel West, Lannan Foundation lecture: "It's not about the win overnight, it's not about the quick fix, it's not about the pushbutton solution. It's about what kind of human being you want to be, what kind of legacy you want to live. It reminds one very much of the blues: 'been down

exceeds the boundaries of logic. Instead, witness requires an imaginative capacity—a capacity to imagine beyond an ending, to imagine life where it is not, in face of the impossibility of a future. This capacity of imagination is ethical and aesthetic. Richard Kearney locates imagination at the intersection of the two. There is urgency to his recovery of the imagination, in a similar vein as Elizabeth Castelli's urgings to recover another dimension of witness. He writes, "Today we rely more than ever on the power of imagining to recast other ways of being in the world, other possibilities of existence."[69]

· The concept of hope is familiar to Christian theologians, and it is linked to the figure of the Spirit. But Lear's call for radical hope turns us to think about hope differently. For Lear, what distinguishes radical hope from hope is the distinctive activation of imagination in the face of an unimaginable future. "It is basically the hope for *revival*," says Lear, "for coming back to life in a form that is not yet imaginable."[70] In Christian theology, hope is often linked to the Spirit of resurrection. The event of resurrection is the promise of new life and new beginnings; the concept of hope has a forward pull. But hope interpreted through the lens of trauma requires an even greater emphasis on imagination. "Imagination" is a more theologically tenuous and suspect term than "hope." In the pneumatology that I have described, resurrection is not guaranteed life, but life that must be witnessed into being. The practice of imagining life in new ways and in new forms is an essential aspect of witness.

Grace Jantzen asks why the term "salvation" has held our theological imaginations captive. We may question interpretations of salvation, but the central framework of salvation and its underlying assumptions still remain intact. Salvation, she says, has always won out over flourishing, a concept that feminist theologians have offered as a synonym for salvation as a way of expanding the Christian vision of God's intention for and movements in the world. Jantzen claims, "The language of salvation is so thoroughly ingrained into Christian theological thinking that we scarcely recognize that we are working with an extended metaphor; it has come to seem like literal theological truth."[71] Salvation itself, Jantzen claims, has been so closely aligned with a particular way of construing the human condition—a primarily negative one. The metaphor of salvation, according to Jantzen, is a metaphor that frames human life in terms of

---

so long that down don't worry me no more, that's why I keep keeping on anyway.' It's not logical. Not logical at all. If you depend solely on the logic, you're in deep trouble."

69. Richard Kearney, *Poetics of Imagining: From Husserl to Lyotard* (New York: Harper Collins, 1991), 228. The full quotation reads, "Today we rely more than ever on the power of imagining to recast other ways of being in the world, other possibilities of existence. Perhaps it is time for the dismembering of Orpheus to be supplemented by a re-membering. Perhaps it is time to put Humpty Dumpty—and other childhood images—back together again. To reimagine, with Joyce, the old Irish dream of Finn-again-awake. To wager once again that imagination lives on in the wake of imagination, that the best response to the post-modern news that 'l'imagination est morte' is: 'Vive l'imagination!'"

70. Lear, *Radical Hope*, 95.

71. Jantzen, *Violence to Eternity*, 208.

death. Although there are multiple interpretations of salvation, the primary metaphor remains in place. We have imagined it in all of its configurations except, in Jonathan Lear's terms, beyond its radical ending, beyond its shattering, in its haunting. What if the concept of flourishing is not an alternative to the concept of salvation but, instead, the vision forged in salvation's collapse? What would happen if, as Jantzen implies, we released the hold of salvific interpretations to imagine Christian discourse beyond the collapse of this particular view?

This is where Lear leaves us, as he imagines the discourse of ethics not only pressed to its limits but, in fact, pressed beyond these limits. What would it mean for Christian theologians to stand in the aftermath of redemption, to witness the collapse of our most familiar frameworks of meaning? This is not a dance at the nihilistic edge of Christian claims; it is, in fact, a trajectory of the gospel's witness as it is handed over in the haunted territory of remaining. "What is it to be one who remains?"

REMAINING, IN LOVE

In our current world, we are witnessing ongoing atrocities and different manifestations of suffering. The invisible forces of global capital and the undetectable effects of new wars and their justifications demand that theological accounts of suffering attend to the elisions constituting traumatic suffering. Although some may say that all "suffering is suffering," there are different expressions of that suffering and its effects that press for renewed theological articulation. I understand this as the increased invisibility of suffering and the power of its erasure. The discourse of trauma engages these invisible realities, continually calling attention to what falls outside the lines of what is, or can be, represented. The challenge of theological discourse is to articulate a different orientation to suffering that can speak to the invisibility, gaps, and repetitions constituting trauma.

As I have shown, a different expression of Spirit surfaces when we read biblical and theological texts through the lens of trauma. A theology of middle Spirit can help us to rethink the theological discourse about suffering, given its new unique dimensions in trauma. Bessel van der Kolk acknowledges that one of the primary effects of trauma is a crisis of the human spirit.[72] This crisis refers to a complete loss of meaning and trust in the world. In religious terms, this crisis goes to the heart of the relationship between human and divine. Determining the correspondence between the divine Spirit and the human spirit is central to pneumatological studies. How does a theology of the Spirit meet this crisis of spirit?

72. Alexander C. McFarlane and Bessel van der Kolk, "Trauma and Its Challenge to Society," in *Traumatic Stress: The Effects of Overwhelming Experience on Mind, Body and Society*, ed. Bessel A. van der Kolk, Alexander C. McFarlane, and Lars Weisaeth (New York: Guilford Press, 1996), 24–46.

I have offered a pneumatology of remaining, suggesting that trauma, in its inability to be located in one space and in one time, moves us onto pneumatological terrain to address the complexities of the aftermath. I have started to envision practices patterned after this testimony, practices of tracking and sensing that propel us to recognize suffering amid its multiple elisions. I want to return in closing to the images that first drew me to the middle and to probing the Spirit in the abyss. I heard in Speyr and Balthasar's rhetoric of the divine depths the language of trauma. The images of Adrienne von Speyr's journeys through hell were images of divine disorientation and forsakenness. The survival to which they both attest is the survival of God; the Spirit witnesses this forsakenness not in triumph but in weariness. Divine love cannot be extinguished. Instead, divine love survives. Spirit is figured both as what remains and as the power to witness to remaining. This is not, however, a contradiction but is suggestive of what takes place between death and life. Divine and human meet in the middle, and there is an intermingling of breath in the abyss; it is the point at which the silent human cry meets the silent divine cry.[73] Spirit meets spirit in the depths.

The tracking and sensing, then, not only unearth and give theological significance to the unknown and unutterable within human experience, but these practices also testify to something of who we understand God to be. The work of the witnesses is to track the undertow and to sense life. But this witness is, as well, a testimony that runs deeper than what we might imagine, to the nature of divine love. In the middle, divine love is witnessed in its remaining. Divine love is not something visible, whose form we must imitate; instead, it is a weary remainder seeking form, the shape of which must be continually imagined. In *The Crucified God*, Jürgen Moltmann provides a Christian theological response to the Holocaust by claiming that God is not removed from the suffering of the world, but rather, God takes suffering into God's being. With his theology of the crucified God, he also provided a counter-claim to protest atheism—death of God theology. Instead of the death *of* God, Moltmann says the cross narrates death *in* God. This theology of the cross challenges the way we understand God's relationship to the world, attempting to speak about the presence of God in a way that accounts for large-scale suffering. Looking through the lens of trauma, the site of the cross is extended into the territory of remaining, a haunted landscape in which something of death remains. With this shift to the middle, the crucified God is now the remaining God, figured in the Spirit. But the Spirit— the weary trickle of love, the fragile breath—finds form in the breath and movements of witnesses. The haunting is also the transmission of the imperative to love, the call for something to be done.[74] The work of tracking and sensing is

---

73. See Simone Weil, "Human Personality," in *The Simone Weil Reader*, 313–39.
74. Gordon, *Ghostly Matters*, xvi.

sanctifying work, the work of making love visible at the point where it is most invisible.[75]

If we read this sacred story as a story of survival, we are pressed to think about what it means to remain in the aftermath of a death that escapes our comprehension. To witness this sacred story is also to receive it for the truth that it tells: love remains, and we are love's witnesses.[76] It is tempting, in the end, to offer a happy ending. One version of the redemptive narrative is so thick in the bloodstream of Christian theology. The story of love's survival is tenuous and always vulnerable to the elisions of our guiding logic.[77] In *Explorations in Theology*,[78] Balthasar images the Spirit traveling the depths of the Godhead, opening up a sphere of the divine that attests to the "unutterable mystery of being."[79] Although expressed in full utterance in the incarnation, there is always the danger that this utterance can become ossified; the living word can become the "letter that kills." The eternal dialogue can shut down. The Spirit always accompanies the utterance, breathing into it lest it become a cold dialectic. The Spirit witnesses, he says, the depths of what is unknown even to the Father and Son. This image in Balthasar's essay, "Unknown Lying beyond the Word," provides vocabulary for the Spirit witnessing to the divine depths. Yet the story of Spirit in the abyss is a love story that Balthasar cannot tell, at least not straightforwardly so. It is, however, a story handed over in the form of an imperative: remain in me, remain in my love.

Spirit is the breath that cannot be cut off, that does not cease. I have argued that this breath is handed over into the depths, and there are middle-day witnesses who receive that breath. In the depths, a transformation takes place. The middle space is the descent into hell, the furthest reaches from all sources of life. Balthasar and Speyr developed an antiharrowing narrative of the descent into hell. The trackless trek of the Son in hell was not active and victorious. The

75. For an excellent articulation of sanctification in response to radical suffering, see the work of Melissa Raphael, *The Female Face of God in Auschwitz: A Jewish Feminist Theology of the Holocaust* (New York: Routledge, 2003). Raphael speaks of the work of women in Auschwitz—their practices of washing and caring for bodies—as the work of restoring (*tikkun*) the divine image.

76. This echoes the line from Cormac McCarthy, *The Road* (New York: Vintage, 2006), where the father and son meet another survivor on the road, and the survivor says, "There is no God, and we are his prophets" (170).

77. In its process of being handed over (its interpretive history), it has enacted multiple forms of violence. Its supercessions and glosses of redemption have covered over. This handing over has been understood as a more secure and stable enterprise. As I have presented it here, the survival of love is more tenuous.

78. The title word, "explorations," can also be translated more literally as "fragments" or "sketches." Such is suggested in the introduction to Hans Urs von Balthasar, *Spirit and Institution*, vol. 4 of *Explorations in Theology*, trans. Edward T. Oakes (San Francisco: Ignatius Press, 1995). Balthasar writes, "As with the previous volumes of *Explorations in Theology*, the general title of *Spirit and Institution* given to the essays in this volume should not be understood as one that intends to indicate a systematic treatment of its topic. . . . This is merely a sketchbook: all it tries to do is approach its main object from different angles. . . . Perhaps some eager soul thirsty for systematics would like to make something out of these fragments. . . . The author, however, mistrusts such undertakings" (11).

79. Balthasar, *Explorations in Theology*, 106.

weary trickle of love was not an image of harrowing. Instead, it was an image of fragile remaining, of love's persistence. It is what is handed over to those who witness in the depths. From this space, a different vision of life can be glimpsed. It is life as remaining. This transformation, this redemption in the abyss of hell, is not about deliverance from the depths but, instead, about a way of being in the depths, a practice of witnessing that senses life arising amid what remains. The middle story is not a story of rising out of the depths, but a transformation of the depths themselves.

Cathy Caruth claims that Freud images trauma beyond its pathology for the truth that it tells. Reading through the lens of trauma, these texts speak to human suffering in its ongoingness. Death persists. They offer, as well, a picture of love in perilous and tenuous form. Love remains. For Balthasar, the divine story must exceed a story of tragedy and survival; it must be theologically rescued from abyss. But what if theologians did not perform this rescue? Perhaps the divine story is neither a tragic one nor a triumphant one but, in fact, a story of divine remaining, the story of love that survives. It is a cry arising from the abyss.[80] The question is: can we witness it?

80. See Cathy Caruth, "Introduction: The Wound and the Voice," in *Unclaimed Experience: Trauma, Narrative and History* (Baltimore: Johns Hopkins University Press, 1966), 1–9.

Index

Acts of the Apostles, 139n65
African Americans, 129, 154n35, 157
aftermath of trauma
  breath and, 163
  Caruth on, 7n8, 27n30
  Castelli on eclipsing in, 41
  double structure of trauma, 7, 7n8, 20,
    20n10, 33–34, 156
  eliding/elision in, 41–42, 43
  flashbacks and, 19–20, 32–33, 156n39
  Herman on memory distortions in, 41
  persistence of trauma in, 2–4, 7–8, 7n8,
    13–15, 18–21, 26, 27n30, 109, 156
  physical body and, 18–21, 25, 26, 41, 42,
    44, 163
  shattering of language and
    communication in, 18–19, 21, 24, 25,
    26, 28, 32, 35–36, 41, 42, 44
  time alterations in, 19–20, 19n9, 25, 26,
    28, 32, 41, 42, 127–28
  See also middle space; recovery after
    trauma; remaining; survival after
    trauma; witness and witnessing
agape, 131, 131n54
Albrecht, Barbara, 61n61
Ambrose, 89n15
Andrew, 90n19
anti-Semitism, 25n26, 82n1. See also
  Holocaust; Judaism
apocalypse, 128
Apocalypse Now and Then (Keller), 128
apostles
  lack of understanding of Jesus by, 93, 100,
    100n31, 162

love of Jesus for, 102, 102n38, 104, 109,
  131–34
paraclete and, 99, 101–5, 101n35,
  103n39, 110, 120–22, 126, 130–32,
  139–40, 162, 163
See also beloved disciple; farewell discourse
  by Jesus; and specific apostles
Apostles' Creed, 45–46, 51
Aquinas, Thomas, 164
Arrested Development, 161
atheism. See death of God theology
atonement theology, 144, 154–55. See also
  crucifixion
Attridge, Harold W., 89n15
Audergon, Arlene, 18, 18n6
Augustine, 71, 130

Balthasar, Hans Urs von
  on between space, x, 138, 160
  on bridge metaphor of middle Spirit, 71,
    72, 72n93, 74–78
  on Christian life, 70n89
  on Christ's descent into hell, 50n13,
    51n18, 53–54, 54nn34–35, 59, 63–65,
    65n74, 74–75, 113, 138n64, 164,
    171–72
  on crucifixion, 49, 55–57, 64–65, 74, 160
  on cruciform love, 134, 160
  on death/life relationship, 34, 42, 61,
    72–73, 77–80, 107
  on divine suffering, 67
  education of, 58
  founding of Community of St. John by,
    52